Extending the Dance
in Infant and Toddler Caregiving

*To the many teachers, parents, and children
who have been our partners and
our teachers over the years*

Extending the Dance
in Infant and Toddler Caregiving

Enhancing Attachment and Relationships

by

Helen H. Raikes, Ph.D.
Professor of Child, Youth and Family Studies
University of Nebraska at Lincoln

and

Carolyn Pope Edwards, Ed.D.
Willa Cather Professor
Professor of Psychology and Child, Youth and Family Studies
University of Nebraska at Lincoln

in collaboration with Lella Gandini

·P A U L·H·
BROOKES
PUBLISHING C⁰®

Baltimore • London • Sydney

National Association for the
Education of Young Children
Washington, DC

Paul H. Brookes Publishing Co.
Post Office Box 10624
Baltimore, Maryland 21285-0624
USA

www.brookespublishing.com

**National Association for the
Education of Young Children**
1313 L Street NW
Suite 500
Washington, DC 20005

Typeset by Spearhead Global, Inc., Bear, Delaware.
Manufactured in the United States of America by
Sheridan Books, Inc., Chelsea, Michigan.

Cover image © Masterfile.

This NAEYC edition is an exclusive printing for the National Association for the
Education of Young Children, 1313 L Street NW, Suite 500, Washington, DC 20005.

NAEYC Order #295

The individuals described in this book are composites or real people whose situations are
masked and are based on the authors' experiences. In most instances, names and identifying details have been changed to protect confidentiality. Real names used with permission.

Library of Congress Cataloging-in-Publication Data

Raikes, Helen H.
   Extending the dance in infant and toddler caregiving : enhancing attachment and rela-
tionships / by Helen Raikes and Carolyn Pope Edwards in collaboration with Lella
Gandini. — 1st ed.
     p.   cm.
   Includes bibliographical references and index.
   ISBN-13: 978-1-55766-859-2 (pbk.)
   ISBN-10: 1-55766-859-0 (pbk.)
   1. Infants—Development.   2. Toddlers—Development.   3. Child care.
   I. Edwards, Carolyn P.   II. Gandini, Lella.   III. Title.
   HQ774.R34 2009
   305.231—dc22   2009013722

British Library Cataloguing in Publication data are available from the British Library.

2013   2012   2011   2010   2009

10   9   8   7   6   5   4   3   2   1

Contents

About the Authors

Carolyn Pope Edwards, Ed.D., is Willa Cather Professor at the University of Nebraska at Lincoln, with joint appointments in the Departments of Psychology and Child, Youth and Family Studies. She received her doctorate in Human Development from the Harvard Graduate School of Education. She has taught previously at Vassar College, University of Massachusetts at Amherst, and University of Kentucky and held visiting research professor positions at universities in Kenya, Italy, and Norway. Her research spans the areas of child development, early childhood education, cross-cultural studies, and teacher preparation and professional development. She is currently studying strategies for strengthening mathematics education and the links between teacher knowledge, attitudes, and student achievement in the early grades and strategies for enhancing young children's school readiness through strengthening literacy education as well as parent and family engagement. Much of her writing describes and analyzes relationship-building practices and pedagogical documentation in the world-renowned infant-toddler centers and preschools in northern and central Italy. She is active on many policy committees at the national and state levels that focus on early childhood curriculum and teacher preparation from preschool to primary and was part of the NAEYC Working Group on Developmentally Appropriate Practice.

Helen H. Raikes, Ph.D., is Professor in the Department of Child, Youth and Family Studies at the University of Nebraska at Lincoln. She received her doctorate in child development from Iowa State University. Previously, she has had teaching positions at the University of California, Davis, and at Iowa State University. Among other foci, she has maintained a career-long interest in secure base relationships for infants and toddlers and first created an attachment-based model while Director of Infant Toddler Programs and Director of Research at the SRI/Saint Elizabeth and Gallup Organization Child Development Center in Lincoln, Nebraska. She was also a Society for Research in Child Development Executive Policy Fellow at the Administration on Children, Youth and Families at the time the Early Head Start program began and co-directed the national research for that program. Today, her work focuses on programs for children in poverty, with special emphases on infants and toddlers, children at greatest risk, and optimal timing of intervention as it relates to developmental trajectories, school readiness, and later success, as well as on innovative continuous program improvement efforts using research and evaluation. She is a board member of the Nebraska Early Childhood Endowment Board, the Buffett Early Childhood Fund, and the Nebraska Children and Families Foundation and is a member of the National Forum on Early Childhood Program Evaluation.

ABOUT THE CONTRIBUTOR

Lella Gandini, Ed.D., is Adjunct Professor of Education at the University of Massachusetts at Amherst and Visiting Scholar (2007–2009) at Lesley University in Cambridge, Massachusetts. She taught as lecturer at Smith College and Mount Holyoke College in Massachusetts and was a visiting researcher at the National Center of Research in Rome, Italy. She received her master's degree in child study from Smith College, her doctoral degree in education from the University of Massachusetts, and, in 2004, an honorary doctorate in humane letters from the Erikson Institute. She is the U.S. Liaison for the Dissemination of the Reggio Emilia Approach on behalf of Reggio Children, Italy, and a correspondent for the Italian educational magazine *Bambini*. She is Associate Editor of *Innovations in Early Education: The International Reggio Exchange.* Her research and writing have focused on parenting and on the philosophy and practices related to care and education of young children in Reggio Emilia and Pistoia, Italy. Her study and exchange supporting the professional development of North American teachers requires frequent periods of direct observation in those Italian cities.

Acknowledgments

The authors of this book have contributed equally to it, and we take the opportunity of rotating our names in the About the Authors section to acknowledge our equal contributions. We also would like to recognize the invaluable contribution of Lella Gandini, U.S. Liaison for the Dissemination of the Reggio Emilia Approach, in coauthoring Chapters 5 and 6 (with Carolyn Edwards) and informing our thinking on many issues we discuss, such as space and environments.

We wish to acknowledge the many colleagues and graduate students who read drafts and otherwise contributed to this book, notably present and former graduate students at the University of Nebraska at Lincoln: Cassidy Housh Baum, Jennifer Benson, Julie Jones-Branch, Keely Cline, Anh Do, Lisa Knoche, Eunju Jung, Jennifer Leeper-Miller, Maggie Ortmann, Yinjing Shen, Martha Ostrom, Cixin Wang, and Linda Willis. We also are grateful to our many colleagues who generously contributed to telling the story of relationship-based programs from their experiences and work with infants and toddlers, including Jenny Bowen, Wen Zhao, Janice Cotton, and Jeronia Muntaner, Half the Sky Foundation, China; Mary Jane Chainski, the Ounce of Prevention Fund; James Elicker, Purdue University; Carol Fichter and Linda Esterling, Nebraska Early Childhood Training Center; Jana Gifford and staff, Child Development, Inc., Russellville, Arkansas; Jeanne Goldhaber and Dee Smith, University of Vermont; Kathleen Feller, Child Saving Institute, Omaha; Donatella Giovannini and Annalia Galardini, City Administration of Pistoia, Italy; Ellen Hall and staff, Boulder Journey School; Joyce Kinney, Colorado Coalition for the Homeless; Mary Reckmeyer and teachers, The Donald O. Clifton Child Development Center of The Gallup Organization; Carlina Rinaldi, Reggio Children, Italy; Nancy Rosenow and Dana Miller, Dimensions Educational Research Foundation; Amy Wolf, Park University; and many others too numerous to mention who have influenced our thinking and expanded our knowledge.

Finally, we thank the educators, parents, and children who allowed us to photograph them and tell their stories. It is for them, particularly, that this book was written.

CHAPTER 1

The Dances of Infancy

Bringing the Relationship Focus to Infant and Toddler Programs

Maria is a 6-month-old girl who attends an infant care center in the southern United States. Maria has had the same teacher since she began infant care 4 months ago. Maria, her teacher Sarah, and her parents have a comfortable set of rhythms. They know what to expect from each other. Most importantly, Maria flows with the rhythm of each caregiving day and the predictable back and forth of interaction (e.g., cooing, caregiving, responding, playing) with both her parents and Sarah. With all of her loving caregivers, Maria visibly brightens and responds to their talk and touch. In some ways, Maria's interaction is like a dance—or two dances, really: the first with her parents and the second with Sarah. Maria has "extended the (parent) dance" by also having an important dance with Sarah, her teacher and caregiver.

Antonio is a 6-month-old boy who lives half a world away from Maria in northern Italy. Antonio attends an infant program with a teacher who also is engaged lovingly and carefully in forming a relationship with both Antonio and his parents. During his first weeks of infant care, Antonio's parents spent a great deal of time at the center to ensure a smooth *Inserimento* (gradual transition into the program). Great care is taken, especially in the beginning, because Antonio's teacher and parents know how important relationships are to infants. If the dance begins well, it will continue to flourish—both between child and caregiver and between teachers and parents. Although Maria and Antonio are living thousands of miles apart, in both of their programs teachers and parents recognize the importance of establishing and maintaining gentle, flowing, reciprocal, and predicable dances between infants and caregivers.

In contrast to Maria and Antonio, 6-month-old Keisha attends a program that does not emphasize relationships. Keisha has four teachers who attend to her needs within a large group of 16 infants. Sometimes her teachers do not interact with her until they hear her whimpering, and she does not always brighten when the teacher comes to her. Soon Keisha will be moved to the older baby room, where she will have four new teachers. Her mother passed on information about Keisha this morning. She was not sure exactly who to tell, but hoped all of the teachers would communicate with each other. Keisha's mother worries about the change that is coming soon. However, Keisha does not seem terribly distressed once she gets home, so her mother wonders if her concerns are necessary.

Relationships provide the framework for infant development. When relationships are contingent, responsive, and reciprocal, they help children break down the incoming stream of information from the outside world so that they can assimilate and understand it, while also providing predictable responses so children can trust it. The rhythms of close relationships with parents, caregivers, and teachers—back and forth, need and response, with gentle rhythms moving to a synchronous inner beat—support emotional, physical, cognitive, and language development. Relationships provide the context for early development. Development takes place in and through relationships (Josselson, 1996). In some respects, relationships provide the setting, medium, and motivation for early development.

RELATIONSHIP AS A DANCE: THE FIRST DANCE

Many infant psychologists have noticed how much the reciprocal responsiveness between parent and child seems like a dance. Thoman and Browder (1987) developed the dance metaphor beautifully in their book for parents called *Born Dancing: How Intuitive Parents Understand Their Baby's Unspoken Language*. They describe the back-and-forth quality of parent–baby communication and how each seeks to fit into the other's actions and needs. Infant and parent develop a unique style in their ongoing pattern of interaction made up of sounds, expressions, and movements.

Colwyn Trevarthen, a British psychologist, added another important dimension concerning dance, music, and song when arguing that mother–infant communication begins with "sympathy between moving minds and bodies" (2002, p. 10). He emphasized the importance of mothers' singing to their babies, rocking them, and dancing with them in their arms in ways that build on babies' innate capacities to experience rhythm. Infants come into life equipped with a natural sensitivity to *musicality* (the flow, shape, and patterns of language, music, and dance) that constitutes the very heart of human sharing, forms the beginnings of cognitive perspective taking and joint attention, and animates and motivates the process of learning. To Trevarthen, natural music is vital to the child— not when it comes out of an electronic source such as a CD player, but instead when it comes from a living person who invites the child to join in the motions of vocalizing, clapping, or bouncing with the adult. The metaphor of the dance— reciprocal, with gentle rhythms and sensitive pauses, moving to a synchronous beat (Thoman & Browder, 1987)—wends its way through this book.

EXTENDING THE DANCE

Parents are usually their child's first and most important partners in the dance of interaction, but extending the dance of primary relationships to other relationships—child care teachers and caregivers, grandparents, friends—is also important. Through all of their strategies and educational practices, educators can be seen as serving the goal of extending the dance begun between children and parents by entering into their own dancelike relationship with the child and supporting the parent–child dances. When an infant enters the teacher's care, the teacher must take the initiative and become attuned. The teacher must get into a rhythm by following the infant's lead. Because a newcomer enters the program "in the arms" of parents, educators enfold families into this process. Gradually, as the dance between educators and infants becomes smooth and familiar, the teacher encourages each infant to try out more complex steps and learn how to dance to new compositions, beats, and tempos. The dance partnership can also widen as both infants and adults try out new partners and as new peers or adults are added to their group. As each baby alternates dancing with one or two (or more) partners, the dance itself becomes a story about who the child has been and who the child is becoming—a reciprocal self created through close relationships.

RELATIONSHIP-BASED INFANT AND TODDLER PROGRAMS

In the United States and other countries, a number of infant and toddler care programs have been designed to be more relationship oriented—intentionally building on what is known about the dance of relationships. In some approaches, educators in infant and toddler care apply principles of attachment theory and research in their work with children and families across several program types and venues (Honig, 2002). Other approaches build on principles long used in European programs. We seek to integrate the underlying principles of these various relationship-based approaches in this book, in particular those of the United States and Italy. We discuss special ways of orienting children and parents when children begin child care, keeping teachers and children together through-out infancy, creating space to support small groups, building close relationships with parents, supporting parent–child relationships, hiring relationship-oriented staff, observing and extending children's learning, and documenting children's growth and development. We look not only at contemporary approaches to in-fant and toddler care but also at the past and traditional cultures of the world, in which extended families have handled child care and women's work through the ages. Caregivers in the modern era did not invent the relationship-based ap-proach to infant care. Rather, mothers and fathers throughout the world use age-old wisdom to expand their infants' world of relationships with caring family and friends. This book draws deeply on the universality of the dances, grounding it in cultural practices that characterize caregiving throughout the world.

Infant and toddler programs increasingly emphasize the importance of the teacher–infant relationship. In the United States, the *Guidelines for Developmen-tally Appropriate Practice* from the National Association for the Education of Young Children (Copple & Bredekamp, 2008) underscore the vital importance of relationships for the development of infants and toddlers. Similarly, the *Revised Head Start Program Performance Standards* (U.S. Department of Health and Human Services, 2002) and the *Statement of the Advisory Committee on Services for Families Serving Infants and Toddlers* (U.S. Department of Health and Human Services, 1994) emphasize the importance of relationships in Early Head Start programs, encouraging primary relationships that endure over time for infants and toddlers. Early Head Start and Head Start Educare programs in the Bounce Learning Network, such as Educare Chicago operated by the Ounce of Prevention Fund, aim to keep teachers and infants together throughout the first 3 years of care (see also Box 4.1). However, one study showed that more program directors in typical U.S. infant and toddler programs wanted to implement continuity models than were able to do so due to implementation challenges

(Cryer, Hurwitz, & Wolery, 2000). Nonetheless, increasingly, U.S. child care programs stress continuity of care over a period of several years. Many Western European infant and toddler programs have been applying such relationship-centered principles for decades. For example, early childhood programs in Italy, which have been in widespread existence for more than half a century, emphasize the relationship-based approach characterizing birth-to-3 programs. The Italians are known throughout the world for excellence in many aspects of early childhood programming.

MODEL FOR DESCRIBING RELATIONSHIP-BASED PROGRAMS

Extending the Dance identifies the core dimensions of relationships in birth-to-3 early childhood programs (see Figure 1.1). In our model, the many elements of the system are created by the players—child, parent, and teacher, considered individually and in relationships—for a total of nine reference points:

1. The child

2. The parent

3. The teacher

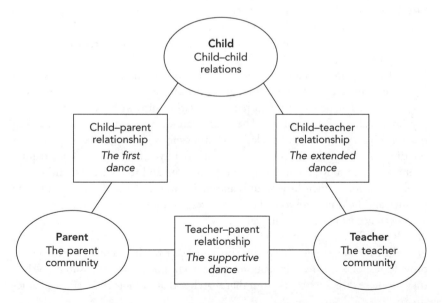

Figure 1.1. A model of relationship-based programs. The corners of the triangle represent the players in relationship-based care: children, parents, and teachers. The connectors (apexes) represent the pairwise relationships between types of players: child–parent, child–teacher, and teacher–parent. Within each set of players (the oblongs) are important within-group relationships: child–child, teacher–teacher, and parent–parent.

4. The child–parent relationship

5. The child–teacher relationship

6. The teacher–parent relationship

7. The child's relationships with other children, creating the peer community

8. The parent's relationships with other parents, creating the parent community

9. The teacher's relationships with other teachers, creating the teacher community

Each of the relationship elements gives rise to a dance in its own right with its own rhythms and steps. In the next section, we take a closer look at each of the nine elements in the model.

The Child

How can one create relationship dances that best support each child's development and sense of well-being? All of the relationship dances emphasized in this book are for the purpose of ultimately supporting the optimal development of the individual child, beginning in infancy. Infancy is a unique period of life. The infant is vulnerable and still needs to develop many systems and skills. Development includes enormous brain growth, language, and formation of the sense of trust and security that guides subsequent relationships. In all these areas, the caregiver plays an immensely important role—the importance of which inspired this book.

The relationship-centered approach to infant and toddler child care is based on the importance of close attachments and relationships to early development and learning. The newborn infant relies on relationships with parents to regulate psychologically and emotionally. The infant cannot exist outside of close, caring relationships. An adult may be relatively autonomous in eating, sleeping, and responding to work and love. Infants, however, are physically helpless. They require caring adults to move them when restless, to come and feed them when hungry, to pay attention to their little sounds and make meaning out of them, to provide warmth and holding, and to replicate the prenatal motion to which the baby has long been accustomed (see Chapter 2).

Research has replicated the methods of nurturing young children that are intuitive to many people. Caring parents and other family members or caregivers provide responses, care, stimulation, contact comfort, talk, and smiles. When they do these things with a rhythm that matches that of their children, the babies thrive.

As their needs are met, babies begin to realize that the world is predictable. They learn from interactions perfectly pitched to their abilities, attention spans, and levels of emotional intensity. Such interactions increase the odds of desirable outcomes—building healthy brain architecture that provides a strong foundation

---

BOX 1.1.
Child who appears secure

Bianca is a very busy 11-month-old girl. She plays happily and with animation; when she gets tired or stressed or just needs to check in, she crawls to her parents and lets them know that she needs them. When her mother comes in the room, Bianca smiles at her and will usually crawl over to greet her. However, after a moment or two of snuggling, Bianca is ready to be off and exploring again.

---

for learning, behavior, and health (National Scientific Council on the Developing Child, 2007). Moreover, if the baby's needs are met, the infant forms a secure attachment that helps to create a foundation for healthy development in early childhood and beyond (Thompson, 1999).

How can you recognize when an infant around 9 months of age or older is developing a sense of security (see Box 1.1)?

- The child seems ready to explore but checks back in every so often with the caring adult, using the adult as a secure base for exploring.
- The child seems happy to see the important adults in his or her life.
- The child accepts comfort when needed.
- The child may often look back or show the caring adult something discovered.

How can you recognize when a child around 9 months of age or older may not feel secure (see Box 1.2)?

- The child may need to cling to adults.
- The child may ignore adults or cry when they appear.
- The child may not be able to accept comfort.
- The child may seem to play independently but does not check in with discoveries or to ask questions.

BOX 1.2.
Child who appears less secure

LaMont is also 11 months of age, but he seems somewhat uninterested in exploring. He stays very near his mother and seems to be worried that she will leave him. Sometimes when LaMont's mother picks him up, he struggles to be put down. He spends a lot of his time in this form of conflict and spends far less time than Bianca exploring and learning about his world.

Children who are secure also have better language, problem solving, and social-emotional development during the preschool years (Sroufe, 1988). A secure child gives energy to learning and checks back in with the caregiver for more information, often hundreds of times every day. Thus, there are more opportunities for learning. An insecure child misses these valuable chances. Furthermore, in infant and toddler development, many systems work together. Good experiences put the child on a positive trajectory for later childhood. Every stage of development is important and must be carefully tended in ways that are appropriate for that stage. Infancy is particularly important for development. Therefore, programs for babies must be carefully designed. Chapter 2 explores the research on infant development. It further explains the importance of relationships and why enormous care must be taken to ensure that all of the processes are well supported.

Parents

A number of important studies have demonstrated what parents can do to assist infant development. Some behaviors are common sense, but it is helpful to know exactly what they are and to learn more about how to promote them. The most important thing parents can do is to be responsive to their child—something that seems to be universally true. Mary Ainsworth, who documented so eloquently the ways parents develop security-promoting relationships, found similar patterns of sensitivity and warmth between parents and children in Uganda and Baltimore (Ainsworth & Bell, 1970). Chapter 2 discusses more of Mary Ainsworth's studies.

Certain parental behaviors can promote infant development:

- *Contingent responsiveness*—When adults respond quickly enough so that infants learn to associate a need with a response, the infants learn that a caring world responds by bringing relief or pleasure.

- *Eye contact and face-to-face play*—Mothers who talk to their very young babies (less than 1 month of age) using exaggerated facial gestures, excitement, and energetic responses have babies who are more secure and contented. Such mothers show interest in their babies and also learn how to read their babies' cues in ways that are fun for both mother and baby.

- *Touch*—Babies need to be held, rocked, and stroked. A very famous set of experiments by psychologist Harry Harlow showed the importance of contact comfort (Harlow & Zimmerman, 1959). Although the subjects in these experiments were baby primates, the studies demonstrated the extent to which the infant was comforted and derived security from a familiar, cloth monkey.

- *Stimulation*—Throughout infancy, appropriate stimulation is an important component of positive relationships. Babies are typically excited about learning when it is matched to their current stage of development. Parents should think about what the child is learning at each stage of development and offer experiences that give the baby a chance to imitate and practice emerging skills in all areas, from sound play to concept development.

• *Promoting a secure base*—The parent should act as the baby's secure base. The mobile baby goes out to explore, returns to check in with the parent, may get some hugs or show the parent what has been found in the explorations, and then heads out to explore again. This pattern repeats itself over and over, with the parent providing an anchor for the explorations.

• *Sensitivity*—Studies show that parental sensitivity strongly predicts infant–parent attachment (e.g., Isabella & Belsky, 1991; Maccoby, 1980; Rosen & Rothbaum, 1993). Sensitive parents are tuned in to their babies; when the baby expresses a need, the parent responds appropriately (i.e., matched to the need the child expresses). Sensitive parents listen and wait, phasing their interactions with the infant's and organizing the interaction so parent and child take turns.

What affects parental sensitivity? Many studies of parental behavior toward infants have been conducted. They demonstrate that a number of factors influence whether parents are able to respond with sensitivity to infants. Most mothers want to be good parents, but they may not be able to do so for various reasons initially beyond their control. For example, if a mother is depressed, she may miss many opportunities to respond to the infant (e.g., Tronick, 1989). When interacting with a "still-faced" parent, a young infant eventually gives up attempts to get the parent's attention (Toda & Fogel, 1993). In these experimental studies, the parent first interacts responsively and then suddenly becomes still by looking straight ahead and ignoring the child. The child demonstrates engagement during the responsive period and becomes disorganized when the parent withdraws. Parents encountering high levels of stress, instability, or other responsibilities may also find it difficult to consistently respond sensitively to the baby. Frustrations may cause parents to inadvertently respond with impatience, with distraction, or not at all.

Some parents did not experience positive relationships as children. These parents therefore lack a road map or a deeply understood sense of how to respond. They must learn how to become sensitive. In some such cases, the relationship with the child's teacher, home visitor, or, in the case of fathers, the *father coordinator,* whose job is to engage fathers in the program and as a parent, is the first accepting relationship the parent has personally experienced. Chapter 8 discusses how infant and toddler programs can help parents become aware and effective in developing consistent responsiveness to their infants.

How can you recognize a sensitive parent?

• The parent responds contingently when the child cries, talks, or expresses joys.

• The parent responds with warmth and animation.

> ### BOX 1.3.
> ### Emerging sensitivity in a new father
>
> Edgar is a new father. His own father died when Edgar was 8 years old, but they had a good relationship before his early death. Edgar then formed a good relationship with his grandfather. Edgar is thrilled to now be a father himself and finds himself responding to and watching little Teddy, his infant, so carefully. He marvels at Teddy's fine features and enjoys holding and feeding him. He is so pleased to be providing for Teddy and cannot wait to get home each evening to see him.

- The parent molds his or her body to the child's and touches the baby often.

- The parent is aware of his or her role in promoting the child's security.

- The parent is generally sensitive in other aspects of life.

Box 1.3 provides an example of a father who is off to a good start in developing sensitivity. Box 1.4 describes a parent who has issues in her life that may interfere with her ability to be present and sensitive when interacting with her infant.

Teachers

Researchers have found that sensitive *teachers* and *child care providers* (terms that are used interchangeably in this book) are similar to the sensitive parents described previously (Howes & Hamilton, 1992). A sensitive teacher promotes good outcomes for children in child care settings. (Also, see Box 2.2 for more about the research that has focused on measuring the characteristics and effects of sensitivity- and security-promoting teacher–child relationships. Chapter 10 discusses which teachers are good candidates for a relationship-based infant and toddler program.) Child development researchers who have developed instruments for measuring quality in infant care environments have also identified features of sensitive teachers with little disagreement (e.g., Arnett, 1989).

> ### BOX 1.4.
> ### Mother experiencing obstacles
>
> LaMere is a new mother, but she finds herself at odds with motherhood. No one told her how tired she would be. She lacks support and finds it hard to catch up on sleep. LaMere pays close attention to the baby some of the time, but other times she ignores little Martin. LaMere thinks that she will probably like Martin better when he gets older.

BOX 1.5.
A sensitive teacher

Brenda is a sensitive teacher who cares for four toddlers. With all of them, she responds when they call, knows them well, and quickly meets their needs. Brenda listens carefully for their words and gestures and replies quickly. She smiles and hugs them often and is patient when they become frustrated. She tries to understand what each child needs in such situations.

How can you recognize a sensitive teacher (see Boxes 1.5 and 1.6)?

- The teacher listens carefully to understand children's communication.

- The teacher is warm and encouraging during interactions.

- The teacher gets on the children's eye level and maintains good eye contact with each child while interacting.

- The teacher is empathetic.

- The teacher is not harsh, intrusive, or punitive.

The Child–Parent Relationship: The First Dance

The three principle players in our model of relationship-based programs—child, parent, and teacher—can also be considered in terms of the relationships that develop between them: child–parent, child–teacher, and teacher–parent (see Figure 1.1). The following sections focus on what is happening *between* the players, beginning with the child–parent relationship. Much has been written by many fine authors about the child–parent relationship (e.g., Brazelton & Cramer, 1989; Thoman & Browder, 1987). Particularly, it is understood that the child's sense of

---

BOX 1.6.
Teacher less likely to display sensitivity

Susan really did not want to be a toddler teacher, but it was the only job she could find. Her own parents raised her with firm discipline, an attitude that she even applies to babies. Her director told her that they do not spank children, so Susan does not spank. However, when the babies misbehave, she speaks sharply to them because she thinks that will teach them what is expected.

BOX 1.7.
Positive infant–mother relationship

Antonio is 10 months old. When his mother comes to the center to pick him up, he looks up, brightens, and with great animation crawls to her. She stops midsentence in her conversation with the teacher to respond to Antonio. She picks him up, and they gaze into each other's eyes. He snuggles close to her, and she molds her arms and shoulders around him and hugs him. It is so clear they are very happy to see one another; when they are together, each is the most important person in the world to the other.

---

security described previously emerges as a result of the interactions that occur early in the child–parent relationship (Ainsworth, 1979).

How can you recognize relationships that are developing well between children and parents? The features of good relationships are very similar to the characteristics of securely attached children and sensitive parents because they are interrelated. However, there are some distinctions. Actions and behaviors of the child outside of the parent–child relationship, response of the parent to people in general and to the child specifically, and relationship between the child and the parent when the two of them are together can be observed.

Features that reflect positive relationships between infants and parents include the following (see Boxes 1.7 and 1.8):

- The child and parent seek eye contact with each other.

- When the child and parent are reunited, both seem very happy to see one another.

- The child and parent adjust their responses to one another.

- The child and parent mold their bodies to the other and seek physical contact with one another.

BOX 1.8.
Parent–child relationship at risk

Marisa is also 10 months old. Her mother has had some difficulties with depression. Marisa plays silently at the center. When her mother comes to pick her up, she talks to the teacher about the day and then goes to pick Marisa up. Marisa comes willingly but does not extend her arms; her mother holds her somewhat stiffly. This relationship needs support to infuse it with vitality to help mother and child each bring and obtain energy in the relationship.

The Child–Teacher Relationship: The Extended Dance

Although much is known about the child–parent relationship, less has been written about the child–teacher relationship. Therefore, ways to promote child–teacher relationships are emphasized in *Extending the Dance*. The child–teacher relationship may be seen as an "extended dance" because, from the child's point of view, this dance extends on the child–parent relationship dance. Although many features are similar to the child–parent dance, the child–teacher dance is unique in some ways.

The child–teacher relationship is a security-promoting relationship resulting in attachment relationships for the child (van IJzendoorn, Sagi, & Lambermon, 1992). Researchers have compared the child–parent relationship with the child–teacher relationship by systematically examining all of the features of attachment in both sets of relationships (Howes & Hamilton, 1992). They have concluded that the child–teacher attachment relationship functions in ways that are similar to how a child–parent attachment relationship functions by supporting the child's development. (Also, see Box 2.2 for more about child–teacher relationships as attachment relationships.)

From the child's point of view, a secure relationship with a teacher in a child care setting replicates the function of a secure parent–child relationship in the home setting. Children use the teacher as their secure base throughout the day. They appear to explore and play more if they are secure with the teacher and if the teacher is present during their playtimes. Children have increased opportunities for language and cognitive development during these explorations, as well as more opportunities for teacher input on what they are learning, when the child–teacher relationship is a secure one. When children are secure in this relationship, they turn to the teacher for comfort when they are upset or stressed. This is important because a child who is comfortable turning to the teacher for comfort does not suffer alone. Such a child is comforted by contact and physical comfort when the teacher holds, rocks, pats, and sits beside the child. A child who is secure with the teacher is somewhat comfortable leaving the parent in the morning. If the relationship with the parent is also secure, the child is happy to see the parent when he or she returns.

The security-promoting relationship with a teacher develops in the same way that a security-promoting relationship with a parent develops. Teachers who are sensitive, respond contingently, interact with animation, provide contact comfort, and are consistent and predictable throughout the day encourage secure relationships with children (Goossens & van IJzendoorn, 1990; Howes, 1999).

How can you recognize child–teacher relationships that are developing well (see Boxes 1.9 and 1.10)?

- The teacher and child seek eye contact with one another.
- The teacher and child brighten at the sight of one another.
- The teacher and child adjust their responses to the other.

BOX 1.9.
Positive teacher–child relationship

Susie is 18-month-old Amity's teacher. In the morning when Amity's mother is dropping her off, Susie has a deep sense of respect for the relationship between Amity and her mother and gives them time to say good-bye. Amity is generally happy to then turn to her teacher. Susie and Amity seem to genuinely enjoy one another during the activities of the day. They look at each other often and smile and laugh frequently. When reading, Amity curls up for a few moments in Susie's arms, Susie strokes Amity's arm, and Amity pats Susie's arm. At naptime, Susie pats Amity's back and provides comfort when she is distressed. Amity uses playtime productively. She engages throughout the room with the materials and uses Susie as a secure base—occasionally looking at or coming to Susie to check in. During those moments, Susie may talk to Amity and extend on her thinking so Amity is growing in language and cognitive development through her explorations. The teacher–child relationship is a positive one; Susie is promoting Amity's sense of security and competence through the relationship.

- The child relaxes when held by the teacher, and the child and teacher seek physical contact with one another.
- The teacher's presence is comforting to the child.
- The child plays productively when the teacher is in the room, using the teacher as a secure base.

The Teacher–Parent Relationship: The Supportive Dance

There is still another dance in our model—the supportive dance between teachers and parents. In an infant and toddler program, the relationships between teachers

---

BOX 1.10.
Teacher–child relationship at risk

Jaren is also 18 months old; his teacher is Michelle. Michelle does not want children to get "too attached" to her so she is careful not to encourage Jaren to come to her during playtime. She gets up when he comes to her and turns him around so he will go play again. When he cries, she leaves the room. Throughout the day, she tries to leave the room often so she can "break him" of his attachment. The relationship between Michelle and Jaren is not a positive one for Jaren and increases his insecurity.

---

and parents are extremely important; good relationships are needed to support the development of the child. The three dances (child–parent, child–teacher, and teacher–parent) are interrelated. The teacher–parent relationship is extremely important for supporting the other dances between the players. Because infants cannot represent their own needs and daily histories to teachers and parents, parents and teachers need to communicate well and work very closely together. The teacher–parent dance provides the infrastructure for good things for babies.

In an infant and toddler program, the teacher–parent relationship dance occurs multiple times throughout the day. On arrival, the parent passes on information about the child's previous evening and day so far. The teacher can set a positive tone for the rest of the parent's day by listening carefully, taking cues from the parent and infant regarding how much they want to talk and cuddle before the separation, and giving the parent a confident sense that the infant will be attended to carefully. Throughout the day, the teacher records information so that the parent can get a clear sense of the infant's day. This information is thoroughly conveyed to the parent at the end of day. Sometimes, it may be necessary for the teacher to communicate with the parent during the work-day (e.g., when it is time to breast-feed, if the child has spiked a fever). These calls express just the right amount of concern and empathy for both child and parent. In addition, parents often have many questions about child rearing, whereas teachers often have helpful views about how to solve everyday problems (e.g., teething, behaviors) because of their experience with many children. Parents also can extend on learning if teachers provide them with observations of children's learning, including what subjects excite the children most. Finally, the teacher and parent often need to work very closely together for consistency around issues such as the use of a pacifier, bottle feeding, toilet training, or biting.

Features of a healthy teacher–parent relationship include the following (see Box 1.11):

- The parent and teacher both seem comfortable and honest in sharing information with one another.

- The parent and teacher go out of their way to build communication.

- The parent is comfortable in the infant care room and center.

- The teacher does not talk negatively about the parent. Rather, the teacher has empathy for the parent's issues.

- The teacher honors the parent's values and child-rearing preferences.

- The teacher recognizes the concerns that most parents have about parenting and helps the parent to gain confidence and skill in parenting.

- The teacher positively portrays the child's good qualities and cognitive, language, and social-emotional interests and growth. This information helps the parent to gain confidence and skill in promoting the child's development.

BOX 1.11.
Supportive teacher–parent relationships

Jane is an infant teacher; Mary is the new parent of Nate, who is under Jane's care. The first day in the center, Mary brought 15 pages of written instructions sharing all of the many fine points about caring for Nate. That day she was teary and fearful of leaving him, even though she had visited four times and Jane had come to their home. Jane fully understood Mary's normal feelings about separation and was gentle and supportive. She said she would call Mary the second she thought Nate was ready to nurse, and Mary could call or come over anytime during the day. Jane has helped many parents return to work and understands what parents need. She is pleased that she can provide that support and continuously works to make changes in advance of children's start at the center to make the transition smoother.

————————————

Carla has been caring for Hannah for 2 years now. She has gotten very close to Hannah's parents, who regard her "almost like a member of our family." They have been through a lot together—like when Hannah had the chickenpox and later when Hannah spiked the high fever when her mother was out of town. Another time, Hannah's mother broke her leg, and Carla helped the family figure out how to navigate this problem.

————————————

Sue is 9-month-old Mandy's teacher. Jessica is Mandy's mother. Each month, Sue and Jessica talk about Mandy's development and plan activities and interactions they will both do with Mandy. They are beginning to introduce baby signs to her and have coordinated which ones they will use and which ones they will emphasize. Sue reports through a portfolio —with photos and narrative—about Mandy's developmental encounters, particularly those they have tried to emphasize this month. Through this exchange, Jessica is learning a great deal about child development.

Children's Relationships with Other Children

Children's relationships with their peers are also important in relationship-based programs. Children who remain together over time in programs are sometimes referred to as *nursery (crèche) mates,* but more often they are called *peers.* As children gain security from predictable relationships with teachers and parents, they also derive joy and continuity from the children they see each day. Some people may not think that infants and toddlers have sophisticated relationships with one another. Although it is true that the more complicated dimensions of relationships do not appear until later in the preschool years, babies become accustomed to each other and derive comfort from the presence of familiar children. Babies as young as 3 or 4 months are often delighted by the cherub faces and antics of other babies. They quickly pick out both babies and adults with whom they are familiar. At 9–10 months of age, infants have been observed playing Peekaboo and other simple games with each other. By 2 years of age, children may play in parallel with one another, such as in the sandbox or with pretend materials (e.g., holding dolls and pretending they are "babies").

When children in a relationship-based program who have been together through birth to age 3 years move to preschool as a group, the children do quite well in preschool, possibly because they provide each other with a sense of security in the new adventure of preschool. Continuity and familiarity seem to promote the quality of young children's peer relations. One study found better peer relations among children who had been together as a group and who had secure relations with their teachers (Erickson, 1991).

In the same way, parents of children who stay together through birth to 3 years become quite connected to each other, often sharing weekend child care and convening children for playgroups or birthday parties. One group of peers who eventually attended different elementary schools in Lincoln, Nebraska, intentionally played on the same soccer team through all of elementary, middle, and high school. The first author attended a shared high school graduation celebration for a group of children who began an infant program together, even though the children graduated from multiple high schools. The bonds formed among children and parents remained strong over the years, even after children were dispersed across many schools over 18 years. Chapter 9 further discusses children's peer relationships.

The following positive behaviors between children may help teachers and parents note when strong peer relationships are forming (see Box 1.12):

- Children seem to brighten when other children in their group appear. As they get older, they routinely greet others.

- As they gain language, children learn to recognize and speak the names of other children. The teacher may help in promoting this process in many ways.

- Children play little games with each other, even if briefly.

- As they get older, around age 2–3 years, children may show empathy or recognition of the distress of another child and may try simple things to help.

- Children may move to be closer to other children.

- As they get older, children may require teacher support less when special friends are around.

> **BOX 1.12.**
> ## Peer relationships in a relationship-based program
>
> Two-year-old Sarah watches when Scoutie comes into the center. Scoutie is sad about her mother leaving, so Sarah gives Scoutie her blanket.
>
> ──────────────
>
> Mary and Kelsey are 10 months old. They are crawling on the floor at the center. A little rubber ball rolls away from Mary. Kelsey gets the ball and hits it, and Mary crawls for it. They seem to be playing together.

The Parent Community

A strong relationship-based program offers opportunities for parents to connect with each other. Many riches that are good for children follow from parents engaging with other parents. For example, parents may compare notes about parenting and learn from one another. This helps parents develop a sense of normalcy about the little problems all children encounter during the early years (e.g., not sleeping through the night, difficulties with toilet training). Parents also learn about expectations for children of different ages and techniques for optimizing children's development. Parents form a community and may stage gatherings (e.g., parties, events) that provide children with comfortable settings for further socialization.

Children perceive when parents have a positive and comfortable feeling about a setting. They mirror the attitudes they see in their parents. If parents are happy and engaged with other parents, teachers, and children in the center, the child learns that this is the way to feel about people. Chapter 8 provides more discussion about encouraging relationships among parents.

How can you recognize parent community in an infant care center (see Box 1.13)?

- Parents get to know other parents; they greet and talk to each other.

- Parents are invited to meetings and group sessions where they can talk honestly about parenting.

- Parents may attend social gatherings that include other parents.

- Parents share information about parenting. They support and encourage each other.

- Parents help each other out with children and provide parenting support for each other.

BOX 1.13.
Parent support in a relationship-based program

Mary and Judy check into the child care center with their toddlers early in the morning. As they do so, they make plans for Judy to take Mary's child home with her that evening because Mary needs to go to the doctor.

_____

The parents in the toddler room are gathering for pizza with the teacher. They are all gathering to talk about toddler development and share tips for children's development during this phase.

_____

Parents bring clothing their children have outgrown. They donate these articles, and the center uses the funds for a scholarship.

The Teacher Community

The relationships among teachers constitute the final element of our model. Teachers support one other and help each other learn the expectations within the program. Some of these relationships may be formalized (e.g., master teachers may mentor head teachers, head teachers may mentor assistant teachers), but all teachers can participate in a spirit of learning and support. In such communities, a "we're all in this together" attitude is readily discernable. One program refers to this spirit of openness to learning and growing as their "circle of learning."

In some programs, teachers work in pairs or threesomes over the entire infant and toddler period. With such a close arrangement, teachers' relationships need to be very positive and supportive. On occasion, directors or master teachers may need to help the team resolve conflicts. Disagreements—when handled well—can become a very healthy way for people to learn about their differences, preferences, and strengths. Teams can mobilize around the strengths of individuals as these characteristics become apparent.

Some programs build community among the staff in intentional ways using structured activities that help to identify the personality types of individuals and preferences for different approaches to handling situations. Then, when difficult situations arise, staff may be less surprised at the reactions of individuals. Also, people whose strengths lend themselves to the needed skills can rise to the occasion as natural leaders. Other situations may require another teacher's skills, as

---

BOX 1.14.
Positive relationships within the teacher–teacher community

Shar and Diane have worked together for the past 2.5 years, each with their own small group of toddlers but in the same room together. Their relationship is light and fluid. They seem to sense when to step in with each other's children and when the other needs a break. There is laughter and energy when they combine their groups for music and playground times.

The teachers of the infant and toddler center are gathered in the atrium on a Saturday morning. They are excited because a special speaker has been invited and they will have time for planning for the next term. They look forward to these times when they can talk freely about their work, problem solve, and think intentionally about what they are learning.

---

everyone has strengths that may be applicable in different situations. Chapter 10 talks more about teacher–teacher and teacher–administrators relationships.

How can you recognize community among teachers (see Box 1.14)?

- Teachers help other teachers and problem-solve within teams.

- Teachers help each other grow and learn.

- Teachers know and talk about the strengths of one another.

- Teachers encourage each other verbally.

- Teachers are considerate of other teachers (e.g., they do not take a longer break than entitled).

- Teachers recognize that they are a community and come together for the good of all.

THE PLAN FOR THIS BOOK

Now that we have described the elements of relationship-based programming, readers will naturally want to know how to implement these features. We turn to that theme in the second part of this book (Chapters 4–10), which focuses on practical aspects of implementing relationship-based programming. First, however, Chapter 2 offers a brief review of the relatively new literature that grounds our understanding of the powerful role that relationships play in infant development. Chapter 2 is more scholarly and theoretical than other chapters in *Extending the Dance* and is less concerned with practice. We encourage you to dive in, embrace the literature, and read about some of the fascinating studies that have taught us so much about the important process relating to infant–adult relationships.

Chapter 3 broadens the context so that the cultural aspects of caregiving may be considered carefully. Relationship-oriented programs have a certain connection with human cultural traditions. When programs begin with a focus on close relationships, they evidence many universal features. We emphasize these timeless aspects of relationship-focused work with infants and want the reader to be grounded in this orientation. Also emphasized are the cultural differences in how families raise children. Honoring this diversity is a component of forming relationships with parents and supporting relationships within the parent community.

Chapters 4–7 emphasize how to implement relationship-promoting programs. These chapters include a closer look at features that may define a relationship-oriented model, special ways of orienting children and parents at the start of child care, keeping teachers and children together throughout infancy, creating space to support small groups, observing and extending children's learning, and documenting children's growth and development. Chapters 8–10 return to the supportive dances of the model: building close relationships with parents, supporting children's peer relationships, and hiring and building a culture with relationship-oriented staff. A number of chapters describe outstanding relationship-oriented programs from places around the United States and the wider world, particularly Italy. Each chapter highlights features of relationship-oriented programs through descriptions of model centers or systems. By engaging in this book, we are hopeful that you will find guidance for understanding and implementing a relationship-based program whether you are a teacher in training, teacher in practice, or administrator. We also think that parents may find the book helpful for understanding what to expect from a relationship-based program and for understanding the benefits of the child–teacher dance—a dance that extends on the one they have begun with the child.

CHAPTER 2

The First Dance

Foundations of Attachment
and Development in the Early Years

From the beginning of life, children try to engage and interact with the people around them. When comfortable and fed, they direct their attention and interest outward toward others who seem friendly, exciting, or loving. Children reach out to get responses by sending signals of distress or pleasure as they try to help manage the pace, flow, and intensity of interaction with other people. Children actively strive to participate in the life around them. They are relationship-seeking creatures whose very survival depends on their success at establishing relationships. Without intimate, nurturing responses from others, children become too upset and exhausted to accept food and comfort. They cannot make sense of sensory stimulation or understand, connect to, or care about the world.

Sensitive, emotionally available adults create the framework for this vital interaction in the process of meeting an infant's basic needs. Caregivers respond to a baby's cues, engage the baby in mutual gazes, communicate with gurgles and coos and later with language, move in synchrony, imitate the baby, and respond appropriately when the baby cries. The baby, who is born with a primary ability to share emotions with other human beings and a need to affiliate and "learn a culture," eagerly finds a way to join in and play along. Many infant psychologists have noted how much the reciprocal responsiveness between parent and child seems like a dance.

Parents are usually their children's first and most important partners in the dance of interaction, but other people become partners when the dance of primary relationships is extended to new relationships. In this book, we show how child care providers can play a primary role as educational professionals. Certainly, there is not only one appropriate solution. Just as there are many styles of dancing, so throughout the world, different cultural, ethnic, and linguistic communities have found alternative ways to embed their children in close, rhythmic relationships with caring people. The style, language, and customs may vary, but their essence is similar, and the primary needs and wants of children are the same (Whiting & Edwards, 1988). Chapter 1 outlined the elements of relationship-based programs, acknowledging meaningful variation that is likely to emerge in different cultures and settings. This chapter, which is more research-based and theoretical, delves more deeply into the relationship-oriented literature that underlies the practice of emphasizing relationships in infant and toddler settings.

IMPORTANCE AND OUTCOMES OF EARLY RELATIONSHIPS: A HISTORICAL REVIEW

The secrets of the infant–caregiver relationship have been pursued by many investigators from different disciplines, including developmental and clinical psychology, social work, education, anthropology, and family history. Much has been discovered about how infants and parents together actively shape the formation of their first relationships, the ways in which this fitting becomes the frame for children's learning in many areas, and the organization or deep structure of these primary relationships inside children. This deep structure has its own properties—rhythms that seem to cut across many modalities and patterns that emerge out of others—that suggest the dance metaphor.

The history of attachment concepts takes us back to the beginning of the 20th century. The founder of psychoanalysis, Sigmund Freud (1903/1953), theorized about the long-lasting significance of children's relationships to their mothers. He was followed by several clinicians such as Harold Skeels (1936), who studied child development in orphanages, and Rene Spitz (1965), who made an important film in 1947 about infant grief. However, John Bowlby (1907–1990) was the father of modern attachment theory. Bowlby studied and qualified as a psychoanalyst, but he made a major breakthrough by shifting the arena of study from the traditional focus on people's memories of infancy to a more direct study of infancy itself. He did this by incorporating observational methods and an ethological perspective drawn from biology into his thinking.

Bowlby's interest in early relationships was inspired by work with antisocial adolescents at the London Child Guidance Clinic (Bowlby, 1944). What Bowlby learned about the boys' behavior and histories caused him to believe that many children's problems could be related not to internal fantasies and wishes, but rather to their actual parenting experiences and the separations and losses they suffered due to such situations as illness, hospitalization, incarceration, or parental death. At the end of World War II, Bowlby was asked by the head of the World Heath Organization to write a report on homeless refugee children, who were stranded by the thousands in postwar Europe. After consulting with many experts and reading widely, Bowlby (1951) wrote a major manifesto, *Maternal Care and Mental Health*, which had transforming effects in waking policy makers and the public to the potentially devastating effects of parental loss and separation on young children's emotional development.

In 1946, Bowlby took a job at the Tavistock Clinic in London and became deputy director of the children's department. There he instituted a major change in child therapy by seeing children and their mothers together, rather than the traditional method of sending the child to the psychologist and the mother to the social worker. Thus, Bowlby kept the focus on the relationship itself and how each partner was affecting the other. Bowlby had many important students and close colleagues who added to his work, including James and Joyce Robertson. The Robertsons made a touching series of films, *Young Children in Brief Separation,* that are perhaps the most detailed visual portrayal ever made of how toddlers experience stress and coping when separated from their parents in a strange place (e.g., *A Two-Year-Old Goes to the Hospital, Nine Days in a Residential Nursery*). These films were influential in reforming modern hospital practices to make stays as brief as possible and allow overnight parental stays.

According to Bowlby (1969, 1973, 1980), the child's needs and the parent's caregiving responses are the nucleus of early relationships, culminating in the attachment of the infant to the parent (and the parent's attachment to the child). Bowlby presented the first convincing evidence that early relationships unfold through distinct phases from birth to age 3 years and a theory based in ethology of how attachments function to promote the child's survival. The child's tie to the mothering figure acts as an invisible bond that keeps both child and parent in proximity to each other. Bowlby used a control systems model to argue that the attachment relationship allows the child to maintain optimal emotional comfort. A parent needs to provide appropriate kinds and levels of stimulation to help the baby regulate states of arousal (i.e., to "come down" when overaroused or upset and to "come up" when bored, understimulated, or ready for play and exploration). By helping the child in this way, the parent guides the child to develop comfortable body rhythms, learn how to maintain emotional equilibrium, and cycle relatively smoothly through states of attention, distress, and sleep during the day and night. The parent promotes the child's survival by providing comfort, protection, nutrition, and cultural knowledge.

Bowlby provided the first persuasive theory of how attachments function to promote the child's adaptation, characterizing both the survival aspects of attachments and the grief infants experience when the continuity of caregiving is lost (e.g., when children are hospitalized). According to Bowlby, the child's tie to the mother figure acts like an invisible bond that keeps both child and parent in appropriate proximity to each other. Behaviors like looking, smiling, calling, crying, following, and clinging are concrete indicators of the child's attachment and the practical means by which the child maintains the desired degree of proximity (see Box 2.1).

Another researcher, Mary Salter Ainsworth, was born in Ohio in 1913 and studied psychology in Canada before she went to Britain to work with Bowlby as a researcher on his team. Recognizing her brilliance, Bowlby supported Ainsworth's early studies of child behavior in the natural environment and the

---

BOX 2.1.
Attachment

- *What is attachment?*—Attachment is an enduring tie to a familiar, specific person. It is a formation or representative of a relationship with an inner organization and with outward signs that are called attachment behaviors.

- *What is its function?*—Attachment promotes survival by helping the child modulate his or her level of arousal so that the child can securely explore and learn.

- *To whom is attachment directed?*—Attachment can be to one or a few people, though the child has a hierarchy of preference.

- *How is it evidenced?*—Attachment behaviors include secure base behavior, distress at separation, joy at reunion, and maintenance over a separation.

- *What builds it?*—Attachment is built through sensitivity to the child's cues (responsiveness); availability (adult is there when needed); a cooperating, not coercive, control style; and predictability.

- *What undermines it?*—Intrusive, adult-centered style of interaction; physical rejection (of child's bids to be close); and depression (because it influences interaction patterns) can undermine attachment.

- *Do individual differences affect attachment?*—Different children require very different amounts of time to build an attachment relationship. Some children are more selective and exclusive, whereas others are more accepting and open. Children's temperaments affect what they experience as sensitive care and cooperative guidance, but temperament does not influence the quality of attachment. Children of all temperaments can form secure attachments (including both fussy and cheery babies).

steps she took to create an empirical methodology for measuring the degree to which a child is securely or insecurely attached. Ainworth's observations of how the attachment relationship develops over the first 2 years of life—first in a village in Uganda (Ainsworth, 1967) and then in Baltimore (Ainsworth, Blehar, Waters, & Wall, 1978)—were the basis for her typology for reliably classifying different types of secure and insecure attachment relationships.

Ainsworth extended Bowlby's conceptualization and identified many antecedents and sequelae of attachment relations. Ainsworth characterized attachment as an adaptive mechanism for infants. If parents fulfill a number of now well-identified behaviors, then infants develop security of attachment, manifesting around 9 months of age, which further serves the next phases of development. Ainsworth demonstrated that mothers whose children are later securely attached responded contingently to their babies' communications. For example, if a baby cried, the mother responded quickly. One of the Ainsworth studies showed that mothers who responded readily to their babies' cries in the first 3 months of life had babies who cried less at 6–9 months of age (Bell & Ainsworth, 1972). Another study showed that mothers who responded to their babies' communications with joyful and exaggerated facial expressions had more securely attached babies at a later age (Ainsworth, 1979). Ainsworth also demonstrated that mothers who responded with appropriateness to their babies' communications had infants who were more securely attached than others (Ainsworth et al., 1978). These mothers were able to determine what their babies needed and met the need. Altogether, Ainsworth noted that contingent and appropriate responsiveness could be characterized as sensitivity in parenting, which she believed to be the main mechanism by which children become securely attached. Sensitivity has been frequently studied as a powerful feature of early parent–child relationships.

According to Ainsworth, many benefits for infants emanate from sensitive parenting and later from the security of attachment that forms. Infants' basic needs for survival, touch, and stimulation flow from early caregiving sensitivity, which build to create a sense of predictability in the child that is characterized by some as a *sense of trust* (Erikson, 1950). A hungry infant with this sense of trust or predictability knows that approaching footsteps indicate good things to follow (e.g., warm milk, loving arms, soft talk from the caregiver). This sense of trust also emboldens the child. A number of studies with babies (e.g., Ainsworth et al., 1978) and rhesus monkeys (Harlow, 1958) showed that a secure youngster actually uses the parent as a secure base, staying close by the parent when frightened and checking back when venturing to explore, as if to "recharge" or simply for reassurance that the parent is still there. A child with this sense of security thus is nourished as needed by the relationship but also uses the relationship as a base for further exploration and stimulation. The sensitive parent adds to this process by noting the child's discoveries, supplying information, and providing support so that the child continues to expand his or her explorations.

Ainsworth and colleagues (1978) characterized these secure attachments as adaptations—the result, in many cases, of the infant balancing needs with the sensitive and timely responses of caregivers. As defined by Ainsworth, *secure children* are able to use their parents' presence and proximity as a source of emotional refueling. Children seek contact and interaction from their present parents to sustain their exploration and enjoyment of the environment. When their parents leave, children are distressed. When their parents return, children again seek contact and reassurance to calm themselves down and begin to play again. Once comforted, children jump back into the play that interests them.

Ainsworth further found, in contrast to the secure pattern, that some children's overtures to their parents are treated dismissively, coldly, or with rejection in regards to social and physical contact. The child then adapts by forming a type of attachment that is more avoidant. *Avoidant (insecure) children* are characterized by a more distant style in the presence of their parent (e.g., little eye contact) and by avoidant responses to parents following separation. Avoidant children do not regularly use parents as a secure base. Sometimes these children are seen by outsiders as being very independent; however, on closer inspection, the child's vitality seems to be blunted and the child's opportunities for emotional contact with the parent are truncated.

Ainsworth defined a third pattern of behavior: *Insecure anxious ambivalent children* (also called *ambivalent* or *resistant*) are distressed by separations and very much want their parents back, but yet they resist and push their parents away when they arrive. These children strive mightily to get to their parents but are not satisfied and fully calmed by them, remaining cranky and irritable even as their parents try in vain to console them. Ambivalent children communicate less through looks, smiles, and little interactions than do the secure children. They have a more restricted range of affects that they express and subject matters to talk about (Cassidy, 1988). These children tend to mix their intimacy-seeking behaviors with anger or hostility.

Disorganized and disoriented children were identified by Main and Solomon (1990) as they tried to understand the behavior of children who could not be easily classified into any of Ainsworth's three categories. These children display contradictory and sometimes bizarre behavior that does not involve a predictable and coherent pattern of attachment. In one situation or with one parent, the behavior takes one pattern. In a different situation, the behavior looks entirely different, sometimes in strange ways involving unexpected eruptions of negative emotion. Later studies have connected disorganized and disoriented behavior with experiences of extreme stress or maltreatment.

Research on relationships has expanded enormously in the years since Bowlby and Ainsworth introduced their concepts of attachment. Some aspects of the research are still controversial, such as possible cultural differences and long-term effects of early attachments, but the central theory and findings are widely accepted. The authoritative book on the subject, *Neurons to Neighborhoods*, said,

"Human relationships and the effects of relationships on relationships are the building blocks of health development. Those created in the earliest years are believed to be formative and constitute a basic structure into which meaningful development unfolds" (Shonkoff & Phillips, 2000, pp. 27–28). There is general agreement that relationships formed with secondary caregivers (e.g., teachers, grandparents) have many features that are similar to those of primary attachment relationships. Box 2.2 briefly summarizes the literature as it pertains to infant–teacher attachment.

BOX 2.2.
Child–teacher attachment

The infant's relationships with the teacher or child care providers are sometimes characterized as secondary attachments (primary attachment is the parent). Here, detailed findings are presented from the infant–caregiver attachment literature, including how attachment figures outside of the family have been identified and what is known about development of and effects of attachment relations in child care settings.

HOW TO IDENTIFY ATTACHMENT FIGURES OUTSIDE THE FAMILY

Some researchers proposed that attachment figures outside the family should provide physical and emotional care to the child and emotionally invest in the child continually and consistently (Howes, 1999). Van IJzendoorn and colleagues also proposed that infant–teacher attachment is independent from infant–parent attachment, related to the sensitivity of the teacher, and can predict the child's social-emotional adjustment (van IJzendoorn, Sagi, & Lambermon, 1992, as cited in Howes, 1999).

Multiple studies have supported van IJzendoorn and colleagues' concepts of infant–teacher attachment. For example, studies have found that caregiver–child attachment was not correlated with mother–child or father–child attachment (e.g., Goossens & van IJzendoorn, 1990), which suggests that infant–caregiver attachment is a unique relationship instead of "an extension of the infant–parent attachment" (Cassibba, van IJzendoorn, & D'Odorico, 2000). However, another study found child–mother and child–caregiver security were significantly related (Booth, Kelly, Spieker, & Zuckerman, 2003).

Goossens and van IJzendoorn (1990) found that teachers of secure infants were more sensitive to infants' signals during free play compared with teachers of insecure infants. Similarly, Howes and Smith (1995b) showed that children who were securely attached to their teachers had teachers with higher responsiveness scores compared with children who were insecurely attached to their teachers. Those two studies further

---

(continued)

Box 2.2 (continued)

supported van IJzendoorn's notion that teachers' sensitivity related to infant–teacher attachment.

Researchers also found the security with teachers was associated with children's higher cognitive levels of play (Cassibba et al., 2000), more gregarious behaviors, and less hostile aggression (Howes, Hamilton, & Matheson, 1994; Howes, Matheson, & Hamilton, 1994). The notion that child care providers are a category of alternative attachment figures is thus supported by different empirical studies.

DEVELOPMENT OF ALTERNATIVE ATTACHMENT RELATIONSHIPS

Because the research has shown that infant–teacher attachment relates to positive outcomes in infants, it is of interest to know how this attachment relationship is developed. Using Attachment Q Sorts, researchers found that infants who were securely attached to their caregivers spent more time with caregivers (Goossens & van IJzendoorn, 1990), and security scores increased when children spent more time with the child care providers (Raikes, 1993). Children also directed more attachment behaviors to the long-term staff members and were more likely to be soothed by them compared with short-term staff members (Barnas & Cummings, 1997). Those findings suggest that the formation of infant–teacher attachment is a similar process to infant–mother attachment. When children spend more time with the teacher, they direct more attachment behavior and tend to develop more secure attachment with the teacher. They respond differently to the long-term teacher or caregiver, which might indicate a unique tie between them.

When children get older, they are more likely to see teachers as organizers instead of comfort providers, which influences their attachment behaviors. For example, in the Howes and Smith study (1995a), 50% of the children in the sample were classified as avoidant. Further examination of this avoidant group showed it was a misclassification; one third of those children had a high score on the Avoiding the Caregiver subscale but also had a high security score. The majority of this misclassified group were preschoolers instead of toddlers. As a result, Howes (1999) suggested different processes for older versus younger children, who often seek comfort from the caregiver within close contact. Alternatively, these older children use the caregiver to organize their social and learning environment, instead of spending time in close contact with the caregiver. Also in the Howes and Smith (1995b) study, children with higher security scores with their caregivers were most frequently engaged in competent exploration of the environment and enhanced cognitive activity, even when richness of available activities and teacher facilitation of individual children's play were controlled for. Those two studies support the idea of teacher as organizer instead of comforter for older children.

Box 2.2 (continued)

SUMMARY

Many infants have multiple caregivers outside the family. Researchers have developed criteria to identify particular alternative attachment figures, who may include the child care provider or teacher. (Other alternative attachment figures may include grandparents or foster parents.) There is evidence that infant–teacher attachment is a unique relationship instead of "an extension of the infant–parent attachment" (Cassibba et al., 2000) and that caregiver sensitivity is related to the infant–teacher attachment (Goossens & van IJzendoorn, 1990), which correlates with children's social-emotional development (Cassibba et al., 2000; Howes, Matheson, & Hamilton, 1994). The formation of infant–teacher attachment is a similar process to that of infant–mother attachment.

Children develop attachment with a teacher when they spend more time with the caregiver and when the teacher is sensitive to children's needs. When children get older, they are more likely to see teachers as organizers instead of comfort providers, which influences their attachment behavior.

Prepared by Cixin Wang, Doctoral Student, University of Nebraska–Lincoln.

RELATIONSHIPS AND INFANT DEVELOPMENT

Almost from the beginning of life, quite remarkably, a baby's expressions, natural rhythms, and emerging competencies provide the framework for increasing complexity and connection in relationships with caregivers. These relationships provide the mechanisms through which the baby's needs are met. At each stage of development throughout the infant and toddler years, the baby brings certain characteristics, the parent responds to the child in the context of these characteristics, the relationship grows, and the child develops new abilities that become building blocks for the next stages of life.

Born Dancing: Early Infancy (0–8 Months)

The newborn has characteristics that invite relationships. The parent responds to the infant in ways that promote the infant's ability to adapt and thrive in the postnatal world, draw the infant into a more nuanced relationship, and promote competencies. What are some of these competencies and how do parents respond? What happens to the child when parents respond optimally? To answer these questions, we consider the period from birth to around 8 months of age—an immensely rich period in the life of the infant. During this time, the infant learns the rudiments of physiological regulation, becomes somewhat attuned to important adults in his or her life, produces sounds, and develops expectations about caregiving and having needs met. During this phase, much of what happens in interaction is a function of the sensitivity of the parent or other caregiving adult who uses the child's rhythms as the basis for interaction. This section briefly explores touch, contingent responsiveness, rhythmicity, face-to-face interactions, eye contact, joint attention, sound sequences, and imitation in the infant–parent relationship as building blocks for the infant's development. Many of these features were introduced in Chapter 1. Here we also briefly discuss the research base for each.

Touch   Gentle, rhythmic touch is one of the first ways adults communicate with infants. Infants seem to be predisposed to respond to touch. Tiffany Field and her colleagues studied two groups of premature infants in a neonatal nursery. Both groups received the same number of feedings each day and averaged the same formula intake. One group received 15-minute massage periods at the top of 3 consecutive hours for 10 weekdays. Massaged preterm infants displayed 47% increase in weight gain compared with the infants who did not receive massages. The infants also were more alert and had hospital stays that were an average of 6 days shorter (Dieter, Field, Hernandez-Reif, Emory, & Redzepi, 2003). Most parents intuitively stroke and gently pat their infants, and mothers all over the world have special ways of massaging their infants. In some cultures, massage rituals (sometimes with special oils) are quite elaborate and are passed from one generation of mothers to the next. Field's work and other studies demonstrate what mothers have known for generations—that rhythmic, loving touch is important to infant growth and development.

Contingent Responsiveness   When the infant cries out of hunger, a caring mother provides a breast with warm milk. The infant gains nourishment and may also gain a sense that hunger will be quelled. The person who brings the warm milk provides comfort, and good feelings flood over the infant. Later, when the infant smells, hears, or feels this person, the infant will stop crying because he or she has associated this person with the act of being fed. When an infant's needs are responded to consistently, contingently, and quickly after the need is expressed, the infant begins to build a sense of trust and belief that needs will be met in the future. Continent responding starts at the beginning of a child's life. A number of studies have found that the adult's contingent responding over time strengthens the child's sense of efficacy and competence (Denham, Mitchell-Copeland, Strandberg, Auerbach, & Blair, 1997).

Rhythmicity and Turn Taking   Infants do not "take in" stimulation and nutrients in a steady fashion. Rather, they alternate activity and pauses in a manner that is often highly rhythmic. The pauses seem to invite an adult to introduce warmth, stimulation, or encouragement in tiny "bites" that are manageable for the infant's developing system. During feeding, normal infants will suck, suck, suck and then pause. During the pause, the responsive mother may withdraw the nipple. She may also make eye contact with the infant, smile, caress, or jiggle the nipple to begin the sucking pattern again. The early rhythms show that the infant comes equipped for dancelike interactions. However, what the mother does during "her turn" builds a foundation for later, more elaborate dances between the two of them.

Some scientists have found that the ping-pong or tennis metaphor provides a good way to understand this feature of relationships. They use the idea of "serve and return" to characterize the back-and-forth nature of parent and child (Center on the Developing Child at Harvard University, 2007). Even at a tender age, there are differences among infants. Some have beginning rhythms that will lead to smooth dancing, whereas others barely dance at all. Some parents seem to know how much stimulation and encouragement to provide the infant. These parents help their infants to regulate the flow of stimulation from both the internal and external worlds. However, other parents need guidance on how to provide the regulatory assistance that infants need during this period.

Face-to-Face Interactions, Eye Contact, and Joint Attention

While very young infants are still developing visual acuity, their best focus is at about 10–14 inches—not coincidentally the general distance between the infant's and parent's faces when the baby is held in the parent's arms (Schoetzau, 1979). As their vision sharpens, babies prefer to gaze at faces and will often brighten when encountering a familiar face. Some very young infants are able to imitate parental facial expressions such as tongue protrusions or making a O-shaped mouth (Meltzoff & Moore, 1989, 1992). The parent builds on the baby's fascination with faces by exaggerating facial expressions, moving slowly, and waiting for the infant to make a response. This face-to-face play has many benefits. Researchers have found that very young infants whose parents engaged them in animated face-to-face play were more often securely attached in the latter part of the first year (Blehar, Lieberman, & Ainsworth, 1977). Parents fill in the natural pauses of the infant's actions with their own actions and vocalizations, creating the beginnings of turn taking, which soon the infant can initiate. The infant begins to look in the mother's direction and waits until she responds before smiling or vocalizing. The infant also is disturbed if he or she cannot get a response from the mother (Cohn & Tronick, 1983, 1988). As the infant matures, parents engage him or her in eye contact—back and forth at first and then in locked gazes. This skill builds to joint attention by 6–9 months of age, when the child looks at something in the environment and the parent looks at it, too. With their attention jointly fixed on a common object or event, the infant is in a perfect position to learn myriad lessons about the environment (e.g., naming the object at just the moment mother and child are looking at it together).

Sound Play Researchers have observed that infants have a special response to the human voice, prefer their parents' voices, and can even distinguish subtle differences in sounds (e.g., "ba" versus "pa") within the first few weeks of life. Sensitive parents play sound games and talk to their infants in special ways to obtain and hold the children's attention. Early on, a parent may imitate the cooing and gurgling sounds an infant makes. By about 2 months of age, it is often possible for the infant and parent to exchange coos while the parent listens carefully, fine-tunes responses to match the infant's coos, and makes subtle changes to gradually enlarge the infant's repertoire of sounds and tones. The parent will continue to modify speech, using high tones to get the infant's attention, talking slowly and with exaggeration, and using a form of talking known as "parentese" to impart information about the sounds, meanings, and syntax of the parent's preferred language (Furrow, Nelson, & Benedict, 1979). Thus, many early lessons for language learning are imparted to children in the context of the parent–child relationship. These lessons come in a variety of formats, including language and sound games, simple talk, book reading, nursery rhymes, and songs. All of these methods enhance the infant's growing ability to communicate, particularly when the experiences occur frequently, with joy, and with artful consideration of the child's emerging abilities to understand.

Object Play and Imitation   Adults have many interactions with children using objects, from offering a rattle to shaking, banging, hiding, fitting, pouring, scooping, and measuring. Early understanding about cause and effect, functionality, size, quantity, and space are learned when adults play simple games with infants and objects. At first, infants do not know that objects have permanence (i.e., that they exist even when out of sight) but infants associate their own actions with things that objects do (e.g., the rattle makes a sound when the infant holds it tightly and moves his or her arm up and down). Later, infants' abilities to attune as mentioned previously (e.g., the infant who coos back and forth to imitate sounds) may further enable them to match adults' actions (e.g., The adult pats a drum. The infant lifts his or her hand, and the adult gently guides it to the drum. Then, the adult pats the drum, and the infant pats the drum.). Ina Uzgiris and Joseph McVicker Hunt (1987) showed that infants progress through a complex series of stages in their emerging abilities to comprehend the world of objects. Throughout these stages, the adult synchronously offers toys and introduces their properties. By using object play, the infant's increasing understanding of things in the world grows.

Learning New Steps: Later Infancy (6–12 Months)

During the latter half of the first year of life, the infant continues to depend on relationships for nourishment, love, responses, and information about the world. During this period, many changes occur in the infant: The infant increases intentional communication, begins to understand that things in the world exist in their own right, and demonstrates an idea of a relationship. Another major change during this phase is mobility. The infant now is physically exploring the world, is gaining new understandings of the world, and needs the sense of security the parent provides as a support to navigate this expanding world.

Communicative Competence   At 6–12 months of age, the infant actively plays with sound, often babbling continuously. Interestingly, at the beginning of this phase, infants everywhere make all the sounds in the human lexicon. However, by the end of the phase, they only produce sounds of the language to which they are exposed. This startling finding is testimony to how important language inputs, as they occur in the context of relationships, are to infants and to their active work as language learners. Infants during this stage can also obtain the attention of parents and play many communication games. Most infants produce meaningful words by the end of the period (e.g., "ma-ma"). A relationship-oriented game that many children play during this time is to point and ask about objects, "What's dat?" or "Dat?" This game demonstrates the many skills the infant now has: joint attention with the adult, the notion that things have names, the use of the question in language, pointing as a meaningful gesture, and expectation that the adult will respond. During this and later phases, the vocabularies of children whose parents talk with them frequently and meaningfully increase exponentially. Children whose vocabulary is not expanded in this manner may fall behind their peers in language abilities (Hart & Risley, 1995).

Objects Have Permanence   At about 8–10 months of age, the infant experiences an amazing transformation and begins to understand that objects have permanence. This understanding is enormously important because it provides the underpinning for representing objects using symbols (language) and for the lack of interchangeability of adults in the child's life. For many children, when they know their mother, they will not be convinced that another person can possibly substitute. Stranger anxiety is at its peak. Sensitive adults can provide support during this very dynamic period of the child's life, helping the child to build on the new understandings of the world with all of its implications.

Concept of Relationships: Attachment   In relation to the cognitive shifts occurring, the child's experiences in caregiving and relationships now manifest in a new way—in the child's representation of the relationship. The child now acts in consistent ways as if expecting a loving, supportive response (and thus seeming secure); expecting to be ignored (and thus seeming avoidant); or not knowing what to expect (and thus seeming ambivalent). During this phase, a sensitive parent or caregiver continues to respond contingently and according to the child's needs to provide a sense of trust but also is increasingly cognizant of the need to be a secure base for the child. When the child ventures out to explore, he or she checks back to see if the parent is there. When reassured of the parent's continued presence, the child continues in explorations. Most children venture out to explore but return to the parent as a secure base hundreds of times over the course of a play period. Primate studies by Harry Harlow (1958, 1959) demonstrated the principle that the young explore more freely when in the presence of the reassuring adult as a secure base.

Mobility   Between 8 and 12 months of age, most children begin to crawl or otherwise scoot around, thus changing their entire way of being with the environment. Now, children are active explorers. The adult's new role as an emotional secure base also provides the framework for cognitive lessons. Burton White (1985) demonstrated that effective parents use pauses when children return to the secure base as opportunities to introduce thousands of on-the-fly lessons (one at a time), providing information about the world in warm doses with reassurance and love. White also demonstrated that the most effective parents extended on the child's learning with each new encounter, building on the child's observation by adding tiny, bite-sized lessons in the middle of exchange. Many of these lessons lasted just 10–30 seconds; however, they were effective because they occurred in the context of the child's interest and were often fun. For example, one 11-month-old infant in the study retrieved a small ball, to which the mother replied, "Ball. You have a ball. It rolls," as she rolled it back to him.

Picking Up the Beat:
The Toddler Years (12–36 Months)

Babies make major strides toward independence during the toddler period. By learning to walk, children become capable of getting around by themselves. By learning to talk, they express their own needs and ideas, and by learning to feed themselves and use the toilet, they take care of their own most basic kinds of care. Their parents or big siblings no longer have to carry or hold them all of the time, make guesses as to what they want and feel, nurse or hand-feed them, rock them to sleep, or change their soiled diapers. Cultural communities may differ in the order and timing of these developmental steps, as well as the importance they give to each for describing the maturity of the child, but they all expect children of this age to make big improvements in mobility, communication, and self-care. Accompanying these steps toward autonomy are some less visible but equally significant changes in cognition and emotion: self-concept, communicative competence, cooperation and compliance, empathy and the emergence of standards, and learning about gender and gender roles.

Self-Concept   Between about 15 and 18 months of age, children begin to recognize their own face and to think of themselves as an "I." Extensive studies of children's self-recognition by Lewis and his colleagues (Lewis & Brooks-Gunn, 1979; Lewis, Sullivan, Stranger, & Weiss, 1989) established that toddlers of this age begin to respond to their mirror image as if they know it is their own face they are seeing. Looking at the mirror, they label themselves by name or use personal pronouns such as *I* and *me* (Baldwin, 1897; Kagan, 1981). These behaviors are taken as evidence that children have formed self-concepts: They are aware they are physically distinct from other people and things and know that they are the source (or *agent*) of their own actions, words, ideas, and feelings. However, children do not yet have a sense of the self's continuity and endurance through time, which comes during the preschool years when they acquire an autobiographical or narrative sense of self (Povinelli & Simon, 1998).

Parents help babies to form a concept of the self through play and daily routines. When changing and dressing the baby, the parent may tickle or stroke the child's body in a way that helps the child learn about the different sensations with hands, face, cheeks, tummy, frontside, and backside. This behavior helps the baby develop subjectivity, a prelinguistic awareness of one's own feelings and body boundaries. Likewise, it is often a parent who first holds the baby up to the mirror and points to the baby (e.g., "Look at Jamal!"). The child looks and sees two faces in the mirror, a big face already known and then a little face nearby. Nursery games like Peekaboo and This Little Piggy, which are found in every culture, help children discover their bodies and what they can do.

As infants develop into toddlers, they begin to evaluate themselves. Stipek, Recchia, and McClintic (1992) found that as children approached age 2 years, they showed prideful responses when succeeding with a toy (e.g., pushing shapes into a sorting box, hammering pegs into a pounding bench) by calling their mothers' attention to their accomplishments. Mothers who tended to praise their toddlers more frequently had children who spontaneously showed more pride (even when not being praised) in the laboratory setting. While competitive success at games with rules (i.e., winning versus losing) has little meaning before age 5 years (sometimes later), young children do care about adult approval and disapproval. Parental reactions teach them that some things they do can please other people as well as themselves, as well as the basic rules and outcomes that people seem to care about.

Children also begin to internalize the forms in which the self-conscious emotions of praise, blame, shame, and guilt are expressed to them. The words, bodily postures, and emotional reactions modeled to them become their working models for proper emotional expression in evaluating themselves and others. These complex emotions reveal that toddlers are developing cognitively as well as emotionally because they require children to judge themselves against a standard or see themselves through the eyes of others (Kagan, 1981). Families help the child develop by supporting the emotional language of their culture in a consistent and safe way. For example, in Taiwan and some other Asian communities, it is common to use shame in socializing children. Many parents can be heard saying things like, "Smart boys don't do that. You are embarrassing me." However, benevolent parents do not use shame too harshly, and they balance it with praise and support. In other communities (e.g., many American contexts), parents feel they should use a great deal of explicit praise with their young children. These parents may frequently say things like, "Aren't you great!" and "That is so wonderful," or clap at many baby behaviors. However, it is most effective not to stress this emotion of pride so excessively that the child expects to be praised with every action. Otherwise, the child will become focused on applause for performance and getting praise from others rather than experiencing intrinsic satisfaction from learning to do things.

Communicative Competence   The second and third years of life are a time of stupendous growth in language and communication. The child likes to look at and touch objects that the adult is holding or looking at, and likewise the adult tends to direct attention toward and name the object to which the child is pointing. Together, the parent and child create frames for coordinated joint attention, or *intersubjectivity* (Trevarthen & Hubley, 1978). During these moments, the adult's level of language use and specific words has a strong impact on the child's language development. Mothers who are more likely to combine showing, pointing, and elaborating on the child's words to highlight specific aspects are more likely to have children with advanced language skills (Baldwin, 1995; Zukow-Goldring, 1996). The child's participation in frames of shared book reading at 14 months predicts language skills at age 18 months (Laakso, Poikkeus, & Lyytinen, 1999) and at 24 months (Raikes et al., 2006).

Children usually speak their first words with the intent to communicate between 10 and 16 months, first acquiring words for objects (e.g., *ball, car, bottle*), social interaction (*hello, no, bye-bye*), and some simple concepts (*all gone, up, more*). By 18 months, most toddlers can understand new word meanings easily. Their vocabulary begins to show a rapid increase from a few words a week to a few every day. They also begin to master the grammatical structure of their language, using word order, grammatical markers (e.g., *-s, -ed, -ing*), and little words like prepositions (*of, in, with*) and indicatives (*a, the, this, that*). The average length of their utterances increases rapidly, and they begin to speak in sentences. Although adults rarely correct children when they make mistakes, they do many things that help children learn correct language, such as asking them simple questions, requesting that they speak about things, and responding to the child's questions. The most effective time to supply children with new words or information is when they are showing interest in something and pause to look at the parent. When parents time their verbal inputs to such moments (i.e., frames of coordinated joint attention), rather than interrupting their child when the child is intently playing or trying to get the child to follow their attention, then their infants tend to develop language more quickly (O'Connell & Bretherington, 1984).

Toddlers like to keep close proximity to the adult, rarely straying far. Through this constant shadowing of their attachment figures, they have many opportunities to observe, imitate, and participate in the organized activities of the family and society (Whiting & Edwards, 1988). These learning patterns are impaired when parents are depressed or otherwise unable to respond to their children's desires to share, show things, play, and converse. Psychologists have found many different styles in the ways that children acquire early language (e.g., some comprehend much more than they can produce, some pronounce words very clearly and others do not, some use many gestures to convey meaning, some have large vocabularies of object names, others know many language routines such as songs and rhymes). These variations can be a source of delight to caregivers.

Cooperation and Compliance   During the second year of life, children become capable of learning family and community standards for proper and desirable behavior. They also begin to feel real socialization pressure in most communities around the world (Kopp, 1982; Maccoby & Martin, 1983; Whiting, 1983; Whiting & Edwards, 1988). Children seem to call forth commands and suggestions aroused by their insatiable curiosity in what others are doing, their desires to participate in adult work, and their new abilities to imitate complex adult and peer routines (Kuczynski & Kochanska, 1990; Reingold, 1982; Zahn-Waxler, Radke-Yarrow, Wagner, & Chapman, 1992). They also elicit many commands related to physical dangers, health dangers, and not wandering too far, as well as matters of proper behavior such as cleanliness and hygiene, saying hello and goodbye, and family property. In some places, 3-year-old children even begin to get commands to do simple household and subsistence tasks; however, this can be pleasant for children. For example, in rural Kenya, giving a small child a chore or errand is seen as nurturant and complimentary—a way to flatter the child as being "big" and included in the family group (Edwards & Whiting, 1993; Weisner, 1989).

However, toddlers do not always want to do what adults tell them. They have earned the stereotype of "the terrible twos." Studies have found a peak of resistant and negative behaviors at about 2 years of age, which usually declines by 4 years (Dubin & Dubin, 1963; Spitz, 1957; Wenar, 1982). Across cultures, little girls are more cooperative and responsive to maternal commands and requests and become involved earlier in responsible tasks (Whiting & Edwards, 1988). Toddler boys are more likely than girls to approach hazards that have a risk or injury. They are also less obedient to their mothers' redirections, perhaps explaining why they suffer more accidents and injuries (Morrongiello & Dawber, 1998).

At the same time, toddlers also try to please adults. In play situations, they often comply when they understand a command or ignore it when they do not comprehend what they are supposed to do (Kaler & Kopp, 1990). When the request is comprehensible and timed not to interrupt their ongoing activity, toddlers rush to show what they can do and enjoy any appreciation or attention that follows (Reingold, Cook, & Kolowitz, 1987). However, in nonplayful situations or when the adult forcefully insists on breaking contact or interaction with the child, toddlers may respond to adult requests with loud refusals and noncooperation (Power & Chapieski, 1986).

Toddlers have many ways to express noncooperation. Young toddlers often resort to the simplest strategies of passive noncompliance and direct defiance, whereas older toddlers begin to use more complex strategies like bargaining, negotiation, and direct refusal (Kopp, 1992; Kuczynski & Kochanska, 1990; Kuczynski, Kochanska, Radke-Yarrow, & Girnius-Brown, 1987). Sometimes,

2-year-old children show peaks of crying and tantrums; these may reflect a child's inner struggle between dependency and autonomy. When toddlers become self-aware enough to realize how much they need adults in spite of their desires to do everything for themselves, they may experience a crisis of ambivalence toward their caregivers (Mahler, Pine, & Bergman, 1975). Such struggles around auton-omy are best handled by parents who tolerate ambivalence and respond flexibly to their children's conflicting messages. Similarly, tantrums are best handled by parents who stand back and allow their children to master their feelings and re-gain self-control (Brazelton, 1992). In this way, children demonstrate emotional regulation, which is an important component of self-regulation.

The parent's response therefore makes a big difference in the shaping of par-ent–child relationships during the toddler years. Parent and child behavior often mirror each other. For example, highly negative 2- to 4-year-old children have more negative mothers (Dowdney & Pickles, 1991). The cause-and-effect rela-tions within the cycle of reciprocity are complex. Power assertions by parents (e.g., yelling, punishment) often achieve compliance in the short run because they gen-erate fear and submission, but they are less effective in the long run because par-ents must use them more and more frequently as time goes on. These techniques also may create defiance in the child instead of the desire to please (Maccoby & Martin, 1983). Instead, when mothers use gentler guidance techniques and nonassertive methods of control, their children are more cooperative and less defi-ant (Braungart-Reiker, Garwood, & Stifter, 1997; Crockenberg & Litman, 1990; Donovan, Leavitt, & Walsh, 2000; Lytton, 1979; Power & Chapieski, 1986).

Responsiveness is a quality in children that is created in the relationship between child and adult. A calm and happy toddler helps to create a good atmos-phere in the home. In contrast, a toddler with a difficult temperament—one who is aggressive, unyielding, and unruly in the face of the parent's attempts at guidance—helps to create patterns characterized by high conflict (Patterson, 1982). Parents have the best chance of enlisting their children's willing compliance if they coordinate their behavior with the children's behavior—both in play and in household routines (Westerman, 1990). Parents should apply firm, responsive control within a context of generally positive emotion and a sense of well-being, which leads toddlers toward learning and success.

Empathy and the Emergence of Standards

During the second year, an early moral sense clearly emerges in the toddler (Kagan, 1981). For example, the child may react to flawed objects as "bad" or "dirty" or may be distressed when a standard is transgressed (e.g., "Kitty is on the table!"). Children sometimes get anxious or upset when they see a person hurt, an object broken, or an important rule violated. By age 3 years, children usually show clear moral emotions such as shame and guilt, pride, hurt feelings, the desire to fix things, and the desire to help. The family helps by organizing the child's feelings into constructive actions, such as apologizing, offering sympathy or comfort, seeking to assist or repair, going for help, or inhibiting future transgression. Parental modeling of empathy is certainly important, such as when the parent makes a hurt face and says, "Oh, honey, you fell down. Let me comfort you" (Zahn-Waxler, Radke-Yarrow, & King, 1979).

This early moral behavior is part of the child's developing capacities of coping and self-regulation (Kopp, 1982). From about age 2 years, most toddlers show self-control (i.e., the ability to comply with requests and to delay or stop doing things they know are wrong). At first, children can do this only when an adult is present, but later they will do it even when alone. For example, children will shake their heads, say "no," and refrain from touching the dangerous object—even when their mothers are out of sight. However, the child's mastery of self-control is inconsistent, so a wise parent should not assume that a toddler will remember not to pull the dog's hair when the parent leaves the room. The achievement of self-control comes gradually and involves major transformations in self-awareness, knowledge of social standards, recall memory, and the ability to delay or inhibit responding.

The child's individual personality now becomes important. Different temperaments may call for different parenting styles to ensure optimal development of a moral self and conscience, setting up different dynamics of reciprocal parent–child interaction. Subtle facial responses (e.g., frowns) and gentle correction may work very well with an anxious, sensitive child who responds quickly to parental disapproval. Such a child is easily motivated by shame and guilt. However, a more effortful approach to moral socialization may be required for imperturbable, bold, risk-taking children. These children learn best through strong positive emotions shared between parent and child, such as joyful pride, challenge, and excitement.

Parents who use too much negative socialization with bold children may find themselves resorting to ever-higher levels of anger, yelling, and punishment to control their children. A pattern of increasing and escalating negativity develops. Soon, many times a day, a raging child screams, lashes out, and maybe hits or kicks the mother until she gives in and concedes the battle, a few moments of peace prevail, and then the next round begins again. This is called a *coercive cycle* (Patterson, 1982).

Learning About Gender and Gender Roles During the second and third years of life, children begin to understand that people have a gender. They begin to construct their own gender identity (i.e., the knowledge that one is and always will be a male or female) and learn about male and female roles in their society. Likewise, their families may be becoming more mindful of their child's masculinity or femininity. However, issues of gender are not yet as significant and exciting to toddlers as they will become later. Instead, age groups (e.g., baby, child, adult) are the most fascinating social categories because these concern distinctions that toddlers can see and relate to (e.g., who gets fed a

bottle, who sleeps in a crib, who wears a diaper, who can ride a bike, who drives the car; Edwards, 1986).

By age 3 years, most children become accurate in labeling photographs of themselves and others by gender (Etaugh, Grinnell, & Etaugh, 1989). Toddlers typically master the nouns (e.g., *boy, girl, man, woman*) before the pronouns (*he, she, him, her*) and correctly apply labels to others before consistently labeling themselves. Their understanding of labels does not yet involve the concept of stability over time, however. Three-year-old children sometimes make comments such as, "I'm a girl, but when I'm four, I'll be a boy." By age 3 or 4 years, children are certain about their own gender. They have formed one of the most stable self-categorizations they will make in their lifetimes (Kohlberg, 1966).

Two-year-old children also begin to watch television and look at picture books. From observing the world around them, they begin to construct role knowledge about toys, adult tasks, and behavior roles (Weinraub et al., 1984). Their new "gender schemas" are not tight logical structures, however, but loosely organized clusters of information picked up from multiple sources and connected to emerging concepts of *male* and *female* (Fagot, 1995; Martin, 1993). They also begin to direct more of their social approaches to partners of their same sex. They do not yet exclude or actively avoid opposite-sex children (as they may during the middle school years), but they often show a beginning attraction or preference for others of their own gender, especially when in group play situations such as child care (Maccoby, 1988; Whiting & Edwards, 1988).

What causes these differences? The role of parental socialization in sex-role development has been closely studied and debated for many years (Fagot, 1995). It is believed that the basic processes of gender identification and forming gender preferences are driven by the child's internal cognitive processes more than by external social reinforcement (Maccoby, 1988, 1999). However, the content of the formed gender concepts is strongly affected by culture and family. For instance, in some families, parental gender roles are extremely distinct and fathers never diaper babies or prepare food, which are considered typical women's tasks. In other families, parents cross over and assist each other when needed. Likewise, in some places, toddlers are dressed distinctively in masculine and feminine clothes, whereas elsewhere children's clothing may show little differentiation until later years. Thus, socialization pressure feeds into children's developing self-cognition and provides implicit messages to children about what areas of gendered behavior are most important and how "bad" cross-gender behavior may be. Parents occasionally use external reinforcement as part of this socialization pressure (e.g., "Good girl, feeding your baby doll"). More often, parental emotional reactions subtly steer toddlers toward gender-typed behavior (e.g., Weitzman, Birns, & Friend, 1985). Parents join with the children in influential ways and modify their attention and interest patterns. For example, Caldera, Huston, and O'Brien (1989) found that parents of toddlers (observed in the laboratory) followed their children in play with either same-gender or cross-gender toys, but they became more involved and excited with same-gender toys. The gender-stereotyped toys also elicited gender-typed play: Trucks evoked different, noisier, and more active play than did play with dolls and tea sets—no matter the gender of the parent or child.

Of course, parents are not the only influential adults who influence gender development. Relatives, neighbors, new acquaintances, and especially media models may play heightened roles in creating worlds of gendered meaning for very young children. Furthermore, peers are important in the preschool and school years: boys and girls older than 4 years separate into male and female play-groups in every culture for which children are present in sufficient numbers for choice to be a factor (Whiting & Edwards, 1988).

SUMMARY

Almost from the beginning of life, infants come equipped to respond, engage, develop, and dance in the context of relationships. They look, suck, coo, and communicate using rhythms that burst and pause, go back and forth, and create openings for expansion and information. Reciprocally, these relationships provide the infant with responses and timing that shape and extend skills, attention, and the relationship itself. One of the leading conceptual leaders in the area of infant development, Dr. Robert Emde, captured these dynamic features—bringing to life the sensitive adult and developing child:

> The infant's coherence of experience results from an *emotionally available caregiver* who is continually responsive to an active, self-regulating, emotional infant—an infant who is "getting it right" in the midst of a particular developmental world that is rapidly expanding. (1996, p. 14)

This world expands to include other caregivers, the focus of this book.

CHAPTER 3

An Old Song

Relationship-Based Care in Cultural and Historical Context

In the 1950s, when Ricardo was 4 years old, he lived in the Philippine village of Tarong (Maretzki & Maretzki, 1963). One day, he walked into the kitchen holding a smoked fish. His parents laughed at the sight of Ricardo carrying a fish. They teasingly commented that Ricardo would not share it with his baby brother, Froilan. Upon hearing this, Ricardo broke off the fish head and gave it to Froilan. Ricardo continued to eat but stopped when there was very little fish left. He looked at whether Froilan had any fish left and then gave half to his baby brother.

Around the same time, 5-year-old Rebecca was living in the Kenyan village of Nyansongo (LeVine & LeVine, 1963). She was observed hoeing in a field with her aunt, cousins, and Moriasi, her 1-year-old brother. When Moriasi began to fuss, Rebecca interrupted her work of hoeing to pick him up. She tried jouncing him, but he only cried louder. "Why are you crying?" Rebecca asked. "I don't have anything to give you."

Rebecca became impatient and gave Moriasi a little slap but then self-corrected and put Moriasi onto her back. She carried him into the shade where her baby cousin and his big sister were playing. Rebecca carefully sat Moriasi down. She then turned her attention for a few moments to her baby cousin—a baby she treated affectionately. The two older girls started laughing and wrestling together, drifting away from the two babies. Rebecca's aunt saw this retreat and said to the girls, "Why are you leaving those babies?" Rebecca immediately ran back and proceeded to amuse the babies by singing and dancing (Whiting & Edwards, 1988).

Antonella is an infant teacher at a *nido* (infant and toddler center) in the city of Pistoia, Italy. In Pistoia, community taxes provide funds for outstanding public early childhood services, including child care for children younger than age 6 years of working parents. Community members, city officials and administrators, early childhood professionals, and parents have come together around a common belief—that promoting what they call a "culture of childhood" through an array of educational and cultural programs to serve children and families is a good way to sustain a livable and friendly city. Most babies who attend the nido enter at 9–12 months of age, after spending a long period of government-supported parental leave at home with their mother. At the nido, parents and educators become very close and build relationships, working together with their joint focus on the children over the early years of life (Edwards & Gandini, 2001; Edwards, Gandini, Peon-Casanova, & Danielson, 2003).

Teacher Marcy is working with Native American children at an Early Head Start Center in the central United States. Well-qualified but not a Native American, Marcy listens, studies, and observes carefully so that she is able to provide care for the children in ways that make sense and are comfortable to the parents and community. For example, in caring for the littlest baby in her group, Marcy has learned how to use the cradle board his mother brought from home. She also follows and supports the use of tribal language and music in the program. Most of the teachers in her Early Head Start program are Native American, so Marcy learns from them and the parents about what techniques and issues are most important on this reservation. She also attends to parenting practices that are not necessarily part of a cultural pattern but are individual variations that she should respect.

Beliefs and values provide the context for human interactions and relationships in any historical time or community setting. The importance of beliefs and values regarding young children is easily seen in the first two observations in the chapter opener, which were taken from a famous cross-cultural project called the Six Culture Study (Whiting & Whiting, 1975). The Filipino parents, for example, remind 4-year-old Ricardo of the importance of sharing food with others, and he willingly gives his baby brother two pieces of his smoked fish. The Kenyan adult allows her 5-year-old niece, Rebecca, to try to comfort her baby brother and does not interfere even when the girl loses patience for a minute. However, when Rebecca and her cousin seem to forget about their infant charges, she immediately corrects them and gets them back on task. Like other Kenyan parents, this woman wants to transmit and support the values of shared economic work and child care within the extended family. She allows the girls to practice and improve their skills of child care, but she steps in when they are about to neglect the babies. Rebecca, though only 5 years old, seems to be well on the way to learning competent infant care within a culture that values large families. In northern Italy, core cultural values have led to the development of high-quality child care programs for infants and older children. In the United States, sometimes many cultures come together in a single program. Although programs may seek cultural continuity of teaching staff with parent clientele, it is often difficult to achieve that aim entirely. Thus teachers and parents may be from different cultural backgrounds, or the parent community may comprise representatives of multiple cultural groups.

Relationship-based approaches of infant and toddler care may be of rising importance in the United States, but they were not invented recently. In this chapter, we look to the age-old wisdom of mothers throughout the world. Parents have always needed to find ways of caring for infants while they performed other important work for their families. Thus, they have created ways to enlarge their infants' world of relationships with caring family and friends while they are busy. It has always been to the parents' advantage to have their infants form important secondary relationships that can keep the children well and happy in a close circle of caregivers.

This chapter addresses several questions:

1. What is culture, and how does it come into play in infant and toddler programs?

2. What are the cultural variations and similarities around caregiving?

3. Are there universalities and variations in how infant–caregiver relationships are regarded throughout the world?

4. Are there universalities and variations in the secondary care of children (i.e., care provided to children while mothers work)?

5. How might that awareness affect how one thinks about building an infant and toddler program in which relationships are emphasized?

As you will see, there is a certain universality to the dances that characterize cultural caregiving throughout the world.

DEFINITION OF CULTURE

Culture is a functional design for living that is worked out by an identified community over the course of their history as a people (Nsamenang, 2000). Culture is studied by anthropologists, who learn about people's ways of life by living directly within the community. Anthropologists become participant-observers who experience the routines and interaction in an ongoing way. Their studies have shown that human beings act less on the basis of instinct than on what they have learned as members of a community. From the beginning of life, humans demonstrate an innate motivation to learn about their culture and imitate the ways of acting and communicating that are shared with others. Humans are natural symbol users who grab onto their culture as a way to make the world predicable and meaningful (Harkness & Super, 1996; Trevarthen, 1988, 1995).

Cultures and Caregiving

Cultural patterns of child rearing differ across time and place according to such macro factors as climate, geography, demographics, economics, political systems, and technology. However, they are not totally unpredictable and random. Under-neath the variation, the care of infants and toddlers has many common features worldwide because people everywhere want their children to survive and thrive. Parents face certain similarities in the tasks of caring for, socializing, and trans-mitting culture to their young children. However, their styles of caregiving are influenced by the features of their daily cultural routines, resources, and roles (Harkness & Super, 1996; Whiting & Edwards, 1988).

What parts of the maternal or caregiving role are most widespread from one culture to another? The most clearly universal aspects of infant and toddler care respond to the basic developmental requirements of young children. Infants have needs for primary care related to health, nutrition, and safety if they are to stay alive and grow. Furthermore, their immature bodies need to be physically supported (i.e., held, carried, or contained) much of the day. As their motor systems develop, they need physical challenge and freedom to move and practice reaching, sitting, crawling, and walking. Their perceptual and cognitive systems likewise need visual and object stimulation to promote learning. Finally, children have needs for attachment and social companionship requisite for social and emotional health (Keller, 2002, 2007).

Caregivers in any society must operate within certain basic limits if children are to survive, thrive, and learn. Adults cannot do just anything with babies. The stakes are too high when they make serious mistakes. Instead, caregivers tend to follow visible and known patterns that they have learned from personal experience and observation. Caregivers try to promote their children's well-being by employing practices that are similar to the customs of others they know, as well as practices that seem to "work" in their unique situation.

Research has found three major cultural pathways of parenting (parental scripts) for childhood socialization. Each of these scripts has its own associated set of parental fears and goals (LeVine, Miller, & West, 1988; LeVine et al., 1994). The first type of parental script is *childhood survival,* which predominates in communities where disease and death are serious threats and the goal of keeping the child alive is forefront in the parent's mind. The second script, *economic achievement,* predominates in contexts where the child's survival is relatively assured but economic survival is very competitive. In these environments, making a living is challenging. It is perpetually being threatened by shortage of resources and opportunities. The third type of parental script is *personal fulfillment,* which comes to the forefront under conditions where both physical and economic survival are predictable. Here, the goals of personal fulfillment and happiness, or maximizing self-development, occupy people's attention.

Besides relating to cross-cultural differences, these types of scripts can also apply differently within a culture. For example, American caregivers living in communities beset by poverty and crime tend to stress survival goals in child rearing by trying to protect their children from untimely death. Their capacities to worry about other goals, such as educational success and personal fulfillment, are undermined by their realistic anxiety about their children's health and survival. Families of new immigrants, in contrast, may stress the goal of economic achievement. They worry about economic survival and push their children to study hard, achieve good grades, and get into the highest-ranked colleges. Families with high incomes may have some concerns about physical and economic survival but also focus on personal fulfillment. These caregivers may wonder whether their children are completely happy and developing to their maximum individual potential.

However, despite these superordinate scripts, not everything that adults do with their babies is cultural, in the sense of being part of a shared pattern. Often, people behave in unique and idiosyncratic ways that may be outside the bounds of the usual and expected. For example, they may decorate their infants' rooms in strange colors or dress them in clothing that others find surprising or inappropriate. Most of the time, the deviations are trivial and without important consequences, but sometimes they may result in real harm to children. An educator cannot assume that every time a parent does something that seems unusual, it is "just part of their culture." People may have more than one source of cultural identity. In addition, sometimes what a person does can be idiosyncratic and nontypical with respect to all of that person's cultural identities—perhaps even deviant in the sense of violating respected norms. For example, a parent may punish a child in a way that is considered cruel and excessive by members of the culture that shaped the parent's child-rearing beliefs.

First, it is necessary to observe and talk with members of the culture. The following criteria may indicate that a pattern of caregiving is part of a cultural belief system:

- It is shared among many people who are related to one another and who live in a community of shared language and culture.

- It is passed down from one generation to the next in observable ways.

- It is believed to promote babies' health and nutritional status.

- It is believed to protect babies from harm or danger.

- It is displayed when soothing and offering comfort to babies.

- It is used to stimulate babies and give them social attention.

- It is thought to promote the learning of valuable skills and behaviors.

- It is believed to help children fit into a social group.

Indicators that a caregiving pattern might violate cultural norms include the following:

- Other members of the cultural group seem surprised, dismayed, or disapproving of it.

- The person who does this behavior seems embarrassed about it or denies doing it.

- The behavior leads to obvious harm or unhappiness, without offsetting benefits for the child.

Subcultural Diversity

Learning about cultural aspects of infant care is further complicated by cultural diversity within a society, sometimes called *subcultural diversity* (Lynch & Hanson, 2004). In most contemporary societies—particularly in North America—people from many national, ethnic, and linguistic backgrounds live together. Consequently, most individuals have been exposed to a variety of cultural models that allow them to draw from a pool of values, beliefs, and practices when formulating their own frameworks of parenting beliefs and practices. Cultural heterogeneity is especially prevalent in areas with high levels of immigration and rapid technological change.

People form varying degrees of identification with others to whom they feel similar in important respects, whether it be because of language, race or ethnicity, religion, geographic region, rural or urban residence, socioeconomic class, or some other marker of social identity. Cultural evolution is an ongoing and dynamic process. Individuals and groups change and adapt as they encounter new situations and ways of doing things. In North America, customs about what babies should wear, what they should eat, how they should be carried, and where they should sleep follow the tides of fashion and current medical advice. Young parents often consult their networks of friends and relatives and their favorite media in making decisions about what to do.

Parents in societies undergoing rapid social change are bound to consider what aspects of their childhood or traditional culture they will retain as they learn about new patterns that they think might be beneficial. For example, consider the pattern of child care seen in Nyansongo, Kenya. This pattern certainly has not remained the same since the 1950s. Since securing independence from Great Britain in 1963, Kenya has undergone dramatic transformations from subsistence herding and agriculture to a modern economy based on money, markets, and wage labor. Women have led the way in adopting innovations and new strategies in feeding and raising their families.

Mothers were studied in the Kenyan village of Ngecha in the late 1960s and early 1970s (Edwards & Whiting, 2004; Whiting & Edwards, 1988), and the process of social change was documented. The Ngecha mothers, like those of Nyansongo, had grown up in large rural families where they learned responsible work and shared sibling caregiving from early childhood. They had little or no education in the formal setting of school and therefore no way to directly tutor their children in academic and school readiness skills. Yet, they had found ways to encourage their children to attend school because education was seen as the pathway to success. The mothers put less stress on the values of obedience and respect for elders and praised their children for "cleverness." They put more emphasis on their daughters going to school than on taking care of their younger brothers and sisters. They modeled traits of creativity and individual resourcefulness in finding ways to make money for school clothes and other school-related expenses by making baskets, growing flowers, selling chickens and eggs, or other entrepreneurial activities. In other words, these mothers adapted to changing life conditions by creating new kinds of expectations and patterns of child rearing, involving changes in their children's typical daily routines, task assignments, play and leisure activities, and time spent in the company of close relatives.

Sleeping Arrangements

Duccio is a 2-year-old boy in Antonella's toddler class in Pistoia, Italy. He is now at home, and it is time for Duccio to get ready for bed. Duccio goes down at night at a late but customary time in a country where many people eat their midday meal between 1:00 p.m. and 3:00 p.m. and rest when possible in the afternoon. The evening meal is now over at 9:00 p.m. His father plays with him a few minutes. Then, his mother bathes him and brushes his teeth. She takes a leisurely time with it, chatting and doing things in just the right way and order to make a soothing and calming ritual. She dresses Duccio in his pajamas and grooms and brushes his hair, calling him *bellisimo* ("very handsome"). When he is all ready, the mother gives Duccio his pacifier and lies with him on her own bed until he falls asleep. Then, she carefully moves him into his crib in the next room.

Care of young children is threaded into the ongoing fabric of life in an almost transparent and unnoticed way in any community. One way that cultural values are manifested is in sleeping arrangements (Tronick, Morelli, & Winn, 1987; Whiting, 1994). In regions of the world where it gets cold in winter, babies are usually wrapped warmly and placed to sleep by themselves in a crib or cradle. In traditional times, they may have been placed in a cradleboard to keep warm and close to hand while their mothers were busy, as described for the Navajo of the American Southwest (Chisolm, 1981, 1989). In hot, tropical regions, babies typically sleep next to their mothers in the mother's bed, hammock, or sleeping mat. Both kinds of infant sleeping arrangements lead to normal child development, but they do shape children differently in developing self-regulation. When infants and toddlers sleep alone, they must learn to comfort themselves back to sleep with their stuffed animal or blanket, by sucking their thumb, or using a pacifier—handy strategies to use when they need to get themselves asleep away from their mother. When babies sleep next to their mother, however, they wake up many times throughout the night to nurse or snuggle. These babies rely on physical contact for sleeping and comfort. When they need to get to sleep away from their mother, they have to start finding some self-comforting technique for the first time.

Babies who sleep next to mothers, however, do not grow up spoiled and unable to control their needs for touch and affection. On the contrary, they learn how to sleep without their mother at a later age, when another baby is born. Demoted from the mother's lap, they now become what the famous anthropologist Margaret Mead called the "knee baby," the one who stays close to the caregiver but is not constantly held (Edwards, 1989). This often occurs at the same age as when they are weaned. As the knee baby, the child begins to move out into a wider world of peers and becomes part of the little gang of brothers, sisters, cousins, and close neighbors who play freely together without adult facilitation yet always within earshot or under the watchful eye of an adult's indirect supervision. The knee child usually sleeps next to someone at night, but it may be the father, grandmother, or an older brother or sister instead of the mother. The child learns how to sleep peacefully at night without nursing or feeding and how to find comfort during the day through a variety of means instead of relying exclusively on the mother.

Social Interaction

Cultural styles of caregiving are reflected in the customary ways that mothers position their babies when they are awake and away from their cradle, crib, or bed. In some cultures (e.g., typical North American and European groups), mothers (and other adults) view babies as partners for social interaction, and play and talk with them whenever possible (Whiting & Edwards, 1988; Whiting & Whiting, 1975). In other cultures (e.g., the rural mothers of Kenya and other parts of the developing world), mothers do not view babies as social partners but instead expect siblings and other children to do the playing. Thus, older boys and girls become skilled at delighting babies through tickling, caressing, and bouncing them in order to keep them happy and also just because it is fun. Furthermore, mothers in some cultures (e.g., the United States) favor a face-to-face, intense, dyadic (two-person) style of play and talking. The mother likes to holds the child in her arms or lap and gazes into the child's eyes as she tries to elicit smiles, coos, and talk from the baby in a mutual dance of interaction. In many other cultures, however, a more inclusionary and group-oriented style may be seen, where the mother holds the child facing outward as she talks or works, or passes the baby from adult to adult. The infant watches and interacts with everyone present, not only the mother. In this way, the mother can easily divide her attention between her baby and her work and other people present, and the baby basks in social life without being the focus of group attention (e.g., Martini & Kirkpatrick, 1981).

CULTURAL VARIATION IN WHO CARES FOR CHILDREN WHILE MOTHERS WORK

Cross-cultural studies suggest that having the mother as the *exclusive* caregiver is one pattern of caregiving—but not the only one, or even the predominant one, in worldwide perspective. Instead, shared caregiving that extends the child's circle of consistent relationships is preferred (see Box 3.1). Sometimes these supplementary caregivers are family adults such as fathers, grandparents, or other relatives. In other cases, the supplemental caregivers are older siblings, who first receive cultural instruction on how to care for babies and time to practice under adult supervision before being given independent responsibility of looking after the baby. Today, in many parts of the world, supplementary caregivers are often hired to look after children either in their own or the child's home. All of these patterns demonstrate the range of possibilities for appropriate infant and toddler care and provide strong evidence that sharing care within and beyond the family

BOX 3.1.
Shared caregiving in Ngecha, Kenya

Mothers in many parts of the world carry heavy workloads. The mothers in a Kenyan village were observed taking charge of the family food gardens, collecting all the fuel and water, and caring for the house and yard. For helpers, they often recruited their children, ages 6–10 years. Girls (or boys if no girl of the right age was available) acted as child nurses, carrying the babies as they played or doing other chores for their mothers. When toddlers got too big and heavy to carry, the child nurses incorporated them into their playgroups. Shared caregiving was seen as normal in the community, and it was part of a system of early training in empathy and concern for others in the family.

Adapted from Edwards, C., & Whiting, B. (Eds.). (2004). *Ngecha: A Kenyan village in a time of rapid social change*. Lincoln: University of Nebraska Press. Photos by Frances Cox for the Child Development Research Unit, circa 1970.

is as much part of the human story as is the mother-exclusive pattern. Extending the dance is an expected and natural way to support parents in the tasks of raising their children.

Maternal Workload

Who cares for infants is strongly influenced by the mother's workload (Whiting & Edwards, 1988; Whiting & Whiting, 1975). Mothers in Southern Africa and other parts of the developing world often carry heavy workloads, being responsible for fetching water and fuel, maintaining the family gardens, and caring for the house and yard. They recruit their older children to help them in their daily work when those children are home from school. Girls or boys ages 7 or 8 years may be designated as child nurses. They carry babies on their backs as they play or go about their family chores, as seen in the example from Nyansongo, Kenya, while babies and toddlers are incorporated into playgroups of older children (Edwards, 1989; Edwards & Whiting, 1993; Swadener, Kabiru, & Njenga, 2000; Weisner, 1987). Shared caregiving—socially distributed nurturance and support—is the norm (Swadener et al., 2000; Weisner, 1984, 1987, 1996).

Household Composition and Father Involvement

Beyond the mother's workload, household composition influences infant care. When people live in extended families, with many close kin on the compound or in nearby courtyards, then grandmothers, aunts, and co-wives (women married to the same husband) often assist in childbirth and infant care. Among the Efe (Pygmies) of Central Africa, the baby may even be nursed by women other than the mother (Tronick, Morelli, & Winn, 1987). Household composition especially influences the level of father involvement. When people live in nuclear families composed of the mother, father, and children only, fathers are more likely to become skilled and frequent caregivers of small children than when they live in extended families, where there are many more female helping hands. For instance, among hunter-gatherers in Africa, some tribal groups may spend part of the year in settled villages and part of the year wandering the land in small bands. In the settled villages, surrounded by other adults, fathers are less active in infant care than they are when they are isolated with their wives and children in the bush and their help and support is more needed (Hewlett, 1991; Morelli & Tronick, 1991). Thus, for the Efe, fathers' roles are flexible throughout the year depending on the family's living situation, suggesting that fathers are capable of picking up their level of child care depending on what is asked and needed from them.

Government Support for Parenting

What about societies today where women are part of the labor force but they do not have large extended families or fathers available to share in the tasks of infant and toddler care? Who helps those parents care for their infants? In modern industrialized countries, traditional patterns of care have evolved to include parental leave and child care systems (Clark, Hyde, Essex, & Klein, 1997; Dahlberg, Moss, & Pence, 1999). In many European countries, such as Norway, Sweden, Italy, France, and Germany, as well as in Asian countries such as China, shared caregiving (both inside and outside the family) is fostered by government policies that are intentionally designed to support the family and women's participation in the labor force (see Box 3.2). In Italy, paid parental leave supports the right of the mother to spend at least 1 year at home with her infant. Other policies support the right of families to later find state-supported infant and toddler care that is educational and nurturing for the children and at the same time supportive of adult independence and self-reliance. In Norway, the period of paid parental leave is extended by 1 month for families in which both the mother and the father participate and take time off from their employment, which encourages the father's involvement.

BOX 3.2.
Parental leave in Europe and the United States

The right of families to take some kind of parental leave in order to take care of a new baby is protected in at least 75 countries, including all of the industrial nations. In the United States, the Family and Medical Leave Act of 1993 (PL 103-3) provides parents in firms with more than 50 employees the right to take 12 weeks of unpaid leave without jeopardizing their jobs.

However, many other countries have more generous policies. For example, in Sweden, working mothers receive 6 weeks of parental leave at 90% pay and an additional 6 months of unpaid leave; mothers and fathers also may share the leave. In Japan, working mothers receive 14 weeks of paid maternity leave; in Israel, they receive 12 weeks of paid leave and up to 40 weeks of unpaid leave. In Italy, mothers can take 20 weeks of maternity leave at full pay (8 weeks prior to the birth and 12 weeks after the birth). Plus, mothers have the right to an additional 24 weeks at half pay after the child's birth. Thus, though many Italian mothers work outside the home, they do not return to work until their baby is at least 9 months old.

Research in the United States has shown that a long leave can be beneficial to mothers and children (Clark, Hyde, Esses, & Klein, 1997). Mothers who took off 4 months after their babies were born displayed less negative affect when interacting with their babies than did mothers who took off only 2 months. This contrast was especially true for depressed mothers and those who had babies with a difficult temperament. These mothers were much more positive with their babies and had smoother, more synchronous interactions.

Some patterns of infant and toddler care observed to be common around the world include the following:

- Infants are held and carried much of their waking day, or else placed in a seat or container that allows the child to see and interact with others close by.
- Infants are fed either on demand or at least every few hours. Responsive caregiving matters.
- A few familiar people help the mother care for the baby.
- Babies are magnets for the smiles and attention of others, and people respond warmly to them.
- Siblings and other children do much of the concentrated play with babies.
- Babies are soothed and stimulated by singing, music, and rhythmic movement.
- As infants become toddlers, they face increasing expectations for mature behavior.

Some patterns have not been observed to be normative in any culture. These patterns may be maladaptive in any cultural setting and include the following:

- Infants are subjected to hard spankings and excessive punishment.
- Infants have no regular bed or sleeping place; they are just expected to sleep anywhere.
- Infants and toddlers are fed and put to sleep with no observable routine or ritual and expected to just fall asleep on adult command.
- No one plays with infants and toddlers; they are expected to play alone for long stretches of time out of earshot and view of others.
- Little or no language is heard; children live in a language-silent environment.
- Toddlers are not provided with any rules or expectations for mature behavior (e.g., no tantrums, biting, interrupting, or demanding).
- Toddlers are pressured with high expectations in every area of behavior and expected to be perfect at all times and in all places.

USING INSIGHTS FROM CULTURAL STUDIES IN AN INFANT AND TODDLER SETTING

Our theoretical orientation to infant and toddler care, education, and intervention is a *strengths-based approach,* meaning that teachers and other professionals should always look for things that families are doing right and build on the strengths that are there. Parents have their own styles and preferences for interacting with their children, with many of these styles being culturally based. Professionals can reinforce and build on these strengths at the same time that they encourage parents to learn new things about child development or what helps their child to learn.

For example, if a mother has a nonverbal style of expressing affection (e.g., she kisses or touches her toddler when he does something well), a teacher might observe, "I can see your baby smile when you touch his cheek because he knows he is doing what you want. That is a good way of teaching him." In this way, the educator acknowledges the mother's competence as her child's first teacher and helps the mother feel more confident. If, instead, the educator believes verbal behavior to be the only correct form of parental encouragement, teaching the parent to say "Good boy" or "Good job" as verbal praise may feel forced and unnatural to the parent and could be counterproductive.

Tools for Learning about Parental Strengths

Many early childhood educators favor home visits and parent–teacher conferences as two of the most important tools for finding out about a family's cultural resources and strengths. The home visit provides a window into the whole life context of the family and seems to transport the teacher into their point of view or perspective on the world. The home visit creates vivid memories for the teacher that can help keep the child's reality in the mind's eye of the teacher, even back in the classroom or center. The teacher can then approach the child more compassionately and convey an empathic attitude that makes the misbehaving child more likely to listen. The home visit demonstrates the educator's willingness to go more than halfway in building a bridge with the family. It also increases the parents' desire to reciprocate by coming willingly into the teacher's classroom. These back and forth exchanges put into motion the partnerships that last between parents and teachers and create the magic of the extended dance.

The parent–teacher conference complements the home visit in creating understanding about parents' greatest goals (and fears) for their children. When the teacher takes time to build rapport and lets the conversation develop at a relaxed pace, the teacher becomes able to really listen to the parents' words and attend to their body language. The teacher may sense, for example, that the parents' concerns are more about the child's survival than about the child's achievements or personal fulfillment. This can help the teacher to find effective ways to communicate with the parents on their own terms. For instance, in the parent–teacher conference, the teacher might echo the parents' concerns for the child's safety by talking about the child's developing language with an example that describes how the child is learning to recognize simple signs, such as red means *stop* and green means *go,* and thus knows what to do when crossing the street. Such an example might have more meaning for the parents than telling them that their child can recognize directional words like *up* and *down.* The two concepts are developmentally equivalent, but the first has much more impact to the parents.

If a teacher is seeing parents in terms of strengths, he or she will

- Look at their behavior in terms of many dimensions
- Look for positive moments of parent–child interaction

- Listen for and use the exact words of parents when talking about their children

- Be able to laugh with parents and enjoy the present moment

    If a teacher is focusing more on deficits, he or she will

- Dwell on things that feel disturbing or annoying

- Want the parents to do things in a certain "right" way

- Feel judgmental when speaking with parents

Everyone has cultural "hot buttons," but knowledge of the many ways that parents and families express their child-rearing strengths can be helpful to the teacher in focusing on strengths rather than deficits. For example, if a teacher is replaying exchanges with a difficult parent over and over, the parent has hit the teacher's hot button. The next step in this situation is to take a deep breath and try to figure out why. For example, a parent's lateness may be very difficult for a teacher. Reflection may help the teacher to realize that this behavior is bothersome to her because the teacher herself is held to very tight punctuality on the job. Reframing differences in cultural terms gives the teacher a way to step back from the situation. After all, behaviors such as being relaxed about time and interrupting the speaker are considered normal and appropriate in many cultural groups. Teachers can therefore master their hot buttons through a little humor and detachment and then take appropriate steps.

The same principles apply in developing a strengths-based approach with children. For example, a teacher may react negatively to a certain child who pulls on clothes to get attention instead of speaking a name, or to a child who seems to push away a teacher who seeks to help or comfort. However, these are not character deficits on the part of the children but simply differences in conventional or polite behavior. The world's communities have found many diverse ways to communicate; no single way is correct. But underneath all of this surface diversity, there are certain prevailing truths. Young children must try to read and interpret adult intentions at an emotional or intuitive level so that they can get their needs met. Likewise, loving adults must try to read and understand children so that they can know how to care for them. Therefore, when teachers slow down, attend carefully, and respond empathetically to the feelings and needs underlying children's words and behavior, they can get beneath the surface of assumptions that make them react instinctively in negative ways to things they find irritating. Children who pull on a teacher's clothes or slap away a teacher's hands are using nonverbal ways of communicating. Without passing judgment, the teacher might simply begin to teach the children a greater variety of techniques for getting their needs met efficiently and effectively.

All parents and families approach child rearing with their own intuitive sense of what is best to do (Aukrust et al., 2003; Rogoff, 2003). Their ideas come from their own experiences, upbringing, and information they seek out from

trusted people in their social network or from the media. How can educators find
out about their own or someone else's parenting beliefs about caring for infants
and toddlers? Participant observation is sometimes used in formal research studies, but that requires special training in field methods as well as informed consent.
Interviews and self-reflection are a less laborious method that can provide at least
a glimpse at parenting beliefs (see Box 3.3). Adults who have gone through a
formal system of education are usually able to describe something about their
beliefs and values when it comes to a domain as important as child rearing. Their
answers tell teachers about their goals, fears, and values for infant development,
their preferred styles of expressing warmth and sensitivity, the strategies they
choose for promoting independence and autonomy, and the approaches they take
to helping their children learn and master the knowledge that will help them be
successful in school.

BOX 3.3.
Interview on parenting
beliefs about infants and toddlers

Every parent and every culture has a system of beliefs about the best
way to care for young children. The following questions can be used to
get a glimpse of your own or someone else's child-rearing beliefs.

1. What are your beliefs about who should take care of a baby? Who is
    the primary caregiver of your baby? Who else helps, and what do
    they do?

2. What are your beliefs about babies and crying? What do you do
    when your baby cries? How quickly do you try to tend to your
    baby? How about when you are busy? How about at night? How do
    other members of your household feel about the baby crying?

3. What are your beliefs about breast versus bottle feeding? How do
    you feel about toddlers still nursing? How about toddlers still taking
    bottles? Do you have any limits or rules on where the child can
    have, or carry, his or her bottle?

4. What are your beliefs about babies and food? How do you feed
    your baby? Are there any mealtime rules? Who eats together at
    mealtime? What is the best way to introduce solid foods? Are these
    purchased or homemade?

5. What are your feelings about dressing babies? How do you feel
    about sending a child to an infant and toddler center in fancy
    clothes? Do you mind if his or her hair gets messed up? How do
    you feel about toddlers going naked?

Box 3.3 (continued)

6. What are your beliefs about babies and sleep? Does your baby sleep in the same room or the same bed as others in the family? Is there a set bedtime? How do you get the baby to sleep? Are there any methods of putting a child to sleep that you don't approve of?

7. What are your beliefs about babies and emotions? Do you feel that babies should express all of their feelings? What do you do to keep your baby quiet? How about the baby laughing and getting really excited? Screaming and crying? Not wanting to share you with others?

8. At what age do you think babies should be toilet trained? How will you go about that process? How about other self-skills like feeding and dressing? Do you try to teach your baby to do these things, or should the child just learn by him- or herself?

9. Do you expect your baby to obey immediately when you ask him or her to do something, or do you give the baby a little leeway? What if the baby dawdles or delays? Do you always follow through on commands, or do you sometimes let things go?

10. What are your beliefs about giving praise to young children? What about special food, gifts, privileges, praise, or other rewards? What are your beliefs about punishment if the child is careless or deliberately does something you don't want the child to do? Who disciplines your child?

11. How much contact does your child have with relatives? Who lives in the household with you? Which relatives do you see most frequently, and which ones do you not see?

12. How much contact does your baby have with other children? Does your child usually play with siblings? Other child relatives? Children outside the family? Do you want your child to play alone more or with a group more?

Parental Styles of Expressing Warmth and Sensitivity

Infants and toddlers benefit from nurturant caregiving that is emotionally warm, available, and responsive. Nurturance can be demonstrated in many ways that seem to promote infant health and well-being. No single cultural group or set of parents uses all of the available techniques, but instead it selects some of them as the customary approach. Parents and communities often use styles that emphasize a physical, social, or cognitive style of expressing warmth and sensitivity (although these styles can be combined).

Certain kinds of parents may emphasize a physical style of nurturance; for example, they focus on their children's desires for food, holding, and responsive touch. Through their provision of food and nurturing primary care, these parents communicate to their children that they love them and are devoted to them. Their gentle touch or use of massage may communicate nurturing feelings and comfort to their children.

Instead of emphasizing primary care, parents may take greatest pleasure in a social style of nurturing by grooming their children's hair, dressing them up, taking them on visits, and teaching them social words and gestures (e.g., "bye-bye," "thank you"). In many cultures, adults take great delight in the social forms of nurturance and communicate their affection through beautifying their children and teaching them the rudiments of good manners.

Still other parents may emphasize a cognitive style of expressing warmth and sensitivity by responding to their children's developing interests and preferences, offering them objects to look at and manipulate, and following their eyes to see what they are looking at, in order to label those things and expand on children's exclamations and words. These parents often are verbal in their interaction with even the youngest children. They treat their babies as conversational partners and intelligent beings who wonder about how things work and what causes things to happen. Of course, parents can combine all three styles.

In today's postindustrial societies, the third style, focused on cognitive- and language-stimulating interactions, seems to lead to the optimal outcomes for children's school readiness and academic success. Warm interactions with family members that include the exchange of words and reasons provide the foundation for compliance and internalized controls in young children. Limit setting and discipline may be less effective in the absence of positive, warm relationships. The expression of positive acceptance through encouragement of listening and speaking skills has been found to be associated with school readiness. These skills translate directly into the preschool or kindergarten setting, where they help children fit into the group and cooperate with the teacher and the flow of the school day.

When teachers recognize all of the ways that parents convey their love and caring to their children, they become sensitive in a deeper and more profound way that reaches out to others and creates a climate of genuine welcoming and acceptance of differences.

Parental Styles of Promoting Autonomy and Independence

Children cannot remain babies forever and must learn to do things for themselves so that they can get along without constant supervision. Thus, promoting autonomy becomes important during the toddler years when children begin to say "no" and want to do things independently. Some families encourage motoric (physical) autonomy by allowing their children lots of opportunity for active movement. Others might allow their children to explore independently in a carefully childproofed home or yard or may take the children outside for regular vigorous exercise. Still other parents might encourage physical autonomy by being exceptionally patient as the children struggle to climb stairs, use a fork, put on shoes, wash their hands, pour cereal and milk, or put things away.

Some parents may emphasize social autonomy because it helps children to function in a social group without constant parental intervention. Parents orient their babies toward social autonomy, for instance, when they help them learn to remain patient and pleasant during a long family meal, use polite words, or to master their jealousy of the attention given to a smaller baby visiting their house (Edwards, Gandini, & Giovannini, 1996). Socially oriented families might also encourage their children to enter a playgroup of same-age peers, to freely share their toys, or to accept another adult's care to join an outing to the park or swimming pool.

Still other families put a premium on cognitive styles of autonomy. They demonstrate this by encouraging early mastery of language skills so that children can use words to express their needs. They might even teach their children some simple signs to communicate with—a practice that seems to be catching on with more and more parents today. Or parents may emphasize the cognitive aspect of independent behavior by putting special energy into helping their children use words to solve problems (e.g., "Tell him no," "Ask for what you want"). Children may also be guided to make sustained and self-directed use of the stimulating materials in the children's bedrooms or playrooms—stocked by parents with books, art materials, and constructive toys—instead of hanging out underfoot of the busy parent.

The pressure for autonomy—whether physical, social, or cognitive—sometimes originates from the child, who suddenly wants to do things independently. Sometimes the pressure comes from the parent, which may arouse distress that can easily be misread and misinterpreted by the cultural outsider as unresponsive parenting. However, what the outsider misreads as unresponsive parenting, the cultural insider recognizes as a painful but necessary phase that will soon be over.

Sometimes the need for autonomy from the toddler starts with the mother, who needs to make her toddler more independent so that she can devote her attention to a new baby. The mother is not unkind, but instead she shows a caring concern for her toddler by giving the child a gentle—or not so gentle!—push to move the child along in a way that is necessary for family survival. The mother controls the timetable. She decides when to wean her toddler from her breast (and the frequent need to nurse) and from her back (and the need to be carried) in anticipation of her next baby's arrival. Her push to change the level of physical contact and care she gives her toddler may precipitate a difficult period of transition for the child, characterized by disturbances such as clinging, refusals to respond, aggression toward the mother, finger sucking, repetitive rocking, fretfulness and crying, disturbed sleep, tantrums, and/or apathy. Following the period of disturbance, however, the toddler "grows up" and acts with the maturity expected of older children. The child now gets praise and approval for orienting toward older brothers and sisters, helping with household tasks, showing increased facility in speech, and generally being more independent of adult support. The child begins to function without constant maternal attention, plays well, and gets most social needs met within a multi-age playgroup composed of siblings and cousins (Edwards & Liu, 2002). Box 3.4 provides an example of what this transition from infancy and toddlerhood looks like in a rural cultural group in Mexico.

BOX 3.4.
Transition from infancy to toddlerhood in Zinacantan, Mexico

Are the "terrible twos" universal? Not necessarily. In many of the world's communities, the transition from infancy to early childhood does not typically involve resistant toddlers demanding and asserting control over toileting and other self-help skills.

For example, in the Mayan community of Zinacantan, located high in the spectacular mountain regions of Chiapas, Mexico, families earn their living growing corn and raising sheep and other livestock; young children are watchful, imitative beings who learn most of the skills of self-care with a minimum of fuss. Their clothing is simple; floors and yards can be easily swept; and toilet training is not particularly a matter of shame, guilt, or pride because children can easily learn what to do by imitating their older brothers and sisters. Children here are not commonly seen asserting their separateness from their mothers and pushing away. Instead, they are more likely to do the opposite and seek to be close to their mothers during their second year. It is their mothers who sometimes need to push for autonomy so that they can devote themselves to care for a new baby.

The toddlers struggle hard to cope with the undesired distancing initiated by their mothers, who up until then had kept them calm, quiet, and peaceful by carrying them under a shawl on their backs and by nursing them frequently. Displaced—and often appearing listless and dejected—the toddlers hover in their mothers' vicinity. They face the twin shocks of being weaned from the breast and weaned from the back. They find that they are denied the pleasures of nursing, of close physical contact with mother by day, and of sleeping next to their mother in the parents' bed at night. After a few-day or few-week period of adjustment, however, these children seem to accept their change in status and to rebound as active members of the children's multi-age courtyard playgroup.

Box 3.4 (continued)

> Mothers in Zinacantan, as in other similar cultures, do not see themselves as playmates or conversational partners for their infants and young children. Instead, they delegate these roles to siblings and other family members. Their infant care practices may lay the groundwork for the development of mature preschool-age children who watch closely, imitate adults and older children, and learn many cultural skills through guided participation in the daily life of family work, leisure, and eating and sleeping routines.
>
> *Source:* Edwards (1989).

Cultural values about autonomy influence the manner in which parents and other family members evaluate and set limits with their children. For instance, there are many ways that parents can express praise and approval for what a child is doing. Some parents and cultural groups tend to use applause and cheers to encourage small children to show off and do little performances. In other cultures, parents do not want their child to seek attention or be boastful, so instead of giving overt praise, they comment to another adult how well the child is doing, give the child another responsibility that indicates success with the first one, or wordlessly display the child's lovely picture to share it with the family. The child notices what the parent is doing and feels a quiet pride that does not make him the center of attention.

Parents' values about appropriate autonomy also influence what they see as too indulgent and as spoiling a child. The following behaviors are points of family and cultural variation in the promotion of autonomy:

- Allowing a toddler to have a bottle or pacifier
- Carrying around a heavy toddler long after the child can walk
- Rocking a baby to sleep instead of leaving the baby to wind down alone
- Nursing a baby many times throughout the day
- Allowing a toddler to throw a tantrum in public
- Letting a child interrupt adults who are talking

All cultures have some areas in which they expect early attainment of autonomy and mature behavior and other areas in which they are relatively lax and indulgent. When people are looking at families from other cultures, they tend to notice those areas of child rearing where the other culture is either much stricter or more indulgent than their own. However, they are unaware of the aspects of their own culture that others tend to find either overly indulgent or overly strict.

Parental Styles of Supporting Learning and Literacy

Just as they vary on the other dimensions of infant and toddler care, parents in different cultural communities have distinctive beliefs about what they believe children should learn. In a general way, these parental beliefs match the demands of the cultural context. For instance, many cultural environments contain physical dangers for young children (e.g., drowning, getting run over, getting lost). These dangers correspond to the earliest words that children need to learn to avoid these dangers (e.g., "Don't run in the street," "Don't pat that mean dog," "Stay close to me"). Furthermore, economic context sets the stage for the child's earliest introduction to physical skills. Gross and fine motor physical skills will always be of paramount importance for infants and toddlers in any cultural setting. Children must learn to move efficiently through the world and to begin to handle and manipulate necessary tools and implements, whether they are spoons, digging tools, or crayons.

The social realm of language and learning is also important to most families. Parents promote their children's incorporation of social skills and knowledge by letting them participate in household work and including them in the joyful celebrations and rituals that are most meaningful to the families. For example, little girls in the Mayan community of Chiapas, Mexico, are drawn gradually into the women's intricate world of weaving blankets, shawls, shirts, and other products for commercial sale through an age-old process of cultural apprenticeship, which first involves carefully watching, then a gradual increase in active involvement (Greenfield, 2004). Parents in many societies today achieve similar effects of stimulating language and learning by incorporating their youngest children in events that give the whole family pleasure, such as sporting events. For infants and toddlers, sitting with the family on the sidelines through long games can be either barren and boring (when they are primarily pacified with food and drink) or rich in learning and literacy experience if family members take time to draw them out in extended conversation, teach them meaningful routines (e.g., the rudiments of the game), and show them all of the numbers, letters, and words on the scoreboard, food containers, programs, and uniforms.

Today, the preacademic or cognitive side of early learning has become at least as important as the social and physical sides because of its connection to readiness for school success. Explicitly symbolic learning that promotes emergent learning in the domains of literacy, math, science, and creative arts reaches all the way down into the infant and toddler years. Parents set the stage for their babies' later school readiness by treating them as conversational partners. Parents echo and expand their children's vocalizations and utterances (e.g., saying "You want more milk in your bottle?" after their child says, "Bottle"). Likewise, parents expand their children's future command of language by modeling and encouraging the pleasure of using words, whether in naming, describing, explaining, rhyming, joking, telling a story, singing, counting, comparing, or computing. Parents also support an early love of language and learning by introducing their children to the cultural arts (e.g., providing drawing and listening materials; taking the child to a puppet show, library, public garden, swimming pool, or park). Finally, parents cultivate a pleasure in reading and future literacy by reading stories to them from infancy and providing a rich supply of books, literacy tools, and imaginative play materials in their home.

The preacademic methods of fostering school readiness are very desirable as part of the "curriculum of the home," but they are not everything. Any and all of the parenting styles of promoting language and learning—physical, social, and cognitive—have their own merit and are positive supports to young children's present and future socioemotional and intellectual growth and development.

SUMMARY

This chapter described some cultural aspects to the ways that parents and family members have responded to infants and toddlers. Adults can use many styles to create a nurturing and caring context of relationship that meets children's basic needs and provides them with adequate warmth and nurturance, opportunities for autonomy, and participation in learning and literacy. Secondary providers who care for children while mothers perform other duties are present in cultures the world over and have been for untold generations. Thus, we call this chapter an "old song." The tune that underpins the dance of relationships has been playing for hundreds—perhaps thousands—of years.

Societies devise their own approaches to secondary care, but nearly all cultures recognize the value of warm adult–child relationships. Beyond this nearly universal recognition of the importance of relationships, providers bring their own conscious and unconscious assumptions about children's patterns of eating, sleeping, speaking, dressing, and forming attachments. Many of those routines, assumptions, and expectations come to be part of a person because of where he or she grew up. A person thus may not always fit smoothly with people who come from other backgrounds. We believe, however, that these different styles and values reflect alternative kinds of community wisdom about child rearing, so it is not necessary to judge them as better or worse. Instead, it is important for educators to become more knowledgeable about their own cultural beliefs and values in order to become more open to other people's perspectives and choices. Cultural self-knowledge can become the foundation for the professional's cultural competence to seek out every parent's and fellow provider's nurturing intentions behind his or her actions, respect diverse cultural styles, and determine how different ways of child rearing promote strength and adaptability.

In the remainder of the book, we describe many specific ways in which secondary caregivers can support parents in extending the dance of relationships. We draw on cultural lessons to suggest ways to promote continuity between children's first relationships and those they begin to form as they move out into a wider world outside the home. This kind of continuity indicates cultural respect for many kinds of caregiver–child dances and promotes a broad view of culture appropriate for an increasingly diverse society.

RESOURCES

Althen, G. (1988). *American ways: A guide for foreigners in the United States.* Yarmouth, ME: Intercultural Press.

Childhood. (2006). Video series produced by Thirteen/WNET, distributed by Ambrose Video, 2006 (http://www.ambrosevideo.com). Three individual programs in the series focus on infancy, with much cross-cultural footage: "Great Expectations," "Louder than Words," and "Love's Labors."

DeLoache, J., & Gottlieb, A. (2000). *A world of babies: Imagined childcare guides for seven societies.* New York: Cambridge University Press.

Gonzalez-Mena, J. (2004). *Diversity in early care and education programs: Honoring differences.* New York: McGraw Hill.

Lynch, E.W., & Hanson, J.M. (2004). *Developing cross-cultural competence: A guide for working with children and their families* (3rd ed.). Baltimore: Paul H. Brookes Publishing Co.

Ramsey, P. (2004). *Teaching and learning in a diverse world: Multicultural education for young children* (3rd ed.). New York: Teachers College Press.

CHAPTER 4

Step by Step

Learning the Moves of the Relationship Dance in an Infant and Toddler Program

Rachel is an infant and toddler teacher in a metropolitan, high-quality, center-based child care program. Although it is early morning, she hurries to the center because she knows her three children will be arriving soon. She missed them over the weekend. Rachel smiles as she thinks about "her" three toddlers, now almost 2 years of age, for whom she has been the primary caregiver since they were about 3 months of age. Rachel's program practices a relationship-based approach. Teachers stay with the children through the infant and toddler years. She contrasts that to the program she worked in several years ago where babies "graduated" every several months. This new system has challenges, but Rachel reflects on how much better it seems to her than the previous program.

Ulrika is an infant and toddler teacher in a northern European, small, good-quality, center-based child care program. She also is enthusiastic about work. Her "family" of infants and toddlers ranges in age from 6 months to almost 3 years. The multi-age approach works well in this small program. Ulrika and the children's parents know that she will be with the infants and toddlers through their infant years.

Mary is a family child care provider. She also cares for several children younger than 3 years. In many ways, her approach to infant care offers benefits similar to those of Ulrika. Mary is the secure base for her infants and provides support for parents throughout the infant and toddler years.

In contrast, Micky works for a program in which infants are "graduated" when they reach developmental milestones: when they crawl, walk, or become 18 months of age and again around age 2. Micky admits that she does not want to "get too attached" to the babies in her room because she finds it difficult to "give them up." Micky thinks that it is hard on the babies and parents when they graduate if they get too attached. She also does not want the teachers in the next room to be angry with her if the "graduated" babies cry when they see her. So, Micky tries to be a good caregiver and be supportive of the parents' wishes but remains somewhat detached with the babies.

In this chapter, we turn to how to structure a program that emphasizes relationships. The first three anecdotes illustrate different ways that relationship-based programs for infants and toddlers may be structured. Micky's program, however, does not emphasize the importance of caregiver relationships for infants and toddlers. The relationship-based programs emphasize the extension of the infant's relationship dances by supporting the child's relationship with child care teachers and caregivers. Micky's program supports the first dance (with parents) but does not fully extend the child's relationship dance into child care. In this case, for the infant who is "born dancing," as Thoman and Browder (1987) illustrated, the natural tendency to be in the comforting rhythms of familiar relationship dances may be interrupted during child care.

STRUCTURING A RELATIONSHIP-BASED PROGRAM

Many infant and toddler programs want to adopt an approach that builds on relationship research and principles. Staff in these programs must determine how to design such a program. How do they extend the dance to optimize relationships within their program? How do they construct their programs in ways that support children's security and learning by maximizing sensitive, caring relationships in all the possible arenas (e.g., teacher–child, parent–child, teacher–parent)? A number of dance steps or features will move programs in this direction. The remainder of this book details practical features of programs, drawn from the experiences of both authors, that support relationship-oriented programming for infants and toddlers. In this chapter, we identify core program features to consider in designing a relationship-based program.

Before designing a relationship-based approach, the following preliminary assumptions should be considered:

1. *Adopting a relationship-based approach requires a strong belief in the importance of relationships.* A careful read of infant and toddler development literature, as briefly reviewed in Chapter 2, should leave one with little doubt about the importance of relationships to infant development. If staff are not in agreement about the importance of implementing a relationship-based approach, it would be helpful to study the literature first to attain a programwide understanding about why changes are recommended.

2. *All relationships matter.* Greater care is given to reflection and thought in relationship-based programs. For this reason, Figure 1.1 emphasized parent–teacher and other relationships.

3. *A definitive "right way" to develop a relationship-oriented infant and toddler program does not exist.* Like relationships themselves, every program is unique. Each program will have its own dynamic ways to apply relationship-oriented features, reflecting beauty in diversity and creativity. Thus, some components in this book may not fit a particular program. Some programs change their approach to assigning babies to teachers first. Others may feel that they need to begin with teachers moving with children. Hopefully, the reader will feel that we offer alternatives about how to implement a relationship-based approach. Boxes throughout this book offer real-life examples of quite different approaches to our overall theme.

4. *The focus on relationships does not replace the need to develop overall program quality.* The features of quality are important in all programs, including relationship-based programs. Quality in early childhood programs, including quality for infant and toddler programs, has been defined and researched for more than 40 years. Generally, quality is considered to have two overarching aspects: *Process quality* pertains to the components of the program that children directly experience, whereas *structural quality* is more distal and sometimes refers to components that states can regulate (e.g., teacher qualifications). The *Infant/Toddler Environment Rating Scale–Revised Edition (ITERS-R;* Harms, Cryer, & Clifford, 2006), a commonly used measure of infant and toddler center-based quality, includes the subcomponents of interaction, listening and talking, personal care routines (including health and safety), activities, space and furnishings, program structure, and parents and

staff as a diverse set of features that together comprise quality.[1] A comparable measurement for family child care is the *Family Child Care Environment Rating Scale–Revised Edition* (Harms, Cryer, & Clifford, 2007). The features of quality are important in all programs, including relationship-based programs. Thus, relationships-based programs build on a base of quality but go further and emphasize a number of additional features. A relationship-based orientation, however, may influence how some or many aspects of quality are organized.

FEATURES OF RELATIONSHIP-BASED PROGRAMS

A number of features tend to characterize relationship-based programs (see Table 4.1). This chapter discusses the importance of ongoing communication about relationships within the program, primary caregiver assignment to individual infants, small group size, continuity in which primary caregivers and children stay together over parts or all of the infant and toddler years, and a teacher role that highlights the child–teacher relationship. Later chapters discuss other features, including supporting relationships among children, recognizing that children's peer relationships are important even at very young ages, the special focus on beginnings and endings, the opportunity to individualize and document children's growth and development, close relationships with parents, teacher and administrator roles, and the design and use of indoor and outdoor environments to support the relationship-based approach.

Table 4.1 highlights the differences between relationship-based and more typical programs—differences which in some cases may be quite noticeable and in other cases rather subtle. Programs may use some or all of these core features. In general, programs that incorporate more of these features tend to have relationships as the unifying feature of the program. Boxes 4.1 to 4.3 provide examples of programs that incorporate relationship-based core features within their overall program approach—in very different ways.

Communication

In a relationship-based program, there is necessarily considerable conversation about the importance of relationships. Teachers understand the importance of relationships to infants; that understanding is reflected in their communications. They understand attachment and what it provides for infants. Thus, if a child

---

[1]The ITERS-R incorporates a feature we discuss as a core feature of relationship-based program: continuity. In the ITERS-R, continuity is measured as an option available for a child to remain with the same staff and group for more than 1 year as part of the Parents and Staff subcomponent. The original version of ITERS did not measure this feature. Thus, to some extent, continuity may increasingly be viewed as a component of quality rather than as a feature that goes beyond quality.

Table 4.1. Assumptions about relationship-based features

Features of a child care program	Traditional American infant and toddler programs	Relationship-based infant and toddler programs
Communication	Program emphasizes other features.	Emphasis placed on the importance of relationships in program communication materials.
Teacher–child assignment	Program may involve multiple teachers for each child.	One teacher is primary caregiver.
Group size and teacher-to-child ratios	Often group sizes and ratios are what licensing laws allow, with several teachers sharing responsibility for multiple children.	Attempts are made to keep groups small, often lower than licensing requirements. Ratios are also often lower than licensing laws specify.
Continuity	Children graduate to new rooms at times of developmental shifts (e.g., when they crawl, when they walk, as 2-year-olds).	Teachers and children stay together as long as possible—throughout infant and toddler years.
Role of teacher with children	Teacher tries to have positive interactions with children.	Teacher tries to provide secure base and responsive relationships with children as well as to have positive interactions.
Peer relationships	Children may be placed in classrooms according to multiple criteria.	Teachers make every attempt to keep compatible nursery mates together.
Beginnings and endings	Children are expected to adjust to the new program and teachers; beginnings and endings may or may not be treated as needing extra support.	Special care is taken to help children adjust to the program and new teachers; special attention is given to separations.
Individualizing and documenting	Planning and the curriculum may be focused on the group. Documentation may focus on group activities, and/or individual portfolios may record how individuals responded to group activities.	Planning is motivated by interests and the development of individual children. The curriculum is used to plan for individuals. Progress of individuals is documented (e.g., individual notebooks, portfolios, diaries).
Relationships with parents	Teacher emphasizes good communication with parents. There may not be as much investment in building a long-term relationship with parents.	Teacher intentionally helps parents build their own relationships with children. Teacher invests in building a long-term relationship with parents as well as emphasizing good communication.

(continued)

Table 4.1. *(continued)*

Features of a child care program	Traditional American infant and toddler programs	Relationship-based infant and toddler programs
Staff relationships	Teachers are committed to a room. Career changes may not be related to when children graduate. Turnover may be higher.	Teachers are committed to specific children. Turnover may be reduced. Administrators work to support the relationship model.
Environment	Space is designed to accommodate the group size of the infant and toddler program.	Space is planned to accommodate teachers and children staying together over time.

BOX 4.1.
Ounce of Prevention Educare

The Ounce of Prevention Educare program in Chicago, Illinois, implements continuity of teaching. "The Ounce" is a well-known Early Head Start/Head Start program that also receives state and private funds to serve more than 150 low-income children ages 0–5 years each year. The program is located on the south side of Chicago.

At the Ounce, continuity of care refers to the practice of keeping infants and toddlers together with their same peers as well as with the same teachers. The children and teachers are usually together from the time the child enters the program to about 3 years of age.

In this program, there are six infant and toddler rooms with same-age cohorts (two infant, two toddler, and two 2-year-old rooms). There are also two mixed-age classrooms. According to Illinois state law, children have to be at least 6 weeks old to enter the program. The classroom teachers are required to have a bachelor's degree, and teacher assistants need an associate's degree. Classroom aides (not expected to have degrees) typically have had some early childhood experience, courses, or a Child Development Associate credential. Every staff member completes an interview process before being hired. The Ounce looks for people who have experience, are passionate, are reflective, and want to do the hard work.

Continuity models are important for any program but especially for programs that serve low-income families. "Children develop relationships, good or bad. What they really need is predictability more than anything but they need love and tenderness as well," said Dr. Mary Jane Chainski from the Ounce.

This program has overcome many challenges in implementing the continuity philosophy. Because the model depends so greatly on

Box 4.1 (continued)

This teacher of older toddlers has been with her group since the children were infants.

keeping children and teachers together, continuity of staff is also an important matter. Good supervision and support for the staff have been essentials at the Ounce for keeping staff and to successfully implement this program. Funding is also important.

Both parents and teachers receive support in understanding the premises and research about secondary attachment relationships. For example, parents have had concerns about the development of attachment with teachers. Teachers also have concern and some have worried about a baby getting "too attached." They have expressed concern about fairness to the other babies who need attention as well as fairness to the teachers in their work load. Supervisory staff help parents understand the literature that clearly shows children's primary attachments are with parents and that teacher attachments supplement this primary attachment to provide security for children while they attend care.

Another challenge has been keeping the children in the program because of family mobility out of the program area. Through the relationships that are developed at the Ounce, the support that is offered to the families, and the value that is placed on the development of every individual child, the Ounce staff hope that families who do move from the area will continue to use their services, even though it may require a longer commute.

Benefits of this model are extensive. Teachers really enjoy the continuity aspect of this model because they are able to be with the same children for a few years, developing relationships with them as well as their families. Transitions to new classrooms and strange situations, which otherwise may be traumatic, are easier for the children because they have come to rely on the consistency and expectancy that the primary teachers provide at the Ounce. Transitions to new

(continued)

Box 4.1 (continued)

classrooms in the building as the children age are handled with care, leaving the children with a feeling of acceptance that they are moving on versus the thought that they have been left behind.

Relationships between staff members, children, and parents are all very important in this model. The Ounce sees that it is important to be clear with the parents as well as to be readily available to them. The Ounce staff provides a very thorough orientation for the new parents to the center.

The design of the building influences the development of these relationships, as it provides a comfortable place for parents to just hang out and talk to people that they see. It gives staff the opportunity to tell parents about something they saw their child do that day or recognize the parent for showing interest in their child's development. Good documentation is another key to developing and keeping those relationships. This gives the parents an opportunity to see what is going on in the classrooms as a learner with their children.

At the Ounce of Prevention Educare program, each child has a primary caregiver.

Ultimately, a program has to be based on the needs of the community and the people that it serves. The Ounce of Prevention program serves as an educator for policy makers, both on the state and federal level; the program serves young, at-risk children and their families and provides a safe, healthy, and predictable environment for everyone involved in the program. The Ounce recognizes the importance of the early years in the development of each child; through their continuity and relationship-based models, it is providing a rich early experience for children and families who need it the most.

Adapted by Martha Ostrom, Lecturer, University of Nebraska-Lincoln, from an interview with Mary Jane Chainski, Director of the Bounce Learning Network at the Ounce and former Interim Site Manager at Educare, Chicago. She has been involved with this program for 8 years and has been in the early childhood field for 37 years. More information can be found at http://www.ounceofprevention.org

BOX 4.2.
Early Head Start Child Development, Inc.

Early Head Start, a Child Development, Inc. (CDI) program headquartered in Russellville, Arkansas, is a center-based Early Head Start program (as is the Ounce of Prevention Educare program featured in Box 4.1). It serves approximately 180 infants and toddlers in centers located in a number of rural counties in Arkansas. As is true for all Early Head Start programs, a primary caregiver is assigned to each infant; infants and teachers at CDI stay together until children are 3 years old.

In this program, teachers and parents begin their relationship even before the child is born. As the photos show, teachers meet with pregnant mothers before birth. During these early meetings, the teachers establish their relationship with the expectant parent, review important information about infant development and caring for an infant, and generally reinforce the prenatal care and information the parent is receiving.

Teachers make prebirth visits to mothers whose children will be attending their program.

The teacher reviews aspects of prenatal development and care, birth, and postpartum plans with the expectant mother.

(continued)

Box 4.2 (continued)

Some of the prenatal visits occur in the child care setting that the baby will later attend, enabling the mother to become comfortable with the setting. After birth, the teacher may visit the mother in the hospital and will do home visits weekly until the child comes to the center. This early relationship between the teacher and mother facilitates the relationship building between teacher and child and creates a base for continuing the teacher–parent mutual commitment to the child.

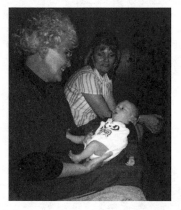

Shortly after birth, the new baby is introduced to the teachers in the center.

A new mother brings her infant son to the center for his first day of care, but his teacher already knows him.

As time progresses and the child spends time in the center, mother and teacher continue to grow in their mutual effort on behalf of the child and the teacher's support helps to support the important relationship between mother and child.

cries during separation from parents, a listener is likely to hear a teacher explain that the child may be having normal separation anxiety. The teacher is empathetic in language about the separation. A listener would *not* hear that the child is too attached, is spoiled, or needs to be "broken" of his or her attachment.

Parents receiving an initial tour of the program will hear about the importance of relationships in the program. In the materials the program publishes, such as brochures and web sites, the importance of relationships is emphasized. The program materials tell how relationships are promoted and why. Boxes 4.4 and 4.5 illustrate language that directors and teachers may find helpful in explaining the program.

When teachers or parents are having problems with a child, directors or other teachers may talk with the teacher or parent about the child's relationships.

BOX 4.3.
Continuity of care at an institution in Hungary

In 1946, a physician named Emmi Pikler opened the Pikler Institute for orphaned and abandoned infants in Budapest that became famously known by its street name, *Lóczy*. The methods of the Pikler Institute have been very influential in France and other parts of Europe because of the fact that children leaving the institution showed surprisingly positive outcomes (e.g., high physical motor skills, low levels of aggression), as well as few of the negative outcomes (e.g., attachment disorder) often associated with institutional experience during the early years. Pikler was the teacher of Magda Gerber, who brought the ideas to the United States and founded Resources for Infant Educarers (RIE), an organization that offers trainings and resources to parents and infant providers.

The Pikler Institute still operates today under the direction of Emmi's daughter, Anna Tardos. What is the secret of its success? Pikler set out to find feasible, replicable, cost-effective ways to eradicate the main cause of neglect in orphanage life, which she saw as the frequent changes of environment and caretakers; impersonal methods of care; lack of significant attachments and affective relationships; monotonous, nonstimulating, and restrictive environments; and lack of contact with the outside world. Pikler developed a theory and set of practices that promoted the following:

Continuity instead of change. Infants live in small groups where they are cared for by the same four nurses (caregivers) throughout their whole stay in the institution. Each child builds a significant, favored, affective relationship with one nurse. Extreme care is taken to limit the number of adults caring for any one child, to ensure their continuous presence for the duration of the child's stay in the institution, and to establish a consistency in their caregiving and educational approach (e.g., their style of speaking and handling children). The small group of children becomes emotionally attached to one another as playmates and companions.

Treating the child as a person, not an object. Nothing is done with haste. Instead, nurses provide personalized attention to each infant in a relaxed, set order that lets each child know exactly when to expect to be fed, bathed, and changed. Caregiving is done with close individual attention, soft touches, sensitive and gentle handling, continual talking with the child about what will happen next, and seeking readiness from the child before continuing (e.g., "Here's another bite; are you ready for it?" or "I am taking your hand to put your shirt on"). A child's feeding or other routine care is never interrupted once it has begun; barring an

(continued)

Box 4.3 (continued)

exceptional situation, the nurse always finishes what she has started with a child. Care is also taken to make the child an active, cooperating participant every time that someone comes into contact with the child. Through these techniques, a child learns that needs will be met in turn and that he or she can trust in predictable, one-to-one, satisfying provision of basic needs.

Safeguarding psychomotor and intellectual development. Good physical health is promoted by trained medical personnel and by sound health and nutritional practices. Regular medical examinations and detailed observations are carried out to monitor the child's development. The necessity of fostering the children's self- and environmental awareness is fostered. From the earliest age, children discover the pleasure produced by free physical activity. They are not restricted in walkers, strollers, infant seats, or other mechanical devices but instead learn to sit up, crawl, creep, and walk through their own independent exploration and effort. For example, a child is never placed in a sitting position until the child can sit on his or her own. Except when the child is being fed, bathed, or changed, he or she is left to explore stimulating objects and play with peers without restriction in a safe but challenging space, under the nurse's watchful eye. After children become fully mobile, they take regular walks in pairs around the neighborhood with a trained adult (often someone from the neighborhood) who helps the children become part of the community. The adult follows the small children's wishes for the pace of the walk, where to go, what to look at, and what to talk about (e.g., they may spend their whole hour playing in a puddle or they may walk for blocks, depending on their mood)—all to support their curiosity and initiative.

Sources: David & Appell (2001); Sussna Klein (2002).

Infants are not blamed for their behaviors. Rather, clues to misbehavior are sought in the context of relationships (e.g., Is the child feeling insecure in one or more relationships?).

Teacher–Child Assignment: Primary Caregiver

In many programs, two teachers are assigned to each room to care for 8 infants or toddlers (a common ratio in many states). Some programs may have three teachers caring for 8, 9, or 12 infants. Traditional programs may share care of all the babies. Programs may even suggest that this is a good approach because all of the teachers know all of the babies (and vice versa) and all of the teachers help each other out.

BOX 4.4.
Language to parent about continuity

Teacher to parent: "Our family will be moving to the 2-year room in a couple of months. I will move with (child) and the other children in our family so the children should feel very secure with the change. We'll also visit often so it is familiar to them before the transition."

Director to parent: "We emphasize children and teachers staying together in this program based on attachment theory, which shows that children develop best and are most relaxed and able to learn when they have secure attachments. We believe the parent–child attachment is the most important attachment but that a secure teacher–child attachment is important too—it helps the infant feel safe and secure while here."

In a relationship-based program, each infant is assigned to one of the two or three teachers, although other teachers help with the infant as needed. The assigned teacher is referred to as the baby's primary caregiver. A casual observer might not be able to tell the difference between the two types of programs at first glance. However, over time the viewer will see how the primary caregiver plays a special role with the baby. Parents know that this is the caregiver who is ultimately accountable for their baby. This is the caregiver the baby should be handed to in the morning. This primary caregiver provides information about the child's day. Over time and with consistency, the relationship among the primary caregiver,

---

BOX 4.5.
Director-to-teacher language about continuity

Director to teacher: "I know you especially enjoy caring for the younger infants but we want to promote secure attachments that are really deep and meaningful, so it is important for you to stay with them for 2 years at least—preferably until they are 3 years old and ready to enter preschool."

Director to new teacher: "I would like you to consider very carefully whether you think you can make a 3-year commitment to these children. Of course, things come up, but generally we like to keep children and teachers together throughout the infant–toddler years. Think carefully about this before making the commitment. We will help you think about your next steps consistent with your professional development plan when your children get close to age 3 years. We think that is the time to make a professional change."

---

infant, and parents deepens. The child develops a secondary attachment (see Chapters 1 and 2) and hopefully gains the benefits of secure attachment during child care. In some programs, the small group of children assigned to one primary caregiver is called her *family* or *family group*.

The Revised Head Start Performance Standards emphasize assigning infants and toddlers in child care settings to a primary caregiver (U.S. Department of Health and Human Services, 2002). Both the Educare program (see Box 4.1) and the CDI Early Head Start program (see Box 4.2) are relationship-based programs that follow the Revised Head Start Performance Standards.

In many programs where a primary caregiver is assigned, a large investment is often made in building the relationship. Parents and teachers meet together to get to know each other and to learn about the parents' values in regards to parenting. This may not be a formal process. Parents may invite the teacher to dinner or teachers may spend extra time with parents at drop-off and pick-up times. As children get older, events may be planned for all the parents and children in one teacher's family to gather socially.

How are primary caregiving assignments made? If a parent requests a particular teacher who is available, it is a good idea to respond to the parent's preference. However, the teachers themselves are important for the success of these relationships. Teachers should have a history of good personal relationships and understand the importance of relationships. Chapter 10 talks about the importance of hiring teachers with these qualities. Directors and master teachers should also work with teachers and parents to reflect on and build positive relationships.

Some children, even at a very young age, come with troubled relationship histories to their child care settings. Their teachers may need support to practice the relationship patterns that will help the children to acquire trust in the world. Fortunately, in the early years, parent and teacher relationships are often independent (see Chapters 1 and 2). Even a child who has a very insecure home relationship may be able to form a secure relationship with his or her teacher. Thus, it may be more important for the child and teacher to "go through" the child's resistances—with considerable support from the director and other staff or mental health consultants—rather than continuously switch teachers.

Group Size and Teacher-to-Child Ratios

Programs emphasizing relationships may tend toward relatively small group size, allowing teachers to concentrate on getting to know their own group of infants. Relationship-oriented programs often have smaller group sizes or teacher–child ratios than is allowed by state law. For example, in one relationship-based program, the state specified a teacher-to-student ratio of 1:4, with up to 12 infants allowed in one room. However, the room for the youngest infants usually had 8 or 9 babies with three teachers. From this team, one teacher with her family moved on to the next room (to begin continuity until age 3). The focus on relationships and desire for the new teachers who would be moving on with their families of infants to form good relationships caused the program to use smaller overall group sizes than the state allowed.

Another relationship-based program formed smaller groups and lower ratios than the state allowed for toddlers. The state allowed a 1:6 ratio beginning at 18 months, but the program often kept smaller families and maintained ratios of 1:4 or 1:5. This was possible (and affordable for the program) in part because families were willing to pay an unchanging infant and toddler rate from when children were 6 weeks until age 3, due to their satisfaction with having the same teacher for this time period. In another case, a relationship-based program built a new facility. Each teacher had individual rooms for her family of four children, which remained as their room throughout the infant and toddler years, from early infancy until children graduated to the preschool. The relationship-based program dictated the design of the space. The small, single-family rooms were "home" to the group of four children and their teacher for 3 years.

Early Head Start specifies both a primary caregiver for each child and group sizes of no more than eight children throughout the infant and toddler period. Educare relationship-based Early Head Start programs place three teachers with groups of eight children.

Continuity: Time with Teacher

Continuity of teacher–child relationships may be the heart of a relationship-based approach. Continuity involves infants staying with their primary teacher over the infant and toddler years (or at least for a significant amount of this period). Continuity with a primary caregiver is believed to allow the time and consistent interactions between the child's signals and the caregiver's responses necessary for a secure attachment to the teacher to develop. There are many ways to implement continuity of relationships between infants and teachers. Continuity in infant and toddler programs has a kinship with the practice of looping in elementary schools. In schools that use looping, the same teacher may stay with children from kindergarten through first, second, or even third grade.

One program emphasized children and teachers staying together from early infancy until children were 36 months of age. In this program, teachers and children moved together several times into spaces designed for the children's developmental level. These moves had an air of excitement about them. Children enjoyed the relatively new materials and spaces, and they were secure with change because their teacher and peers remained with them in the new space. When children were 3 or older, they graduated to the preschool. Educare of Chicago (see Box 4.1) follows this type of 0–3 continuity model.

Early Head Start in Russellville, Arkansas, begins its continuity approach even before children are born (see Box 4.2). The teacher who will care for the child visits the mother before birth, sometimes in the hospital after birth, and at home before the child begins child care at 6 weeks of age. By the time the child is ready to start child care, this teacher (who will be with the child for nearly 3 more years) already knows both the parent and child. Another relationship-based program keeps children and primary teachers together throughout the first year. Then, when the children become toddlers, they receive another primary teacher who is with them until they are 3 years of age.

There are different ways to consider age in infant and toddler programs: multi-age grouping, same-age grouping, and modified same-age grouping. Each of these approaches supports infant relations with teachers over time. Programs can be structured in other ways, but most cases are likely a variation of these three methods.

Multi-age Groups   With multi-age groupings, a single teacher may be responsible for three or four children (or the equivalent number if there are part-time children). Within the group, children's ages may vary from young infants up to 18 months or even up to 3 years. For example, in one program, the teacher cares for four children: a 2-month-old, a 9-month-old, an 18-month-old, and a 32-month-old. When the 32-month-old child graduates, a new younger child comes into her family.

The upper age of the group is often related to state teacher-to-child ratios. In some states, the infant period extends to 12 months. In other states, it is 18 or 24 months. Some programs, such as Early Head Start, require similar ratios across the entire infant and toddler period. Thus, multi-age groups may include children within the entire range of entry to 36 months.

Some teachers prefer multi-age grouping to same-age looping because they believe that the children learn a great deal from the older children. They also think that the older children learn more pro-social and nurturing skills by supporting younger infants. Other teachers prefer this approach because they think that children's variable schedules over these ages enable them to give each child more individual attention. Multi-age grouping also has some drawbacks, such as the difficulty in equipping a room for children of variable ages. For example, a 30-month-old toddler benefits from small toys that are unsafe for a 9-month-old infant. However, an inventive teacher can usually figure out ways to work around this problem.

Same-Age Groups   With the same-age group approach, children are fairly similar in age within the infant and toddler range. For example, one teacher's family was assigned to her when the children were quite young, between 2 and 4 months of age. The children's birthdays are all within 6 weeks of one another. They will stay together until the children are 3 years old. With same-age grouping, teachers become highly attuned to each developmental stage. The investment in preparing materials and activities is well received by both children and parents. Children may have highly complementary interests and form a tightly knit peer group. Although parents may compare children's developmental milestones (e.g., which child rolled over first), a good teacher can emphasize and celebrate individual differences to minimize this problem.

Modified Same-Age Groups   Programs using a modified same-age approach may group children by age during the first year or so of life. Children then move into a multi-age toddler room where family groups range from 12 or 18 months to 3 years. There is considerable variation in continuity programs, often for very good reasons intrinsic to the program or facility. One program used a same-age approach for only a year because one teacher could not commit to staying with children until age 3. Therefore, the same-age continuity system for a 0–3 system could not be fully implemented, even though other teachers were able to make this commitment. Variability among teachers is not uncommon, particularly when the continuity system is first being implemented. Because of space, personnel, or other reasons, it sometimes makes more sense for teachers to stay with children of one age group (e.g., 0–18 months or 18–36 months) but not over the entire time period of 0–36 months. Continuity systems seem to work best if programs feel they have some flexibility when implementing, particularly in the early stages.

Role of Teacher with Children

The relationship-based model builds out directly from attachment theory, described in Chapters 1 and 2. In high-quality infant and toddler programs, teachers respond to infants in ways that are sensitive and contingent, consistent with the research by Ainsworth and Bell (1970) and others. In a relationship-based program, the teacher also intentionally invests in the relationship with the child and works to build the attachment relationship; the teacher understands features of relationships with infants that might not be taken into account in a less relationship-based infant and toddler program. For example, a teacher in a relationship-based program acknowledges and cultivates the role as secure base for the child. The teacher knows that his or her presence gives the child an anchor for exploration and is of service to the child in this way, being consistent in interactions but also in space and time. In such a case, when the child looks to the teacher from across the room, tentative about touching a new object, the teacher may smile, thus signaling that it is okay to proceed. A good teacher of infants would know to maintain communication with the child during exploration, but a teacher in a relationship-oriented program incorporates such secure-base awareness into the conceptualization of his or her role as teacher. The teacher will be caring for this child for a long time, so investments in establishing a good relationship are well worth the inputs. Thus, in a relationship-oriented program, teachers may go further in investing in relationships with children and the teacher–child relationship dance.

As noted previously, relationship-based programs provide a specific way to view children's developmental problems. For example, if a child were demonstrating behavior problems in a relationship-based program, teachers might take a look at the teacher–child relationship or the parent–child relationship earlier rather than later in deliberations in an attempt to understand what the child might need. Perhaps the child's father has been out of town for an extended period or the mother and child have been experiencing conflict over bedtime. As a solution, if a child appears to be under stress, teachers are certain to give the child big doses of secure base, contact comfort, and highly contingent responses—all components of good relationships. Thus, often the teacher's quests for sources of and solutions to problems are sought in relationships.

Peer Relationships

When children are together in a family group with the same teacher over time, they become quite familiar with and attuned to one another. They learn to respond to each other in ways that are contingent and develop some ways of communicating with one another even before they can talk. Skillful teachers who know children well also scaffold interactions between children, teaching them relationship skills that increase their bonds with one another. For example, a skillful infant teacher can be seen encouraging infants to pass toys back and forth, to show one infant how to be gentle with another one, and to engage infants in empathetic responses to one another.

Studies have found that children who are secure in their caregiver relationships also are more effective in peer relationships (Erickson, Sroufe, & Egeland, 1985; Lieberman, 1977), possibly because they have learned good relating skills or because the adult attends to and scaffolds effective interactions. Another study found children who were secure with their teacher and who had been with their same group of children longer had better peer relationships than their counterparts (Erickson, 1991).

Both the child–teacher relationship and children's experiences with one another contribute to children's growing understanding and relating to peers. Sensitive teachers in relationship-based programs are aware of both their roles and the other children's roles in creating peer relationship skills and security. Thus, it is not surprising that in many relationship-based programs, children move as a group to preschool, even if the teacher does not accompany them. Children typically adjust very well with their secure base of peers around them. In such a model, children often become very attached to one another and may develop pro-social behaviors long before such behaviors are usually seen in infancy. They also may develop important and long-lasting friendships. For example, 9-month-old Mary would toss a ball towards Kelsey (also 9 months of age), giggle, and wait for Kelsey to react. These girls remained best of friends through elementary and high school, even celebrating their high school graduations together.

Beginnings and Endings

Beginnings—how the program experience starts and the handoff from parent to teacher—are important in relationship-based programs. Endings also matter—how a long-term experience with a teacher is completed and the reverse handoff from teacher to parent each and every day. Chapter 5 elaborates on beginning and ending program involvement.

In relationship-based programs, it is important to support both parents and children in the new child care experience. Program beginnings set the stage for long and productive relationships. Parents prepare by meeting the teacher, learning how the program works, having opportunities to visit, and forming a relationship with the teacher prior to the start of child care. For an infant, the preparation includes an adjustment period that allows parents to provide security until they are comfortable with the teacher.

Once the relationship with the teacher is comfortable, the beginning of the child's day involves greeting the teacher he or she has come to know and feel safe with. Avoiding rushing and pressure, teacher and parent allow the child to embrace the teacher and peers each morning and provide support on days when the child may feel conflict about separation. Relationship-based approaches bring strong relationships with teachers to the infant's natural reluctance to separate from parents, which mitigates stress for children and parents.

Continuity models, in which teachers and children build strong attachment relationships that serve children well over their infant and toddler years, need to address the anticipated and actual separation that occurs when children are ready for preschool. Parents may feel anxious about losing the predictability and partnership of the teacher to whom they have grown close. They may grieve the end of the child's infant and toddler years. Teachers may lament caring for the infants they have held, nourished, and loved over a period of several years. Children, especially if they move on with peers, may not be as sad as the adults about this transition. However, children may miss seeing the teachers they have depended on so consistently for several years. A sense of loss, as well as excitement about the future, may accompany this transition. In Chapter 5, we see how the Italians provide a capstone in the *diario,* or *diary.* Some relationship-based programs ritualize the transition with such things as graduation programs. Teachers, parents, and children celebrate the time and memories they have had together and acknowledge the natural sense of separation they may feel.

Just as each day should be carefully opened, it is also important to bring closure to child care days. Information about events and the emotional tone of the day are passed from teacher to parents. The teacher helps the child prepare for the transition to home, encouraging the child to greet the parent. As the child grows older, the teacher can help him or her prepare stories and artifacts (e.g., paintings) about the day. In some cases, the primary teacher's workday may end before the child leaves. In relationship-based programs, afternoon teachers are sought following the same principles as for primary teachers—they consistently work with the same group of children, every day if possible. Primary teachers are careful to orient the afternoon teachers so they can pass the parents information about events and the tone of the day. Beginnings and endings are important. They are treated respectfully and carefully in relationship-based programs.

Individualizing and Documenting

Relationship-based approaches to infant and toddler care allow for individualized programs (i.e., tailoring the program to the needs of individuals, particularly in planning experiences that nourish all areas of development and curricula). How does this happen? We find that teachers know children better when they form secure attachments that deepen over time. When teachers are wholly responsible for just three or four children, they are able to focus their attention and more deeply think about each child. A teacher might reflect, "What was Jon thinking about today when he was opening the cupboard doors?" Teachers focus on the development and meanings each child is expressing and about how they can expand and nourish those expressions. The relationships in a small group enable the teacher to approximate the kind of attention that tuned-in parents give to optimally developing infants.

Skillful and creative documentation can enhance a teacher's awareness of the development of individual infants, allowing for reflection about individual children and the overall group process. Through the lens of a camera or intentional observation, teachers become more attuned to the children in their care. By reflecting on what is seen and by preparing portfolios or documentation boards, the fleeting and changing moments of infancy are captured by teachers. Teachers and parents then can reflect together on the emerging development of infants. Documentation is honed to a fine art in Italian infant centers. Chapter 6 further describes individualizing and documentation approaches—both Italian and American.

Relationships with Parents

In high-quality traditional programs, teachers seek to communicate well and consistently with parents about children's activities. However, in relationship-oriented programs, there is often an even stronger investment in building that relationship and in supporting the parent–child relationship (see Figure 1.1). The investment in relationships with parents may have dimensions not seen in more traditional programs.

In one program that also emphasized research, each year teachers and parents both completed Attachment Q Sorts (Waters & Deane, 1985), a measure of the security of the child's attachment relationships that can be used with either teachers or parents. Attachment data were used for research and program aggregate purposes. Teachers and parents also were invited to a conference with the director, who examined the patterns within the Q Sorts to understand how the child was entering into relationships with each parent and teacher. During this conference, the director pointed out patterns of consistency as well as ways that each relationship could be strengthened. Conversation did not center on whether the child had secure or insecure relationships with adults, but rather focused on behaviors (e.g., Why does the mother rate "child seeks contact comfort" highly but the teacher does not?). The discussion was typically rich as the director, teacher, and parents sought to explore dimensions that would support the child in both relationships. Such a quest to build relationships may not be as strong or intentional in more traditional programs and the use of formal data may be unique even for relationship-based programs, although some programs do rely on formal and informal assessment procedures to determine if they are meeting their own goals. We return to the topic of teacher–parent relationships in Chapter 8.

Staff Relationships

Working in a relationship-based infant and toddler program has many implications for staff. First, not everyone can or should be a teacher in a relationship-based program. Hired teachers need to believe in the importance of relationships with infants and work hard to cultivate positive relationships. They need to recognize the healthy features of relationships and know when they are seeing features that are not healthy (see Chapters 1 and 2). For example, when infants do not greet parents or teachers happily, they are signaling some level of discomfort that needs to be addressed thoughtfully. When an infant wants to be picked up and then put down in a confused manner, the teacher knows the child is experiencing ambivalence. When the infant seems afraid to leave the teacher's side during play, there is work to do in helping the child feel secure enough to venture out. Teachers need to understand these often-subtle behaviors. Teachers who form secure relationships with infants are typically those who have experienced good relationships with parents and others themselves. In such cases, forming relationships with babies is intuitive.

Relationship-based approaches seem to bring an important shift in how teachers view their work commitments. One program had a high rate of turnover (not atypical of the child care field) prior to shifting to a relationship-based approach. After the program became relationship based, with teachers and children staying together over the infant and toddler period, turnover was drastically reduced. For many years subsequently, there was little or no turnover among the full-time teachers. In this program, teachers fell into the gentle rhythms of acquiring a new family of children every 3 years and staying with those children until the children were ready for preschool. Then, they reinvested in a new family for 3 more years. When teachers took a new family, it was emphasized that they were expected to stay until children entered preschool. If they desired a career change, teachers were asked to do so at that time. If teachers were unable to make the commitment to stay with their children during the infant and toddler years, then the program asked the teachers to be floaters or substitutes until they were ready to commit. This approach seemed to work in this particular program. Teachers increasingly came to understand the importance of relationships and why the program was structured in that way. When the 3-year time period was coming to an end, the director in this program spent a great deal of time reflecting with the teachers on professional goals. It was emphasized that this was the preferred time to make a transition. After considerable reflection, interestingly, the teachers usually would decide to invest in a new family and repeat the cycle.

A relationship-based approach may not work for all teachers. Intervention also may be needed to help some teachers promote relationships with children. Teachers have their own working models of relationships and bring their own early attachment relationships as ghosts from the nursery (Fraiberg, Edelson, & Shapiro, 1975). Teachers who did not experience healthy attachment relationships with their own caregivers may not be able to promote healthy attachments with infants. For example, Martina did not have a secure relationship with her mother, who abandoned the family when Martina was quite young. Although Martina enjoys very warm relationships with the children she cares for and both children and parents become quite affectionate toward her, Martina is also observed to interrupt children's play to draw attention back to herself. Intensive one-to-one guidance is helping Martina with her behavior, showing where she is strong and where she may be blocking relationships. However, it may be very difficult to change these patterns without Martina experiencing security in relationships or without more intensive attachment work. People like Martina can be good infant and toddler teachers if they have developed awareness of the qualities of good relationships and have had opportunities to form supportive relationships in their adult lives. However, it is very important to carefully hire teachers who will be teaching in a relationship-based program, as discussed in Chapter 10.

Administrators also have unique roles to play in a relationship-based program. Considerable administrative time must be devoted to directing a continuity- or relationship-based program. An administrator must oversee the admission and matriculation of children. When children are ready to move into the toddler room, administrators must ensure that there is available space and a smooth transition. Parents must be clearly informed about what to expect in the system. It is important that the administrator devotes sufficient attention to relationships with staff that sometimes—especially on their first moves—need support and counsel. Administrators must also work with teachers in building new partnerships. When a new teacher moves into a room with ideas about how the space should be used, her creativity and ownership should be honored, but the former team's approach should also be considered. When teachers have completed the cycle, they should receive recognition from the administrator for a job well done. Also, they often may need time to process the experience and grief that sometimes accompanies separation. On some occasions, an administrator must recognize that a teacher is not readily able to carry out this model. This may require close examination of the teacher's own attachment style—a process that may be painful. All teachers require feedback on their relationship-building style, but this process likely will be one that emphasizes growth and excitement about combining skills and awareness. Only an administrator who is highly committed to the approach should embark upon it. The model requires considerable effort and commitment. We return to the topic of staff again in Chapter 10.

Environment

The physical space of an early childhood facility needs to support a relationship-based approach. We think this topic is extremely important, so Chapter 7 is devoted entirely to it. Until then, we stress that teachers need to "own" their classroom spaces. Teachers need to feel a sense of pride and ownership in whatever classroom space is assigned to them. They need to be able to design the environment to individualize experiences, as we have described previously, for their small group of infants. It is important that the space supports children's use of teachers as a secure base. Thus, the classroom needs to have an ample play area so that children can explore while keeping their teacher in sight. In general, the space supports children's growing attachment relationships to their teachers, as well as easy teacher-to-parent communication. For example, children should not be taken to a different part of the building for naps away from their primary teacher. Children also should not be dropped off in a room other than the one where the child's primary teacher is located. This allows the teacher to be available to the parent for communication. The space should relate to the group size and lend itself to continuity. The outdoor environment needs special attention.

SUMMARY

This chapter emphasized some features of relationship-based programs, including communicating about the importance of relationships, assigning primary caregivers, small group sizes and low child-to-teacher ratios, continuity, teachers who provide a secure base, smooth transitions, individualized approaches to planning and documenting children's time in child care, an environment that supports relationships, and positive relationships within the early childhood community.

A continuity or relationship-based approach is not casually implemented (e.g., Aguillard, Pierce, Benedict, & Burts, 2005). However, we have noticed in both American and Italian programs that the deepening interactions and knowledge gained by intentionally promoting relationships among teachers, children, and parents are extremely rewarding. When a relationship-based program is fully implemented, we have observed that both calm and excitement characterize the program. The calm comes from the security that most children

come to feel while in the program; the excitement, from the framework for learning the approach provides.

The first author (Helen Raikes) conducted research in a program that aimed
for every child to have a secure relationship with the teacher. Of children who
stayed more than 1 year with teachers, 91% of their relationships with teachers
were assessed to be secure, using the Waters and Deane Attachment Q Sort
(Raikes, 1993). Because children felt safe and secure, they spent their time focused
on learning and developing, not crying anxiously. The teachers were calm and
secure in their knowledge of the importance of what they were doing. Parents were
typically relaxed and happy, knowing they had strong support during the infancy
years. The program developed rhythms, like life itself, of continuity and change.
The change was manageable because it occurred within the context of continuity.
The program was also characterized by excitement about learning. Freed from
many anxious cares and disruptions of adjusting to new teachers, teachers, children, and parents could concentrate on learning and enjoying each new day. As
teachers came to know children well, they could plan for them as new developmental passions and interests emerged. The rhythm lent itself to readily using an
infant and toddler curriculum that built on children's interests and strengths (see
Chapter 6). Teachers focused on their roles as secure bases. Planned playtimes
emphasized the natural excitements of normal infant and toddler development.

It may take several years to shift from a traditional to a relationship-based
approach. Box 4.6 illustrates how one program made that transition. Making
the shift often means capitalizing on changes and seizing opportunities when
there are staff changes. For example, a new teacher may be hired who is open to
moving up with the infants, thereby creating the opportunity to make a shift.
Each program that embarks on a relationship-based journey will be unique—like
relationships themselves!

BOX 4.6.
One program's story of
transition to a relationship-based program

It may be difficult to see exactly how a relationship-based approach is
different from more traditional, high-quality infant and toddler programs. The following real-life story should help you see the difference.

The story originated about 1980. Helen Raikes was co-director of
an employer-supported child care center serving employees of The
Gallup Organization and a community hospital in Lincoln, Nebraska.
The program was initially not relationship based. Children graduated
from Baby 1 (room for infants from 6 weeks to mobility) to Baby 2 (room
for crawling infants) to Toddler 1 (room for advanced crawlers and
"wobbly walkers") to Toddler 2 (secure walkers) to the 2-Year-Old

Box 4.6 (continued)

Room. With each move, the child changed to a set of new teachers. Parents and children, therefore, were continuously in adjustment mode and—perhaps not surprisingly—there was some teacher turnover.

However, noting what sometimes felt like unnecessary disruptions, we asked, "Why are all of these changes occurring and do they make sense given what we know about how infants develop and learn?" We also asked ourselves, "Does this make sense given what we know about the importance of relationships to the development of infants and toddlers?" Furthermore, the culture of the employer organization was one that studied, analyzed, and sought to improve relationships of all types. Did it not make even further sense to make our infant and toddler program consistent with this emphasis on relationships?

We set to work changing to an approach that made more sense based on what we know about babies and began to invite teachers to move with children. We did not make these changes abruptly but gradually over a period of several years. First, when one group of children was ready to graduate to the next level, we asked if the teacher would like to move with the children. Teachers weighed these decisions carefully. To move with one group meant leaving behind routines and a teacher partnership that may have become comfortable. Teachers may have thought of themselves as "tiny baby specialists" or "toddler specialists." Thus, to move into a new room often meant that they, too, would have to take risks and grow in new ways as teachers. On the other hand, in weighing those decisions, teachers recognized the value of continuing to build the relationships with the children they would move with. Some teachers chose to move, and others did not.

However, when teachers moved with children, we noted important differences. With the supportive teacher as a secure base for the move, the moves were characterized by a greater sense of adventure. Parents seemed less anxious, and there was a general downward spiraling of child and parent tension around changes. Knowing the beloved teacher would be with the child, the parents and (at some level) the children often became excited about the anticipated moves. For example, we would more frequently hear teachers and parents alike stating this group of children was "ready to move." As a result, knowing the teacher would move with children tended to mean that everyone seemed better able to fully embrace the coming new experiences and stages of development.

Gradually, more and more teachers began to "move up" with their children. After about 3 years, we had established an entire system whereby every 6 months or so, there was a shift of teachers and children rippling throughout the program. A teacher from Baby 1 would move with a group of newly mobile infants into Baby 2; a group of advanced mobile and beginning walking toddlers would move with their teacher

(continued)

Box 4.6 (continued)

into Toddler 1; and solidly mobile toddlers who were gaining in representation abilities and organized play would move with their teacher into Toddler 2. Finally, a teacher with new 2-year-old children would move with them into what was known in our program as the "magical" 2-Year-Old Room. This was quite a procession, preceded by visits to the new room, meetings with parents, deep housecleaning and space planning, and intensive meetings among the teachers in new partnerships.

We learned a great deal in those early years of experimentation about what went through teachers' minds as they prepared for such a move. We soon learned that they began thinking about whether they would "move up" far in advance, but we noted both a deepening and relaxing of the investment they made with the children and parents when they knew they would stay together over time. Altogether, the transition to an entirely relationship-based, continuity model took about 3 years.

CHAPTER 5

The Right Foot

Beginnings and Endings

Carolyn Pope Edwards and Lella Gandini

Beginnings and endings—welcomes and good-byes—are very important times in early childhood settings. Beginning moments, when children and their families first enter a classroom or program, set the tone for whatever new experiences will follow. Ending times, when children and families prepare to move to a new classroom or program, are equally important because they provide closure and next steps. Both beginnings and endings represent major transition times for children, and they have received much attention in the professional literature. During these times, the dance of relationship opens up to include the possibility of new people, places, and routines. The child has a chance to learn new moves and dance steps. The opportunity to stumble is also present, so it is important for adults to help children get off on the right foot as they step into each new relationship, as well as to pass off the children well when they are ready to leave the classroom or program and move on to a new one.

The bigger the transition, the more emotional it is for the person going through it; therefore, transitions should be treated with respect and care. A good transition helps everyone get off on the right foot together. The transition to kindergarten in particular is considered a key time to influence the child's and family's attitudes toward the school experience. Intense transitions are emotionally charged with the uncertainty of change. For example, entering a new setting like preschool or child care creates uncertainty for the child and parents about the people, routines, and expectations. The level of emotional arousal increases on transition days, and when the uncertainty gets too high, the child or parent may feel anxiety or even fear. Moderate levels of uncertainty often arouse excitement and anticipation because most people enjoy new situations when they feel in control.

Beginnings and endings are also times of significant learning. Transitions present learning opportunities because people best remember whatever stimuli come first or last in a sequence. In memory studies, this tendency is called *primacy* or *recency.* For example, when introduced to a set of new names and faces at a party, a person is more likely to remember the individuals met first upon arrival and last before leaving, rather than the ones in between. In addition, cultures always commemorate important "firsts." For example, baby books are full of first events that parents want to remember—first laugh, first step, first word, first birthday, first day of preschool. In many cultures, the naming ceremony (e.g., baptism in Christian religions) is a big family event where the child is formally named and accepted into the group. It is an important rite of transition marked by family, feasting, and rituals. Likewise, graduations are very special times.

This chapter considers some ways that teachers can take advantage of the emotional and cognitive significance of beginnings and endings. They can use beginning times to construct a sense of belonging and mutual trust and set up the conditions for the kinds of relationships that they want to form in their setting. They can use ending times to create shared meaning about what happened in the setting and why this history is important for the child and the family. Because Italy is a country that has pioneered and developed to a high level the art of transition in early childhood education, we will take special note of some of its models for beginnings and endings.

A DELICATE TIME OF BEGINNING RELATIONSHIPS: INSERIMENTO

The presence of someone who is very well known to the child for the entire duration of the settling in period is highly valued and supported in Italy. After a series of communications and visits between the family and the center, parents are invited to spend some time at the center with their child. During the first days, the parent and child will remain for a few hours playing, observing, and communicating with the teachers and other families. Day by day, parents and children increase their stay in the center until their full schedule is reached. The center provides flexibility in the way parents can respond most effectively. With a great range of variation covered, parents' full-time presence may last from a minimum of a few days for some families to a maximum of several weeks for others. (Bove, 2001, p. 110)

In Italy, educators give particular attention to beginnings and endings as delicate and significant times in the course of human relationships (Edwards & Rinaldi, 2008; Kaminsky, 2005). They have drawn on attachment theory and worked on developing a gradual, individualized, and respectful period of entry that they call *Inserimento* (pronounced in-ser-i-men-to). Inserimento literally means "becoming inserted," but is better translated as "settling in." It refers to the method of fostering relationships and communication when the child is entering the infant and toddler program for the first time (Bove, 1999, 2001). The concept includes not only fostering a smooth separation from the parent and home, but also the child and family's adjustment into the new community at the program. The adjustment period is interpreted as a delicate event in the child's and family's life. Therefore, it involves a variety of strategies aimed at encouraging parental involvement and begins well before the child's first day at the center. Inserimento requires careful planning and preparation by the teachers. It allows children to use their parents as a secure base while they gain familiarity and confidence in the new setting and to gradually widen their circle of companionship to include new peers and caregiving adults.

Over the years, Italian educators have defined general guidelines and developed variations of procedure for Inserimento (Bove, 2001; Edwards & Gandini, 2001; Gandini, 2001; Kaminsky, 2005). There are two main alternatives. In the first approach, Individual Inserimento, each parent and child unit enters at a separate time so that educators can focus attention on each newcomer. The teachers set up a schedule in consultation with all of the families to stagger the entry points. Many parents (usually mothers) then arrange to take some vacation days from work so that they can be free to be at the center as much as they and their children like. The second method is Group Inserimento, in which a small set of families enter at the same time. In this case, each new family and child gets less individual teacher attention. The families look more to each other right away and begin to care about and find support in one another, as well as in the teachers. Both methods have their advantages.

Prior to the period of Inserimento, the child care administration has already created a foundation of positive expectations. The administration has communicated an image of the programs that will reassure parents and make them feel welcome in the centers. This positive message has been constructed over time (weeks or months) and takes the form of publicity materials, including booklets, posters, and notices widely distributed throughout the town. These sources of information are backed up by the special occasions that are open to the whole town, as well as the informal reports and grapevine communications of families who have used the programs. For the new families, each contact—from the first trip to the Office of Public Instruction for registering, to the first visit to an infant and toddler center, to the encounter with the teachers to plan the child's transition into the center—is carefully and thoughtfully prepared and executed.

The First Entry

The process of Inserimento in the city of Pistoia, Italy, was studied for 12 families in 1995 (Edwards & Gandini, 2001; see Box 5.1). These families were followed for 3 years to determine how the children and families made their first transition into the program, how they "retransitioned" after summer vacation, and how their final transition from the infant and toddler center to preschool was conducted.

In this center, teachers prepared a cozy and friendly area, equipped with pillows and baskets of toys, to welcome each family one by one (on a prearranged schedule). They also made wall displays of photos and notes about each child's initial transition period. In one center, there was a small book for each child that contained written notes on each day by both a teacher and parent. In another center, there was a poster that showed a photo of each child, a plastic envelope that contained a piece of string that measured the baby's height on the first day, and a few notes. Later, these photos and notes were used as pages in the child's memory book.

One year, videos were made by the teachers of their new babies' weeklong period of Inserimento. The heightened emotion of all participants is easy to see. The parents entered the new situation with expectations of pleasure. The children looked at their parents' faces to read their parents' emotional reactions. Mothers only, both parents, or sometimes a grandparent came to meet the teacher who would be the one to guide the family and child through the transition. Parents never left the child on the first day. On subsequent days, as the child felt more comfortable, parents would leave the child for longer and longer periods. The pace of separation was guided by the child's and parent's sense of emotional comfort. Box 5.1, composed of images captured from video, illustrates the story of Chiara, one child who was followed for 3 years in the research study. Her period of adjustment was about as reassuring and gentle as any parent could possibly hope. In fact, when later interviewed about how the Inserimento had gone, this mother commented, "Very well. If my daughter could talk, she would have said, 'Go on, leave, Mommy.'"

The Time of Re-Inserimento

At the beginning of the children's second and third years in the infant and toddler centers of Pistoia, children's readjustment periods went smoothly and easily. Most children were glad to see former playmates and quickly took up old play patterns and familiar toys. The teachers made a symbolic event out of the "Re-Inserimento" by setting aside a day for each child during which he or she formally presented a box of treasures collected with the help of families over the summer. Then, at lunch, that child had the further honor of helping the adults serve the meal. Sometimes the child's mother came to the center to help her toddler hand out little gifts (sweets) to all the children in the group.

BOX 5.1.
Inserimento (settling in)

This box describes Chiara's first week in an infant and toddler center in Pistoia, Italy.

The first day, Chiara (10 months old) and her mother came into the infant and toddler center, *Il Grillo* (The Caterpillar). Chiara's mother invited the teacher, Franca, to hold her baby, and together they went around to look at the environment. Franca said, "Let's show your mommy your room."

They looked at the cubbies where extra clothes and diapers are put, and then Franca pointed out, "Here there will be notebooks compiled by both parents and teachers—a notebook to go back and forth. You can write what you see, and we will respond with what we see."

Franca said, "Why don't we sit down, and your mother will tell me everything about Chiara."

As the adults talked, the baby played. Teacher and mother in turn offered toys to Chiara, which she happily accepted. Chiara's mother told what Chiara liked to eat, how she liked to go to sleep, and why the parents decided to bring her to the center. Asked about her expectations for Chiara in the center, the mother told about one of her hopes: "I don't want Chiara to be one of those little girls who are so shy that they won't talk to anyone. Maybe coming to the infant-toddler center, she will become an outgoing girl."

Just then, Chiara's attention was attracted by the sight of a little boy slightly older than herself and coming around the corner into her area. This little boy was already adjusted to the program. Franca picked up immediately on Chiara's attention and drew a connection to the mother's expressed desires for Chiara. She told the mother, "Chiara is very interested in other children." The mother nodded, "Yes, yes." So, Franca gently carried Chiara close to Lorenzo and introduced the

(continued)

Box 5.1 *(continued)*

two in the affectionate language Italians often use in talking to young children.

The children seemed to enjoy this three-way interaction. Chiara reached out to put her hand softly onto Lorenzo's hand as Franca said that he was *bello* (handsome). Then, Chiara turned to look directly into the face of her new teacher, as if to take in fully who she was. She also looked over at her mother to check with her. Her mother was gazing at her with a smiling face, signaling that she approved of her baby's interest in new people.

Later in the week, Chiara was now comfortable enough that her mother left her for a while each day. One time, her mother intended to return to feed her, but because she was delayed, Franca began to feed Chiara. The baby ate hungrily until she saw her mother arriving, whereupon she burst into tears. Franca sat back to make room for the mother to draw near and handed over the bowl of cereal. The mother tried to feed Chiara some more bites, but the baby was too distressed to eat. Her mother took her out of the feeding chair into her arms to comfort her.

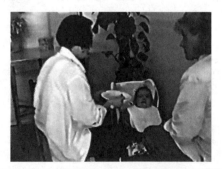

Box 5.1 (continued)

> By the end of the week, Chiara and her mother were now very comfortable in the center. When Chiara's mother arrived to pick her up, Chiara rested in her teacher's arms while the adults talked about the baby's day. Then, Chiara reached out for her mother. As mother and baby turned to leave, Chiara's mother named everyone present and waved bye-bye for Chiara to her friends.
>
> *Source:* This photo essay is drawn from the research project of Gandini, Edwards, Galardini, Giovannini, and the municipal infant and toddler educators of Pistoia, Italy (Edwards & Gandini, 2001).

SUGGESTIONS FOR ORCHESTRATING SMOOTH BEGINNINGS

American early childhood literature is filled with tips for smooth beginnings (e.g., Baker & Manfredi/Petitt, 2004). For instance, there are many songs and games that help children get to know everyone's name. Teachers also know that they must begin the school year by carefully teaching children the routines and rules they will need for the new setting. Educators have worked out effective ways to improve the introduction of children with disabilities and their families. Careful planning is important for infants and toddlers, for whom attachment is such a central part of life. Infants and toddlers have a difficult time with issues of transition and adjustment because they are still constructing internal representations of their primary attachment (see Chapter 2).

The period of separation and adjustment must account for children's fears and anxieties around separation. Careful planning about the parents' feelings is just as important. A program can do many things to create a welcoming atmosphere for new families and to help young children through this period of adjustment (Keyser, 2006). Some educators have taken a hint from the work of the Italians and instituted some of the strategies of Inserimento, as described in the photo essay "Building Relationships in Infant and Toddler Care," in the color insert, and the description of the welcoming process by Pittsburgh infant-toddler teachers (Whipple & McCullough, 2005).

Many of the strategies for introducing a new child to a center revolve around offering parents clear information and providing a personalized first contact and period of adjustment and orientation. In addition, beyond the strategies of "doing things" is an equally important side of "feeling things." The actions to create smooth transitions help educators become sensitive and tuned in to the ways that very young children express their feelings and indicate that their transition period is going well. Teachers then know that all of their efforts are working to make children and families feel comfortable in a new program (Honig, 2002).

A program that focuses on welcoming families into partnership has some or all of the following features:

• Parents are invited to visit the school before enrollment.

• Formal orientation is provided to parents.

• At the first contact, a member of the staff is available to answer questions, listen to concerns, and set up meetings and visits.

• Brochures, booklets, and handouts are offered to inform parents about the program, community resources, and quality child care.

• The administrator and other staff know how to talk to families and offer them reassurance.

• Teachers make home visits to families to learn about the children's daily lives.

• There is a welcoming celebration each year.

• The program helps families get to know one another.

• Two-way communication with families is encouraged.

• Language support is provided for parents with a language difference.

• The program helps parents understand the process of transition and separation.

A program that pays close attention to the emotions of the infants and toddlers who are entering a new program may have the following characteristics:

• Pictures of children and their families are posted in the classroom.

• Teachers talk to children about their families during the day.

• The environment contains familiar, homelike items for children.

• Each child is cared for in a way that is consistent and familiar.

• Children are helped to have a good-bye ritual with the parent who drops them off.

• Children's feelings are acknowledged, and children are allowed to express distress at their parent's departure.

• Individual differences are expected in the way children show they are distressed or missing their parents.

• Each child is told when it is getting close to the time when the parent returns.

Similar to notations in Chapter 1, a child who is forming an attachment to the new teacher may show the following signs:

• Smiling and showing pleasure in greeting the teacher

• Seeking to be held and touched by the teacher

- Snuggling contentedly in the teacher's arms

- Eating and falling asleep easily for the teacher

- Crying or noticing when the teacher departs

- Acting subdued or actively missing the teacher when the teacher is absent

- Smiling across the room and bringing things to show the teacher

- Seeking the teacher's help and reassurance in preference to others

- Playing well and with concentration when the teacher is nearby

- Cooperating with the teacher's requests and directions

THE TIME OF GOOD-BYE: ENDING THE DANCE SO ANOTHER CAN BEGIN

All good things must come to an end. Just as the transition into a relationship can be eased and made meaningful, so can the transition at the end of child care. Because teachers do so much to create extended close relationships in their programs, they also need ways to close them using the emotional language of attachment. Children, families, and teachers want to end their dance together in a graceful and satisfying way—not in an awkward, abrupt way that provides no sense of closure for the dancers.

Certainly, transitions are necessary and routine. Many kinds of transitions have to be managed by children, parents, and teachers in group care, including transitions as children move from one activity to the next and as they depart for the day. The most difficult sorts of transitions, however, are those that involve ending relationships for good—saying good-bye to the people, places, and things that one has grown to know and love. The common tendency is to minimize the feelings of loss that young children experience when they leave a program, but in fact young children have the same kinds of intense feelings that adults and older children do. When children's feelings are minimized and glossed over, it sends the message that they should not emotionally invest in relationships and that their attachments are trivial. Although children adjust to changes, they find them stressful. Therefore, it is desirable to keep the number of transitions to a minimum. When possible, children should make the transition to a new classroom or program with one or more familiar friends or caregivers as a unit.

Teachers can do much to ease transitions and make them constructive and meaningful. The key is to recognize everyone's feelings and allow them to be expressed in some acceptable way. The tendency is to downplay any painful feelings of loss and sorrow and not make adequate plans for the transition. However, transitions that are well planned and that acknowledge feelings are helpful to all parties involved—children, families, and teachers. The children see that their lives are stable and predictable and that their attachments to their beloved caregivers, group, and place are respected (Honig, 2002). Parents are educated about the contribution the program has made to their child's development and well-being. Caregivers get a sense of closure about their time with the child and family and acknowledgment for their caring work.

Family Books as Supports for Transition

Using technologies such as digital photography, creative teachers can find many ways to use pictures and stories to allow parents and children to ease comfortably into their programs. For example, at the Boulder Journey School in Colorado, each new infant has a *Book About Me,* which can be pulled from the shelf anytime a child wants to look at it for comfort or curiosity. The books are created through the collaboration of parents and teachers. Just before the infant enters the program, the parents are given a booklet with titles on the pages but nothing else. Parents fill in the pages with their own words and photos. Pages from one child's book are shown in "A Book About Me": Family Books as a Support for Transitions in the color insert.

Memory Books (Diaries)

In Italy, the teachers draw on the universal symbolism of celebration and gift giving to give meaning to their good-bye rituals. A good-bye gift makes visible the value placed on a relationship and creates expectations of positive reciprocity. Memory books—or *diarios* ("diaries"), as the Italians call them—are the favorite method of many infant and toddler teachers in Italy to say good-bye. They are records of the child's growth and development, but not assessments in the systematic, formal sense of portfolios in the American context (Meisels, 1995). Instead, they are personal and emotional in tone and format. These memory books are widely used throughout Italy in infant and toddler centers and preschools. They are given to a family at a party or special exit interview at the time of departure from the program. Carlina Rinaldi of Reggio Emilia, Italy, describes whom the diary serves:

> *For the educators,* it is certainly a way to refine their abilities to see the events when and where they happen, to analyze and self reflect....
>
> *For the parents,* it is an opportunity to get closer to the child and to study him or her through the eye of the educators... to know more about how the child is while away from home.
>
> *For the child,* awareness is gained through a higher communication, attention, and sensitivity of the environment around him or her, and from being a "subject of love"; the diary documents a personalized educational intervention, a document that when he or she is grown up will enable him or her to read fragments of his or her own story. (Edwards & Rinaldi, 2008, pp. 25–27)

Diaries are not standardized in format. They include such things as photographs that capture significant moments; creative products, such as drawings and constructions; anecdotal records and summary notes; letters exchanged; and schedules or calendars (see Box 5.2). To connect these pieces, the teacher adds simple text that speaks directly and affectionately about the child's experiences and highlights the child's particular strengths and contributions to the life of the group (Giovannini, 2001). The families who receive the diaries treasure them and look at them for years, and thereby they are helped to form a continuing sense of alliance with the early child care system of their city.

BOX 5.2.
The Diario (Diary) in Pistoia, Italy

Constructing a *diario* (diary) requires a great deal of time, continuity, and determination. The preparation for a diary is about building an archive. It is about having a container for each child to store photographs and observations, folders for paintings and drawings, and a box containing the child's three-dimensional work. Other invaluable tools are personal calendars for each child and reflective observation notebooks, both of which provide an excellent support for memory.

It calls for a generosity of attitude and a will to give back to the individual child—and to his or her parents—the events, thoughts, feelings, and ideas that tell the story of the days at the infant and toddler center. It calls for the ability to retell, to place events and small personal anecdotes within a broader history so that a memento of childhood can be given to each child. Beyond that, building such documentation about a single child is a way to offer individual attention and to value and identify individual differences and styles. It allows the teacher to make each child's experiences unique and special.

Teachers begin to gather material for the diario starting at the time the child enters the center, but they compile it only toward the end of the child's stay. There are many ways of preparing the cover, but the identity of the child is always highlighted. The first pages usually contain notes by both the primary caregiver and the parent concerning the earliest encounter, and the accompanying images show the infant or toddler at that time. Words, images, text, and small creations made by the child and teacher can all be included among the pages. The continuity between center and home has a strong presence in the diario. Messages sent by the family, correspondence, and photographs are included. The moment of offering parents the diario is rich with emotion

---

(continued)

Box 5.2 (continued)

and gratitude. Even if the parents expect to receive a diary, the particular one they are given is a complete surprise.

The family of Duccio receives the diary at the end of his third year in the infant and toddler center.

The diaries fit into the system of documentation in the Italian approach to infant and toddler care, described in Chapter 6. However, they are a particular kind of documentation, intended to tell the story of the child's life in the infant and toddler center. As a parting gift, the diary creates a satisfying finale so that the positive (secure) feelings of attachment, so carefully created, are not turned into negative memories by abrupt separation. The diaries provide a positive interpretation of the child's growth and change over time and render each child's place in history unique and special.

Teachers in Pistoia recorded the moments when parents were given their child's diary (Edwards & Gandini, 2001). The researchers wanted to capture and record the parents' fresh responses to the diaries and hear their reflections about their sense of their children's experiences at the infant and toddler center as the concluding moment of their participation in the research. Here is a typical example of what happened, which is adapted from Gandini and Edwards (2001, p. 193).

The parents of Daniele (age 3 years) opened the diary, placed it on the table, and expressed admiration and surprise. Daniele was there with them and started right away to point to his own pictures and the ones of the other children, saying their names and what they all were doing together at the time of each picture. The parents conversed intensely with him, moving slowly through the pages. After a few minutes, Daniele ran away to play with his friends in the other room. In the conversation that followed, the father exclaimed, "You know, we were expecting this, but it is still beyond any expectation." His wife added, "I believe that this can become more and more precious with time." She also talked about how close she had come to feel to the whole group of children. She said, "It is important also because all the children are in there in one picture or another."

Memory Books for Children without Families

The Italian approach to constructing memory books for infants and toddlers can be adapted for many other kinds of programs and situations. They may be particularly important for children who are at emotional risk. For example, they have become very useful and important in infant nurture and preschool enrichment programs for Chinese children in welfare institutions and orphanages (see Box 5.3). There, for vulnerable children with disrupted personal histories and

---

BOX 5.3.
Memory books in Chinese welfare institutions

Half the Sky is a philanthropic foundation created by adoptive parents of orphaned Chinese children in order to enrich the lives and enhance the prospects for the children in China who still wait to be adopted and for those who will spend their childhoods in orphanages. Half the Sky establishes early childhood education, personalized learning, and infant nature programs in state-run Chinese welfare institutions to provide the children with stimulation, individual attention, and an active learning environment.

Every child in Half the Sky programs has a Memory Book. The book serves several important purposes. It is a form of long-term documentation, showing the child's high points of experiences and pathways of growth in the program. It also serves as a tangible form of autobiography, a way for children to develop a positive sense of self and their place in the group and the world.

Children reading a memory book together.

(continued)

Box 5.3 (continued)

The teachers consider the Memory Book to be extremely meaning-ful for the child who has no family to provide that natural source of personal history. For these children, the document serves as personal history, something they can always keep and cherish in later life. Wherever a child goes, she can take her Memory Book with her.

WHAT GOES INTO A MEMORY BOOK?

Teachers are responsible for developing a Memory Book for each child in Half the Sky programs. Depending on the ratio of teachers to students, each teacher may work on several books at once. A child making the transition from the Baby Sisters program to the Little Sisters Preschool takes her Memory Book with her.

On a weekly basis, each teacher should provide *at least* one or two detailed objective observations on each child and/or on the child's work. This means writing down detailed notes about a child's progress and special moments or experiences that seemed significant for that child. A teacher might include a sequence of drawings that reflect a child's learning process. Or, individual drawings might be included that show a child's progress.

Child reading her Memory Book by herself.

The Memory Book should also include some group photos and notes about special events or experiences that were important to all the children, such as an outing or celebration.

In order to develop a quality Memory Book, teachers must observe each child carefully and get to know that child in depth. When a teacher knows a child well enough, she is able to catch the ordinary moments

Box 5.3 (continued)

that show positive changes and growth. Therefore, the Memory Book is a window on each individual child, showing his or her unique characteristics and path of development in the following areas: physical, emotional, social, cognitive, and language.

Entries in the Memory Book should be developed in a systematic and logical way, covering each of these areas. All Memory Books should be updated every two weeks. That way, the observations included in the books should be no more than two weeks apart. In Half the Sky programs, the teacher supervisor checks the Memory Books as part of the regular weekly check of teacher performance.

Child taking a Memory Book from the bookshelf.

From Evans, K. (Ed.). (2003). *For the children: The Half the Sky Foundation's guide to infant nurture, child care, and preschool education in China's social welfare institutions* (pp. 162–163). Berkeley, CA: Half the Sky Foundation; reprinted by permission. Further information in Cotton, Edwards, Zhao, and Gelabert (2007).

without families of their own to talk with them about their past, memory books help children to construct a sense of their own identity. The toddlers and preschool children love to look over the memory books that are continually being created about each one of them. The memory books help the children construct a coherent autobiographical (narrative) memory, which is an important component to the development of a stable identity (Evans, 2003).

For adopted children, who are making a transition not only from one set of caregivers to another but may also be crossing cultural and language boundaries, memory books are of immeasurable value in creating shared meaning about what happened in their early childhood setting and stimulating many conversations about the child's developing identity. The dance of relationships flows more smoothly than it would otherwise. The new adoptive parents eagerly pick up the moves they need to dance along with their children into the next phases of their lives.

RESOURCES

Bove, C. (1999). L'inserimento del bambino al nido. (Welcoming the child into infant care: Perspectives from Italy). *Young Children, 54*(2), 32–34.

Cotton, J., Edwards, C.P., Zhao, W., & Gelabert, J.M. (2007). Nurturing care for China's orphaned children. *Young Children, 62*(6), 58–62. Available online at http://journal.naeyc.org/btj/200711/pdf/BTJEdwards.pdf

Giovannini, D. (2001). Traces of childhood: A child's diary. In L. Gandini & C.P. Edwards (Eds.), *Bambini: The Italian approach to infant/toddler care* (pp. 146–151). New York: Teachers College Press.

Kaminsky, J.A. (2005, Spring). Reflections on *inserimento*, the process of welcoming children and parents into the infant-toddler center: An interview with Lella Gandini. *Innovations in Early Education: The International Reggio Exchange, 12*(2), 1–8.

Whipple, R., & McCullough, S. (2005, Spring). The welcoming process. *Innovations in Early Education: The International Reggio Exchange, 12*(2), 9–16.

CHAPTER 6

Now Really Dance

Individualizing, Documenting, and Planning

Carolyn Pope Edwards and Lella Gandini

Each month, Brenda, a teacher, meets with 20-month-old Marty's mother Jody to discuss emerging developments. They discuss what Marty seems to be excited about, what he has lost interest in that was exciting a month ago, and the progress Marty made the previous month. Brenda and Jody take stock and reflect together about Marty's development—mostly about what Marty may need at the next stage. Brenda consults an infant and toddler curriculum for ideas about experiences that will allow Marty to do more of what he is excited about now. For example, she and Jody have both noted that Marty seems to have acquired rudimentary abilities to pretend and use symbols in new ways. He pretended to drink from an empty cup the other day, and Jody observed him gently rocking his favorite stuffed monkey. Brenda and Jody consult the curriculum about ways to extend his burgeoning ability to pretend. They plan together to use figurines, blocks, and transportation items to represent Jody going to work, returning to pick up Marty at the child care center, and going home together. Each month, Brenda (with Jody's help) individualizes the child care program for Marty.

This chapter focuses on individualizing the infant and toddler program. It draws on a particular process of documentation to support individualization and to provide a mechanism for reflection in a relationship-based program. The documentation process is like dance study in the field of dance—a way to observe, break down, compare, and interpret what goes on when partners dance; to discuss why some dance performances seem so beautiful, satisfying, powerful, stirring, meaningful, and imaginative; and to determine why others seem to fall short and need improvement. The documentation process helps teachers to review, reflect, and plan on behalf of their small dance partners so that they can follow and get into step with them, and then lead them on to master new steps and dance styles.

Individualization is critical in infant and toddler care and education. In a relationship-based program, teachers must seek to know each child in a very complete and intimate way. While the setting involves a group of children, the relationships are with individuals—individual infants and individual parents or guardians. Thus, the program is organized around the needs of individual children; it is driven by the individual infants and toddlers whose needs and interests are recognized and affirmed.

As Chapter 5 made clear, when a new child enters an infant and toddler program, the teachers must help the child and family to find their comfort level in the program. Small groups of children with primary caregiver assignments further teachers' efforts to get to know each child and family very well. Teachers establish routines of changing, eating, and napping by getting to know the rhythms of each child with routines that work for each child (e.g., putting a child down for a brief midmorning nap, feeding a child as soon as she awakens), although they may gently move the group of children toward common times for eating and napping.

A second way that teachers build around children's particular characteristics and needs—or individualize—is by observing each child and planning intentionally to extend the child's interests while planning an emergent curriculum. This method of individualizing is markedly different from planning a different activity each week because it is something the teacher wants to do or because it fits the current season (although some of these activities may occur as well). Individualizing requires thoughtful reflection on each child's inner life—what the child is interested in, curious about, passionate about, and eager to learn about. Children become most excited about learning new skills when they have expressed some beginning skill (or are otherwise "ready"). Thus, this form of careful observing provides children with enriching experiences with respect to their motivations. Children respond to this kind of planning by eagerly noticing and engaging in the learning and play experiences that teachers offer them. A published curriculum helps teachers select interesting experiences for children, although such a curriculum is not followed in a lockstep fashion. Rather, experiences are selected from a menu or set of alternatives matched to the child's present interests. Box 6.1 provides an example of a relationship-based program that is purposeful about individualizing around each child's development.

The notes in Box 6.1 illustrate how portfolios can be part of the planning process as well as a method of summarizing children's strengths and developmental gains. Portfolios document a sampling of children's efforts, progress, and achievements; record some of their key experiences; and showcase strengths (Meisels, 1995). Portfolios are used in parent–teacher conferences to show what

---

BOX 6.1.
Individualizing infant and toddler programs at the Donald O. Clifton Child Development Center

The Donald O. Clifton Child Development Center (CDC) in Omaha, Nebraska, is a relationship-based infant and toddler program. Teachers are assigned to "families" and stay with children from early infancy until children are 3 years of age and attend preschool.

Each month, teachers identify new experiences for each child under their care. Teachers record these plans in each child's developmental portfolio that grows over the course of the child's years with that teacher. Teachers observe the child and, with the parent, select experiences to offer the child for the next month. These experiences are offered at the center, and parents may choose to offer them at home as well. Experiences are selected based on the infant's emerging developments and interests (sometimes passions), or are in an area of development where the child may benefit from additional experiences.

As much as possible, experiences are selected based on strengths, a child's talents, or emerging interests. For example, the teacher may observe that the child is often asking "Dat?" or seems to be pointing often as if to ask about the names of things. The teacher may then decide to intentionally select experiences for the child that focus on labeling things in the environment. The teacher thinks about ways to be responsive to the child's questions and comes back to things labeled often to give the child lots of chances to practice. The teacher identifies labeling as the child's goal for the month, together with one or two other key goals.

(continued)

Box 6.1 (continued)

> At Donald O. Clifton CDC, the teachers select new experiences from the menu provided in *Beautiful Beginnings: A Developmental Curriculum for Infants and Toddlers* (Raikes & McCall-Whitmer, 2006). They select the new experiences following through on careful observation of the child during the previous period. Next, throughout a given month, teachers (and parents) record the child's responses to the experiences offered. They take photographs and write about the child's responses. They also photograph other notable events that occur during that month. All are entered into the infant's portfolio, which parents take home on a weekly or monthly basis. The teacher continues to build the portfolio through the infant and toddler years. When the child graduates to preschool, the portfolio is given to the parents to keep.
>
> The portfolio serves as a memory book of the child's early development in the child care setting, a tool for monthly planning, a way to document developmental activities, and a communication strategy between parents and children.

was used by the teachers in making daily plans and individualizing the curriculum. They spark conversations in which both the parents and the teacher talk about the value of the program experience and all of the changes seen in the child. Conferences are also a time for everyone to acknowledge their appreciation for the relationships that have been developed and discuss any concerns about the future. The conversations hopefully contribute to the family's future involvement in their child's care and education and sense of confidence in their parenting.

PEDAGOGICAL DOCUMENTATION

Documentation is a process of observing and reflecting that improves planning within an educational setting and assists teachers in observing, interpreting, making decisions, and communicating with children as well as adults. This process is sometimes referred to as "pedagogical documentation" to highlight the active participation of the educator in sustaining the learning process and to distinguish it from other types of documentation. It involves gathering pieces of evidence through photography, anecdotal records, samples of children's work, and transcripts of children's comments and conversations (all of these kinds of evidence are important). Then the evidence is analyzed, organized, shared, discussed, and eventually presented in a finished form. Although primarily used by teachers, documentation is useful for all important adults in children's lives. It helps teachers to implement their curriculum to meet every child's needs for timely, stimulating experiences. It also helps them to become better communicators and advocates. When the finished outcomes of teaching and learning are made visible through carefully and clearly designed booklets, panels, or displays, then parents' and the public's respect and valuing of early childhood education are increased.

The activities of observing and reflecting have been part of early childhood practice ever since the field began. However, these activities have been refined in Reggio Emilia, Italy, in influential ways that are spreading around the world. In Reggio, documentation is said to be a kind of *visible listening* based on close relationships between children and adults (Gandini & Goldhaber, 2001; Malaguzzi, 1998; Rinaldi, 1998; Vecchi, 1998). Documentation is a "visible trace and a procedure that supports learning and teaching," making them part of a two-way transparent process (Rinaldi, 2006, p. 100). To make learning and teaching "visible" is a shorthand way of saying these processes should be carefully recorded, reflected upon, and, most of all, respected and sustained.

The Italian documentation process combines easily with teaching practices familiar in North America, such as emergent curriculum (Jones & Nimmo, 1994). With emergent curriculum, classroom activities result from the interaction between teachers and children, with both sides contributing ideas to build worthwhile units of study, and lesson plans are not something set far in advance. Likewise, documentation integrates naturally with infant curricula that build on children's interests and strengths, such as *Beautiful Beginnings* (Raikes & McCall-Whitmer, 2006), in which documentation is used over time to create a learning portfolio that reflects children's individualized experiences and outcomes. It also integrates with planning of toddler-appropriate use of projects to support children investigating a topic over a period of time (Helm & Katz, 2001; Katz & Chard, 1996; LeeKeenan & Edwards, 1992). In fact, documentation can be integrated into any curriculum planning based on intentional teaching that involves an intentional balance of teacher-guided and child-guided instruction (Epstein, 2007; Helm, Beneke, & Steinheimer, 1997). It can also become a regular part of many teacher education programs (e.g., Burrington & Sortino, 2004; Cox Suarez, 2006; Edwards et al., 2007; Goldhaber & Smith, 2002; Smith & Goldhaber, 2004) or staff development meetings (Abramson, 2007).

THE DOCUMENTATION PROCESS

Framing a Question

The documentation process follows a cycle that begins with a question (see Box 6.2). Teachers—no matter how experienced they are—find observing each child in the group to be helpful and necessary in answering the kinds of questions that arise during their daily work. The documentation process is a way to place child observation inside a *cycle of inquiry* that begins with asking a question about the child's thinking and learning in order to plan and take next steps (Gandini & Goldhaber, 2001).

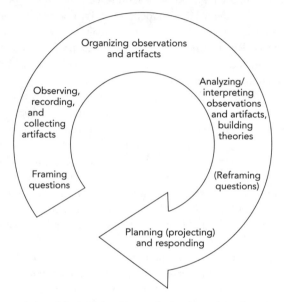

BOX 6.2.
The cycle of documentation

The cycle of documentation begins with framing a question and ends with planning and reframing new questions. In addition to the steps portrayed below, it often also includes a step of preparing finished documentation to share with parents or visitors.

The question should be genuine and researchable (Meier & Henderson, 2007). Good questions often begin with the stem "How can I..." or "What is happening when...?" Some examples of researchable initial questions include the following:

- How can I get Susie to have an easier transition in the morning?

- How can I get Lily more engaged in pretend play?

- How can I support Rinaldo's interest in flowers?

- How can I help Yung Sim have a smoother transition to naptime?

- What is happening when Mark and Maria are struggling over a toy and I jump in?

Some initial questions are too broad for teacher research and need further refinement before they can be addressed. Here are some examples:

- What is the best way to do transitions?

- Why do I have so much crying in this classroom?

- How can I make the children stop hitting and grabbing?

Gathering Evidence

Having established a suitable opening question, the teacher begins to gather evidence to answer it. This kind of evidence can be called *raw documentation* because it is not intended for public consumption. This initial part of the cycle of documentation puts the teacher into the role of an observer (almost a scientist) as data are gathered. The teacher then describes and clarifies these observations of an individual child or a small group of children. A few visual and written records of the children's play and social interaction can be collected using any kinds of observing techniques or tools desired (e.g., camera, tape recorder, video camera, notebook and pencil, computer). In this way, the teacher keeps track of some of the important moments and events that go on related to a particular educational experience.

Reflecting on the Evidence

Next in the cycle, the teacher sits down with at least one other person and studies the collected records to try to understand what they mean and what they might suggest about next steps in teaching. What were the children saying and doing, and how should those actions be interpreted? For example, if the child was frowning and moving slowly, was that because he was lost in thought or because he was upset and tired? If the baby said, "Up, up!" did that indicate she wanted to be picked up and hugged, or carried to the window to look outside? It is always valuable to have another person participate in the discussion, whether it be another teacher, aide, parent, intern, or supervisor. This step of reflection requires a scientific or analytic attitude, as well as a willingness to share perspectives and learn through others' questions and interpretations. Thus, although each child has one primary caregiver, the circle of observing and reflecting on that child widens.

Using the Findings to Make Decisions and Plan

The process of analyzing and discussing leads to decision making. The teacher decides what to do next. For example, suppose the starting question was, "How can I get Susie to have an easier transition in the morning?" Perhaps the notes and photos gathered led to a hypothesis that Susie likes it best when her father follows a set routine with her—first helping her hang up her jacket, then putting her clean clothes in her bin, then sitting in a certain place to play with toys, then handing her over to a particular teacher. The teacher could brainstorm with her colleagues about how to share this insight with Susie's parents, perhaps bringing them in as partners on the reflective process and asking them their interpretation of the notes. Sharing has two benefits: It generates specific suggestions about steps to take, and it creates a dialogue and sense of trust that sets the stage for further cooperation.

Asking Another Question

Decision making and planning often lead to new questions. For example, the teacher may now wonder, "How can I use what I have learned about Susie to help Ralph with his morning transition?" or "What happens when parents happen to be in a special hurry? What can I do on those days to help the children?"

Creating Finished Documentation Products

Finally, to complete the cycle of documentation, the teacher may create finished documentation products to share with others inside or outside the classroom (Hong & Forman, 2000; Kline, 2008). This stage involves a new set of skills: *carefully designed and clear presentation* and *storytelling*. Artistic and literary skills are vital in this step because well-composed documentations draw in the audience and communicate effectively. The finished products that are shared and displayed can take many forms—slide show, panel, booklet, or videotape. They are studied to make new hypotheses about children and begin the cycle again. In whatever finished form, these products usually combine three elements that create the dynamic interplay of perspectives that underlies the documentation process:

- Visual images of the processes and key moments that occurred

- Words said by the children, perhaps along with some sample products such as drawings

- Interpretive or summary text by the teachers that orients the observer to what initial and final questions are being addressed by the work

At the University of Nebraska Ruth Staples Child Development Laboratory, faculty and preservice students use the process of documentation to foster rich experiences for infants, toddlers, and preschoolers (Benson & Leeper Miller, 2008; Edwards et al., 2007). Many teacher educators today are finding ways to help their preservice students gain skills of documentation. A good example, the story of "Two Toddlers Explore Plants," is found in the color insert.

WHAT IS DISTINCTIVE ABOUT
THE DOCUMENTATION PROCESS?

Documentation Fosters
Collaboration Between Teachers

What makes this approach to documentation distinctive from other observation and reflection strategies? For one thing, it starts a collaborative, or relational, process between teachers (Oken-Wright, 2001; Oken-Wright & Gravett, 2002). It fosters professional growth for teachers working in pairs or small groups. Documentation preserves a collective story of a set of children, their parents, and other adults and has implications involving all of these dances among the different combinations of people in relationships (e.g., child–child, teacher–child, parent–teacher). Thus, it extends the dance of life in the classroom from a moment of performance that disappears as soon as it is completed, to a dance that can be reviewed and studied by teachers as they analyze what worked well and where to go next.

Documentation Helps Teachers
Understand Individual Children's Thinking

A second distinctive aspect is that documentation serves as a tool for getting closer to children's conceptions, or explanations, of how the world works. In that way, as described previously, it helps teachers to individualize their work and plan next steps with children as they observe and understand them better. For example, infant and toddler teachers have used documentation to promote the infant cognitive milestone of object permanence (May, Kantor, & Sanderson, 2004) and toddler language development (Logue, Shelton, Cronkite, & Austin, 2007). It has helped teachers unpack the meaning of toddlers' empathy (Quann & Wien, 2006) and their delicate emotional relationships (Doherty, 2004; Edwards, 2004; Edwards & Rinaldi, 2008) and provided a new lens for studying toddlers' exploration of challenging materials, such as glue and clay (Kantor & Whaley, 1998; Smith & Goldhaber, 2004). Box 6.3 provides an example of using documentation for children's emotional growth and well-being.

Documentation Focuses
on Individual and Group Learning

Documentation is used not only for following the progress of an individual child but also for systematically following the child's interaction in a group and for following how the child together with others develops ideas, theories, and understandings (Edwards & Rinaldi, 2008; Helm & Helm, 2006; Reggio Children, Italy, and Harvard Project Zero, 2001). The child's interests and desires do not

BOX 6.3.
Documenting children's
emotional growth and well-being

This story comes from the Centre for Early Childhood Education, Loyalist College, Ontario, Canada, where Alex Doherty was a teacher of infants and toddlers. In her classroom, they were exploring many questions about the children's emotional growth. Two of their initial teaching questions were: *Is the environment giving the children the feeling that they are safe and tenderly held by the caregiving adults? What can documentation tell us about that?*

———————————

We next turned to our environment and asked about its holding qualities. We decided that in order to answer the question, we needed to turn it around and consider it from the children's point of view. How did the children embrace and (be)hold their environment? One example that became important for us involved the children's delight in the warm sunlight coming in the window. They would climb up on a radiator to bask in the sunshine, and then (good caregivers that we were) we would encourage them to keep their feet on the floor. Then one day, we stood back and listened to the silent dialogue between child and window. The question confronted us: "Really, why can't the children sit in the window?" We began to build a structure that would straddle over the radiator and offer a pleasing construction and safe haven for the children to regard the world outside. Our children began to observe the coming and goings of parents, other children, and vehicles.

About that time, the children had begun a relationship with a sea gull that opportunistically visited during their stroller walks. Our babies (and the gull) enjoyed snack during their walks, and sometimes cracker and muffin crumbs would be left behind. What did these trails mean in "relationship language"? Could they be a trail for the children to find their way back to school, a communication for the birds, or both?

It was as if a question was resonating from the environment: What would happen if we placed birdhouses in the window? Would the birds follow the crumbs back to school? Would the birds understand the communication? Putting out birdhouses, we indeed did find that the birds came to meet the children, just as the children had met them on the walks. Many days we enjoyed the luxury of embracing the moments of beak-to-nose encounters, when children and birds beheld each other through the window glass.

Box 6.3 *(continued)*

> We also asked ourselves whether we value tenderness and softening in the children's classroom. How did the environment caress the relationships that were beginning to form? Did the environment embrace, hold, nurture, and regard each child? Our previous experiences with the radiator and the birds allowed us to take the risk of not answering the question immediately. Instead, we attended to the dialogue between children and objects that may not have been speaking out loud but nevertheless would communicate to us if we would listen. This hypothesis allowed us to trust ourselves, and the faces and responses of the children then told us that they felt we also trusted them and considered their knowledge and feelings to be important.
>
> Finally, we again reflected on our documentation. How did it reflect our values about beholding the children in their environment? Again, we discovered that inadvertently by concentrating so hard on illustrating the theories and investigations of children and teachers, we were making the assumption that the basic relationships did not need to be captured. We were overlooking the importance of presenting the tenderness of relationships, whether person to person or baby to bird.
>
> From Joanne Hendrick. *Next Steps Toward Teaching The Reggio Way: Accepting The Challenge To Change,* 1/e. Published by Allyn and Bacon/Merrill Education, Boston, MA. Copyright © 2004 by Pearson Education. Adapted by permission of the publisher.

develop in a vacuum but instead are greatly influenced by what peers are doing. For example, when a baby sees another child pick up a toy, the baby may reach out for it and want to play with something similar. Similarly, when one child watches another trying to put a shape into a box, the child may also want to work on that skill. In this way, children shape one another's emerging interests. The teacher will find that planning small group experiences serves each child's individual needs. In general, the process of documentation turns teachers into action researchers who ask questions and make hypotheses about groups of children under their care. Teachers then immediately use those observations and findings to inform next decisions about program planning.

Documentation Promotes Advocacy and Communication

A final distinctive aspect of documentation is its power as a communication tool. Documentation helps to create understanding and sharing of perspectives between teachers and parents (see Box 6.4; Brown-Dupaul, Keyes, & Segatti, 2001; Fyfe, Hovey, & Strange, 2004). Malaguzzi (1998) said that, "Teachers must leave behind an isolated, silent mode of working that leaves no traces" (p. 69).

BOX 6.4.
Documentation to
promote teacher–parent sharing

Documentation stimulates parents' curiosity and excitement about their children, fosters understanding of what their children know and can do, and provides concrete examples of what parents can do to have an impact on children's learning. Knowing what to do, understanding the importance of it, and having the confidence that what is being suggested is do-able, all increase parents' motivation to engage children. Your documentation can give parents ideas on how to get involved in children's education and learning. It can help parents in:

- Taking advantage of ordinary moments with a child and turning them into special moments of learning or discovery

- Responding to the individual styles that different children use to formulate and express their thoughts and feelings (e.g., some children are more verbal; others "think out loud" in drawings, gestures, or arrangements of objects)

- Supporting young children's initiatives so they can actively test and try out their ideas with adult support and become more purposeful

- Making beautiful things with children out of readily available materials

- Talking with young children, asking questions, and noting details that provoke children into thinking more

- Coming close when children are playing, drawing, and writing, and having conversations about the world (e.g., how things relate, stories, explanations)

- Writing down things a child says, or adding written notes to the child's art, as a way of reinforcing and paying attention (i.e., encouraging them further)

- Connecting with teachers (e.g., knowing topics to talk about at parent–teacher conferences, such as the child's strengths and interests)

- Connecting with teachers in group discussions or committee meetings (e.g., asking about how they use observation in assessment and evaluation)

- Respecting the professional skill involved in quality early childhood education (realizing how it goes beyond protecting health and safety)

- Raising expectations for what should happen for young children in their learning day (wherever they spend it)

He argued that the flow of documentation is important not only for teachers and children but also for parents and outside visitors to the school, to whom it introduces "a quality of knowing that tangibly changes their expectations" and allows them to take a new and more inquisitive approach toward the whole school experience.

THE SKILLS OF DOCUMENTATION

Collecting Information

Becoming an effective observer and documenter involves many skills and takes time to develop. The process of documentation begins with the systematic collection of evidence about children. Two important skills are necessary for collecting information: the ability to listen and observe closely and the ability to use recording tools (e.g., cameras, video, notebooks, paper and scissors) efficiently. In the group setting, it is important to record children's discussions, gestures, and explanations as they talk, play, and work together. The recording can be done with any tool or combination of tools that the teacher chooses.

Written notes are essential, whether in the format of anecdotal notes or some more systematic observational system such as time or event sampling. These written notes, made during or immediately after some events, provide descriptions of what happened, how children responded, what they said, and the observer's tentative interpretation. Sometimes teachers develop specialized checklists, charts, or notations for recording. At an early education program in Lincoln, Nebraska, educators have pioneered the use of "visual notes" for following the visual-spatial work of children from the toddler age onward, such as their block building and outdoor construction skills with natural materials (Miller, 2004; Neugebauer, 2004), as seen in Box 6.5.

BOX 6.5.
Documenting children's visual-spatial work

At the First-Plymouth Early Education Program in Lincoln, Nebraska, educators work closely with children and families to promote learning and development with a special emphasis on their visual-spatial skills. They believe that children today are not receiving the outdoor and constructive experiences they need to develop this side of their thinking. Without visual-spatial competence, children often struggle to develop literacy skills.

Walking through the classrooms, evidence of visual-spatial learning is seen everywhere. Children of all ages, from infancy through kindergarten, play in classrooms equipped with wooden blocks large and

---

(continued)

Box 6.5 (continued)

small, other constructive materials, and replicas of famous buildings and structures such as the Eiffel Tower and the Great Pyramids. Teachers have been trained in a specific documentation technique called *visual notes*. This technique not only helps teachers to strengthen their own visual-spatial skills but also allows them to capture children's learning using a pictorial documentation method. Visual notes depict the specific construction and engineering skills that children are using in their structures. They identify types of materials that children are using, problems they are solving, and the sequence of building. Visual notes, combined with verbal narrative, often convey children's emotions. They help the teachers "listen" to children in a new way. See the provided example.

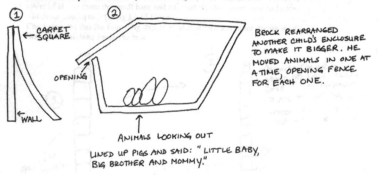

Brock (pseudonym) 2 1/2 year old boy   Observed: February 13, 2003

Lined up blocks

Counted: "1, 2, 3" (unprompted)

Then got wooden animals. Tried to make them stand up on carpet square and was frustrated. We moved carpet square (moved it up against wall). His animals repeatedly climbed the carpet "mountain" (with narration).

① CARPET ← SQUARE

② BROCK REARRANGED ANOTHER CHILD'S ENCLOSURE TO MAKE IT BIGGER. HE MOVED ANIMALS IN ONE AT A TIME, OPENING FENCE FOR EACH ONE.

OPENING

← WALL

ANIMALS LOOKING OUT

LINED UP PIGS AND SAID: "LITTLE BABY, BIG BROTHER AND MOMMY."

In interpreting these notes, the teacher pointed out that the toddler was demonstrating skills of classification (he selected three identical blocks), counting (unprompted), problem solving (he used his carpet square in a different way when his original plan did not work), creative representation (his carpet square became a mountain that the animals could climb), and verbal language (narrating a story).

By Dana Miller, Research Director, Dimensions Educational Research Foundation (http://dimensionsfoundation.org). Copyright © 2004.

Audiotapes are useful tools to capture important discussions and record the way the group and individual children express themselves. Transcribing audiotapes is laborious, but reviewing the exact words that children say often surprises the teacher and suggests the way that memory distorts and simplifies.

Photographs are important for supporting written observations. They offer a natural and visual form of record. Teachers need to learn to take photos that are well composed and sharp and that capture meaningful moments that correspond to other forms of records being kept (see Box 6.6).

Videotapes can show the process of an activity or project and can also record discussions and live action. Just as in still photos, it is important to capture crucial moments and to work toward technical skill in taking images that are well composed, well lighted, and at the right level and angle.

BOX 6.6.
Improving the visual quality of documentation with photographs

1. Keep your camera handy to be ready when the opportunity presents itself.

2. Take photographs from the child's level rather than from above, looking down.

3. Try shooting from different positions: standing, sitting, kneeling, lying down.

4. Get as close as possible to the children when photographing them.

5. Place a reflecting shield on your flash to soften the light on faces.

6. Eliminate ugly backgrounds in your photographs.

7. Make a written note about when and why the photograph was taken and what was happening at the moment.

8. Make sure every photograph has a clean, clear center of interest.

9. Select photographs where every face is at least the size of a dime.

10. Select your photographs carefully—avoid clutter that comes from too many photos.

11. Enlarge photographs to a size with maximum impact (e.g., 4 by 6 inches).

12. Provide each photograph with a simple line border to set it off from the background.

(continued)

Box 6.6 (continued)

13. Try to create a story with your photographs—a narrative series of pictures.

14. Think carefully about to whom your documentation is directed. Who is the primary audience? Is it children, parents, or other teachers?

15. Select one lead photograph that captures the peak moment of the story or symbolizes the entire story.

16. Do not try to cover too much. People's attention span is short.

17. When mounting photographs, think of a poster or picture page as a visual sentence or statement. What is the message of the documentation?

18. Use about six photographs on a picture page, and make one of these an obvious dominant.

19. Be conscious of the white space on your page or poster. Find a balance between including images, text, and white space so that the finished project is visually pleasing to the reader. Try not to overcrowd the page or poster with images and text.

20. Use a uniform font for all headings that is consistent in size and color. You can use different fonts to differentiate other parts of the page or poster from the headings. Use only the number of words absolutely necessary to tell the story: avoid using too many words and overwhelming the reader with text.

Organizing Your Information

After teachers have recorded information, they need to spend time organizing and arranging their observations into a systematic form that will display an individual child's (or group of children's) growth and change. Selecting, organizing, and arranging activate teachers' thinking to deeper levels of understanding as they seek to interpret what they have collected. To bring together the information and make sense of it, there is no cookbook series of steps. Instead, the most important thing is to create a structure for the teacher to work with others to compare perspectives and interpretations. Multiple perspectives are not merely helpful—they are absolutely necessary to get beneath the surface of things because an educational experience always has many layers of meaning and many angles from which it can be viewed. It is a collective story composed of many voices. The documentation process unpacks this complexity and suggests the richness of some of the perspectives from which an experience can be viewed and some of the many levels from which it can be analyzed.

Documentation has great value in promoting partnership with parents (Fyfe et al., 2004). The value of using documentation to communicate with families is seen in Box 6.7, about a toddler program in which teachers used their notes to foster discussions with parents about their children's language. The teachers then used the knowledge they gained from parents to help them extend their own conversations with children because they could better understand what the children were trying to say.

BOX 6.7.
Strengthening partnerships with families through toddlers' stories

Carrying clipboards and digital cameras, we observed children's play and documented their use of language associated with objects. We created computer folders for each child, recording the language, reflecting on our interpretations, and attaching photographs to jog our memories. We quickly realized that the toddlers in the 18- to 24-month age span were using single words to tell stories, so we needed families' help to better understand the context of the stories.

Baby could mean "I'm tired and I want to sit on your lap and suck my thumb" or "I'm pretending to rock the baby to sleep" or (to a mother with a new baby) "Where is the baby you brought yesterday?" *Mitten* could mean "I'm ready to go home now" or "Look at my red mittens; my grandmother gave them to me" or "I can't find the other one that matches."

Most parents were used to their children using words to label or request something, but they had not thought about words as signaling stories. Sharing our documentation of the words their children knew piqued their interest and strengthened our own.

Together, teachers and families began to collect stories. Sending home photographs of children engaged in meaningful activities and e-mailing messages back and forth, we created books for each child, using the words they understood as well as the words they used. With parents' help, teachers saw increased opportunities to extend children's play by building on their home stories. When a child said, "Ball," rather than extending that language by saying, "It's a red ball," the teacher could say, "Roll the ball, just like Daddy." Knowing that *ball* was a story about rolling a ball back and forth with Daddy, the teacher expanded the story, the language, and the game.

Adapted from Logue, M.E., Shelton, H., Cronkite, D., & Austin, J. (2007). Strengthening partnerships with families through toddlers' stories. *Young Children, 62*(2), 85–87. Reprinted with permission from the National Association for the Education of Young Children.

Presenting an Interpretation
Through the Finished Product

Teachers also need the help of colleagues when they are creating a documentary product that represents and communicates their summary and interpretation of the experience. The goal is to create a product that communicates effectively and allows the audience to hear the voices of the children. Many rounds (drafts) are necessary when selecting and arranging photographs, adding labels to create a display panel or booklet, writing the project narrative, and putting together the entries for a memory book. Creating final products allows teachers to improve their artistic and writing skills and to learn how to give critical feedback constructively to each other. Teachers really appreciate honest suggestions from others that help them improve the appearance of their documentation.

Excellent documentation creates a relationship with the viewer. It draws the viewer into the inner world of children and increases respect for them. It also increases respect for the teachers. Excellent documentation tells a clear, concise story about learning, development, or mastery. It also supports attitudes of curiosity and interest about young children and their learning.

Documentation products can be created in many different formats, including the following:

- *Panel displays* are favored by the Italians in Reggio Emilia, who treasure them as a primary vehicle for transforming the look of their classrooms and creating products that can be part of exhibits such as *The Wonder of Learning: The Hundred Languages of Children,* which toured North America under the direction of the North American Reggio Emilia Alliance.

- *Memory books* were explored in Chapter 5 (see also Edwards & Rinaldi, 2008; Giovannini, 2001).

- *Project narrative books* include the published story of toddlers and fish (Reggio Children, Italy, 1996) and exploration of clay (Smith & Goldhaber, 2004).

- *Videos* with material on infants and toddlers include *Bambini*, about the family-centered early childhood system in Pistoia (Edwards, Gandini, Peon-Casanova, & Danielson, 2003) and videatives (http://www.videatives.com).

- *Slideshows, program newsletters, and other published documentation products* provide rich resources to study and discuss.

Finally, participating in school study tours and professional conferences is one of the best ways for teachers to learn about how documentation is done and how it can support the ongoing process of quality improvement. These contexts create a special kind of respectful and open relationship in which information and experiences can be exchanged among colleagues.

Strengthening Relationships Through Continuity of Care

Continuity of care is promoted through small group sizes, low child–teacher ratios, cultural continuity, and teachers who stay with children for several years. This model is followed at the Ounce of Prevention Educare, located on the south side of Chicago, and provides a framework for responsive relationships. Educare Chicago is one of a growing number of Early Head Start/Head Start programs in the Bounce Learning Network committed to excellence in care and education for children birth to age 5. (See also Box 4.1.)

Building Relationships in Infant and Toddler Care

"As an educator I feel attachment is very important with the infants as well as the toddlers. Many children when they start at our facility are quite hesitant to stay with teachers and children they do not know. There is no attachment there. It takes time to develop a bond and attach."
—Missouri infant and toddler teacher, June 2004

In a program in Kansas City, Missouri, infant teachers developed their own Inserimento ("setting in") process for welcoming new children and parents and for supporting the babies' prior attachments as part of building new ones with the caregivers.

DAILY JOURNAL
WEDNESDAY, SEPTEMBER 10, 2003

Today was a lot like yesterday. We did not get a morning activity off the ground because many friends were sleeping and the ones awake were too crabby.

This afternoon we did have two friends that felt ready to take on an activity. Tyler smiled when he saw the flour on the table and quickly came over to feel it. Max was a little less eager; he preferred to touch it slowly with just a couple fingertips first.

Finally Max decided to really get his hands in the flour, which now had water mixed with it. He was very curious and examined it when it began to stick to his hands. Tyler found out that the flour would slide easily on the table. He worked to spread it out around him and cover his part of the

table. After the fun of that wore off, Tyler decided to eat all his flour...

Hopefully the rest of the day will work out so the friends that were sleeping earlier can play with flour and water as well.

Acknowledgments: This photo essay is drawn from the research project of Amy Wolf: Wolf, A. (2007). *Building relationships: A study of families, children and teachers.* Ph.D. dissertation in Education and Sociology, University of Missouri–Kansas City. The research was presented at the 2006 annual convention of the National Association for the Education of Young Children.

"A Book About Me"
Family Books as a
Support for Transitions

Teachers discover that pictures and stories can support children, families, and faculty as they initiate and develop relationships. For example, at Boulder Journey School in Boulder, Colorado, each new family creates "A Book About Me" for their child that is displayed in the classroom. These books provide comfort for children and opportunities for families to learn more about one another, while offering teachers information about the children with whom they work. Families fill the books with anecdotes and photographs about their child and family, their child's favorite experiences, and things that give their child pleasure and comfort, and they share the books during the first weeks of school. Books are passed on from year to year so that children can reflect on their growth over time.

Here are two sample pages from the book that Caleb's parents created for him when he entered Boulder Journey School.

Reprinted with permission from his parents and his grandmother, Ellen Hall, Executive Director of the school (http://www.boulderjourneyschool.com).

The Generous Space for Children

In Pistoia, Italy, educators believe in making space favorable to the child and the group. They want the space to transmit to children a sense of belonging to a community with a history, in an inclusive way that reaches out to all the new arrivals. For example, most rooms contain recognizable pieces, such as wicker cradles woven by local craftsmen, and furnishings coming from children's homes. The space is also evocative in encouraging connection to the local culture through imagination and fantasy. Each infant and toddler center features puppets and a stage. Through pretending, stories, and fairy tales, children and teachers begin to explore imaginary roles together, confront emotions, and create a collective imaginary world.

The teachers pay great attention to the presentation of materials and resources as a way to offer children an intense, absorbing experience. What they call a *generous environment* is one in which the generosity derives not only from the richness and the variety of materials provided but also from the teachers' attitudes, implicit in the care with which materials have been sought out, selected, and offered to children. It is a generosity of attitude characterized by attention and listening by adults who know how to observe, offer things, and pace their offerings at the right moment. In this way, teachers sustain children's attention and co-involvement, reanimate their interest when necessary, and value what they do.

Nature Explore Classrooms for Infants and Toddlers

The outdoor environment can illustrate the principles of relationship-based care as well as the indoor one can. Here we see some of the areas outside at the Child Saving Institute in Omaha, Nebraska, one of many programs in the state dedicated to nature education.

The climbing area

Digging in the sand area

Social play in the
hammock area

Rolling down the
small grassy hill

Inspecting flowers
in the garden

The water feature
in the "messy area"

Photos by Linda Esterling and Carolyn Edwards.

Here is another Nebraska Nature Explore Classroom, this one part of a family child care center called Hand in Hand, in Lincoln, Nebraska. Teacher, Jane Kreifels, uses her attunement and sensitive relationship to infant Olivia to introduce the child to the wonder of nature through sensory explorations.

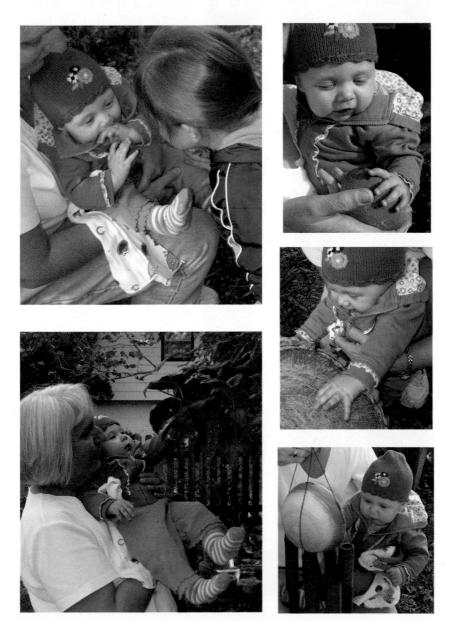

Photos by Linda Esterling.

Two Toddlers Explore Plants

Children explore nature and practice skills of self-regulation through peer interaction.

Sofia was out on the playground. She discovered a leaf on the ground and lifted it up to her face as if investigating the texture. Then she searched for her friend.

"Kya, where Kya?" Sofia found Kya and walked over to her with her leaf in hand. She pushed the leaf toward Kya's face. "Look, Kya," Sofia insisted.

Sofia walked Kya over to the plant where she found the leaf. Kya reached and touched the leaf. Sofia took her own leaf and placed it on the plant. Kya and Sofia looked at each other and smiled.

"Look, Kya," Sofia instructed to Kya as she explored a new part.

"Here, Fia," Kya responded and handed Sofia a different part of the plant. Kya then reached up high to a new part, pulled it down to her face, and tried to lick the plant.

"NO, Kya!" directed Sofia. She wanted her friend to explore, but not by tasting.

In this episode, the two little girls built on their friendship to practice and display self-regulation skills as they made discoveries and shared the joy of exploring plants. Because of their close observation of each other, their use of words, and careful listening, they were able to focus together without intervention of the teacher.

Adapted with permission from J. Benson & J. Leeper Miller (2008). Experiences in nature: A pathway to standards. *Young Children, 63*(4), 22–29. Reprinted with permission from the National Association for the Education of Young Children. Photos taken at University of Nebraska Ruth Staples Child Development Laboratory and reprinted with permission of Jenny Leeper Miller.

SUMMARY

Documentation produces many benefits that are not separate. They are connected in a tight system in which each aspect enhances the rest in a positive feedback loop. Adult dance teams who wish to become more sophisticated and complex in the dances they can perform employ self-study strategies such as video photography and notational systems to study and talk about what they do. These methods allow them to focus on the choreography of their dance and work on the whole story of the dance, its musicality (matching of dance and music), and how the sequence of dance moves fit together. They can study their individual artistic expression, execution, footwork, and other techniques. They can also consider how each dancer is moving in position and interaction with the others.

In just the same way, teachers who wish to improve their teaching skills use strategies of pedagogical documentation to enhance their moves of observing, planning, and communicating. They can look at the teaching and learning process as a whole and see how it is progressing and fitting together in the big picture. They can also break down and analyze each step and skill in the documentation cycle and focus on any particular ones they want to improve, from questioning, to observing and recording, to planning. Finally, they can consider how the different participants (i.e., children, parents, teachers) are getting along and interacting with one another. Their programs will benefit in the following ways:

• **Relationships between teachers and children are improved.**

During the process of documentation, teachers have to pay close attention to each child so that their observations can be objective and realistic. As teachers become better listeners and observers, they also change their teaching behaviors with children.

• **Children's learning is extended.**

As teachers observe and document the children's active engagement and involvement, they become more familiar with the children's interests and better able to encourage them in the right direction. When activities are closely related to the children's interests and questions, the children become more active and eager learners (see Box 6.8).

• **Children's sense of identity is enhanced.**

When children experience themselves as seen and understood by adults, they come to believe that they are being taken care of emotionally and that their ideas and feelings are being taken seriously. They increase their trust of other children and adults. Children love studying the raw and finished documentation that is continually being updated all around them. The documentation helps them construct a coherent sense of their own capabilities and ongoing development over time.

BOX 6.8.
Excerpts from a nanny's diary

During training to become a nanny, Half the Sky caregivers hone their observation skills so that they can identify the children's interests and shadow them. They learn how responding to these interests promotes development. The children make remarkable progress, as documented in the anecdotal notes that become part of their memory books prepared by the nannies with the help of the nanny supervisors. Children who once lay in beds all day with dull, flat expressions become ones who move their bodies eagerly, jump with joy when they see their nannies arrive in the morning, reach for toys to explore, and babble and laugh with glee. The children's health and physical development are carefully monitored, but the most motivating evidence of changes for the *zumu* are those she observes and documents. In one case (just one of many similar stories), a child with cerebral palsy named Lian Genhui went from being nonreactive, nonspeaking, and nonwalking at 20 months; to smiling, crawling, and standing with support at 28 months; to speaking at 29 months.

LIAN GENHUI'S DIARY

May 2005. I met Lian Genhui, a 22-month-old toddler who has cerebral palsy and floppy muscles. She became one of the children under my care. I observed that she was emotionless, unaware of the outside world and did not react when I tried to make contact with her. She was quite weak and drank only milk; she could not hold the milk bottle herself or eat anything solid. When I held her in my arms, she felt so soft, and she had no strength in her muscles at all. She could neither speak nor crawl. Most of the time, she lay in her crib. She didn't know how to play with toys or other children.

November 2005. It has been 6 months since I began work with Genhui. I was determined to change her environment. Every day I massaged her muscles while talking and singing to her. I gave her my warm smiles and made eye contact with her to let her know of my existence and my love for her. I often spent time playing with her on the floor. Now, she can smile at me and can even recognize the people and objects around her. She can make a sound like, "Enenahah," to communicate with me, and she understands some simple words. She learned to crawl, stand up by holding on to something, and move her feet. I frequently encourage her to try new moves and little bits of progress and she loves it! It makes me feel we have built trust between each other. I hug her a lot because she has become part of my daily life now. When there is a stranger visiting, she will be scared and only I can calm her down.

Box 6.8 (continued)

December 2005. Lian Genhui brings me joy every day. Many times I put her back up against my chest so that we were facing the same direction. In the beginning, she didn't cooperate and would refuse to put her feet down on the floor. So I gently held her up and moved my legs against hers to push her forward. In this way, she was actually practicing walking as I walked. Day after day, she could even move a few steps forward with me though she still had to hold my hand. Now she can imitate some simple gestures, for example, "good-bye," "welcome," and "blow a kiss." She can also point out the location of her nose, eyes, and mouth. She seems to trust me and gradually has begun to take my advice and eat new foods.

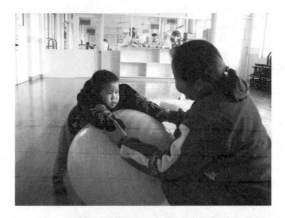

Prepared by Janice Cotton, Director, Infant Nurture Program, Half the Sky Foundation. Further information in Cotton, Edwards, Zhao, & Gelabert (2007) and Zhao (2003). Printed with permission of Janice Cotton and Half the Sky Foundation.

- **Children's learning is guided.**

Documenting helps teachers intentionally work with children as they explore and learn. The documentation serves as the basis for discussion between teachers. It helps them uncover the meanings and concepts behind what children do and then make plans and choices for what to do next. Teachers can guide the children's learning step by step, always monitoring the activities to make sure they meet the children's interests and allow them to progress and develop.

- **Families are drawn in.**

Documentation, whether raw or finished, provides the perfect medium for conversations with parents, provoking questions such as: What happened here? Isn't it fantastic? What do you think it means? Have you seen anything like it? What do you think was behind the children's behavior? What learning strategies did they use? What does it all mean, in your opinion? Parents delight in such conversations focused on their children. They are drawn into a lasting concern with the process of learning and what adults can do to facilitate it.

- **Teachers are empowered.**

When teachers begin to reflect in an organized way on their own learning, they use documentation to compare perspectives and refine their approaches and activities. They become more skillful at assessing children's knowledge and learning. They become self-motivated to set higher expectations for themselves. As teachers document their goals and successes, they gain support from administrators and other staff at their program. When other people can see clearly what goes on in the classroom—by looking at the project panels, booklets, or videos of the classroom activities—they come to better understand and appreciate the value of the education and care children receive (Abramson, 2007).

- **Bridges are built to the community.**

The children begin to gain confidence, knowledge, and social skills that they can use to interact with their community. Documentation becomes a way for children to explore the relationship between themselves and the larger world. Furthermore, it helps the public better understand and appreciate the children. Documentation creates a relationship with viewers that increases respect for children and teachers. It tells eloquent stories of the children's (and teachers') triumphs and creates anticipation about further stories to follow.

RESOURCES

Edwards, C.P., Gandini, L., Peon-Casanova, L., & Davidson, J. (2002). *Children of the world's societies: No. 5. Bambini: Infant/toddler care in Pistoia: A child-friendly city* [Video]. Lincoln, NE: Great Plains National. Available online from

Teachers College Press and Learning Materials Workshop at http://www.learningmaterialsworkshop.com

Gandini, L., & Goldhaber, J. (2001). Two reflections about documentation. In L. Gandini & C.P. Edwards (Eds.), *Bambini: The Italian approach to infant/toddler care* (pp. 124–145). New York: Teachers College Press.

Katz, L., & Chard, S. (1996). The contribution of documentation to the quality of early childhood education. *ERIC Digest*. (ED393608) Available online at http://www.ericdigests.org/1996-4/quality.htm

Peaslee, A., Snyder, I., & Casey, P.B. (2007). Making our thinking visible: Using documentation for professional development. *Young Children, 62*(4), 28–29.

Reggio Children, Italy, & Harvard Project Zero (2001). *Making learning visible: Children as individual and group learners*. Reggio Emilia, Italy: Reggio Children.

Smith, D., & Goldhaber, J. (2004). *Poking, pinching, and pretending: Documenting toddlers' explorations with clay*. St. Paul, MN: Redleaf Press.

CHAPTER 7

A Beautiful Dance Hall

Space and Environments

Marcy arrived at her toddler program one morning holding her father's hand. They stopped to hang up her coat at the row of cubbies in the hall, identified by a photo portraying Marcy's whole family. Her father read a note from the teachers telling all about what the children did yesterday and another inviting him to an upcoming family celebration. Coming into the room, they went immediately to their favorite place—a couch and low table set up to have the feel of a living room in the middle of the classroom. With a nearby bookcase and a few books arranged on the table, the area also served as the book area, but it was more homelike in appearance. It invited Marcy and her father to sit and snuggle a moment. Marcy's father read her two stories, and then she was ready to play. She kissed her father good-bye and happily waved to him as he went out the door.

It was outdoor time one crisp autumn day at Jane's family child care home. Livia and Brianna, both 2-year-old girls, headed with enthusiasm into the backyard with the other children. They immediately headed over to the low platform and ramp that Jane had recently installed. Brianna led Livia up the ramp and then ran down. She turned to encourage Livia, who was reluctant, to come down also. Finally, Brianna ran back up the ramp and showed Livia another way to come down, sliding on her bottom. Livia loved that method. Then Brianna and Livia ran off to an area of the yard called the "messy area," filled with woodchips and autumn leaves. The two girls sat on a log and shuffled their feet in the leaves and woodchips. They dug their hands in, and Livia looked up and said, "Brrrrr, cold." Brianna imitated, and they both giggled happily. Next, Livia and Brianna headed off to the wood cookies and stepped from one to the next, finally settling down to dig through the sand and leaf bits. They used their fine motor coordination to carefully pick up and examine tiny bits of material. Livia got the idea to carry handfuls of sand back to the ramp, and then she and Brianna began to go up and down it again, making rough, scraping sounds as they ground their shoes against the sand and wood.

These examples suggest the key ingredients of relationally based environments for infants and toddlers. These places create an immediate feeling of welcoming and discovery. They extend the dance begun between children and parents by creating beautiful invitations that cause everyone to feel like entering the dance of relationships. The environments also encourage each child to try out more complex steps and learn how to join in new arrangements of play and learning with other children. Greenman defined an environment as the following:

> An environment is a living, changing system. More than the physical space, it includes the way time is structured and the roles we are expected to play. It conditions how we feel, think, and behave; and it dramatically affects the quality of our lives. The environment either works for us or against us as we conduct our lives. (1988, p. 5)

What kinds of spaces promote the dance of relationships? Environments—whether indoor or outdoor—must be safe, developmentally appropriate, and individually appropriate (Isbell & Isbell, 2003). Environments for infants and toddlers should be totally different from spaces for preschool children and furthermore suited to the mix of children in the program. Young infants (0–8 months), crawlers and walkers (8–18 months), and toddlers (18–36 months) use space and materials very differently. Therefore, it is important

---

BOX 7.1.
Environments in relationship-based programs

The following are principles for environments in relationship-based programs serving infants and toddlers.

1. They create an atmosphere of peacefulness and joy by both soothing and stimulating the senses.

2. They invite complex exploration and social play.

3. They inform, document, and teach.

4. They create a sense of identity and belonging.

5. They reinforce the message that children's individual needs will be recognized and met.

6. They are welcoming and inviting.

7. They are safe, developmentally appropriate, and individually appropriate.

---

to plan the environment around the developmental needs and capabilities of the children served.

But more than basic safety and appropriateness is required. Our focus in this book is on fostering relationship-based programs that welcome and invite, create a sense of identity and belonging, stimulate the senses and promote complex social play, and are visually informative (see Box 7.1). This chapter discusses these principles and shows how educators can provide warm, beautiful environments that create community, are reassuring and comfortable, and excite children's minds and imaginations.

INDOOR ENVIRONMENTS FOR INFANTS AND TODDLERS

The transition from home to an infant and toddler program can be a difficult one for young children and their families, especially during the first transition. Too many centers and child care homes present an extremely intense collection of bright lights, loud primary colors, and hard surfaces that contrast strongly with the familiarity of home. Such an environment does nothing to create a calm, intimate, and cozy environment.

Create a Warm and Welcoming Environment

A welcoming and inviting environment begins with the presence of homey elements and soft features, such as carpets, window coverings made of natural materials, ceiling hangings, pillows, and stuffed toys that absorb sound (Curtis & Carter, 2003, 2006). A mix of comfortable child-sized accessible furniture coupled with an adult-sized couch or rocking chair for reading and cuddling make for an inviting surrounding. Soft classical music played in the background and heated floors add to the soothing and comforting effect. Attention to attractiveness and harmony in design suggests an attitude of caring and love. These values are evident in softly colored floor coverings and furnishings, sunlight pouring through the windows, green living plants, and cleanliness and order. Lighting and carefully chosen and balanced colors can create a unifying feeling and make people want to enter and stay. A physical space always reflects the culture and identity of the people who create and use it. Regional and local touches are very important to making a space feel welcoming in the right way. In the United States, for instance, a southwestern look is very different from Midwestern or New England style—each has its own charms.

Provide Adequate Storage

The environment must also contain places for parents to store children's things, such as their extra clothes and diapers, and for parents and teachers to exchange notes and information. Charts attached to cubbies where parents can record when the child woke up, what the child ate, and other notes relieve parents' anxiety that the teachers will not know what they need to provide the best care for their child that day. All of these things provide parents with a sense of security that their child's individual needs will be met while they are away. In addition, the program needs adequate storage for its toys, materials, extra equipment, and supplies so that these items are well organized and accessible. Without adequate storage, an environment looks cluttered, messy, and chaotic, which is tiring and depressing to the staff and children.

Promote Identity and Belonging

Children and adults love to see their identity displayed in positive and individualized ways, such as through a set of family photos on the wall or taped onto the windows of the classroom so that light pours through and illuminates them (see Box 7.2) (Wein, Coates, Keating, & Bigelow, 2005).

Displaying images from children's home and family lives in the early childhood environment creates a continuous reminder of the home-to-program connection. These photos can be displayed in a variety of ways, such as plastic sleeves placed in cribs, photo stands and frames, notebook binders, bulletin boards, or handmade books. Some of these images should be portable so that children are free to move them around and incorporate them into their play or turn to them when they need comfort or reassurance. (Curtis & Carter, 2003, p. 37)

BOX 7.2.
An amiable space in Reggio Emilia, Italy

At the Peter Pan infant and toddler center in Reggio Emilia, Cristina Bondavalli has worked to strengthen each child's primary attachment to family; yet, at the same time, she widens children's opportunities for new relationships and connects their lives at home to the center. For example, the entryways to the center and to each classroom are set up to give entering parents many ideas about what happens inside. Beautiful, carefully designed displays inform parents about the rhythm and content of their child's day. A display composed of little notebooks and journals about each child, decorated and encased in transparent envelopes, conveys a primary message of belonging and openness.

Coming into the classroom, parents find an inviting place formed of homelike rather than institutional pieces of furniture, where they can linger and talk. Other focal points for parents are the set of framed photographs of each child arranged on a chest of drawers; the collection of treasure boxes where children have placed their mementos collected with parents last summer (to be shared with the group on a special occasion during early fall); and the large folders containing children's work, placed in an inviting spot to share with peers or parents. The environment is emotionally and physically safe yet also amiable to encouraging encounters, communication, and relationships.

Adapted from Edwards, C.P., & Raikes, H. (2002). Extending the dance: Relationship-based approaches to infant-toddler care and education. *Young Children, 57*(4), 10–17. Reprinted with permission from the National Association for the Education of Young Children.

Mirrors at the children's eye level reinforce the message that the program intends to promote children recognizing themselves and growing their own unique personalities. Instead of feeling impersonal and anonymous, the environment individualizes the experience of coming into the center. The children find their names, faces, personalities, connections, favorite things, and preferences reflected not only through the ways that teachers greet them but also through the space and routines. In the infant room at the Boulder Journey School in Colorado, a set of stiff white cards hangs by strings from the ceiling of the infant room, each one decorated with photos sent in from a child's home. When an adult holds an infant, they can stand and look together at the child's card and talk soothingly about the family members.

Create a Soothing and Stimulating Atmosphere

Too many program environments today create a jarring, loud, overstimulating visual impression through the use of hard surfaces, harsh lighting, and blaring primary colors. People sometimes assume that young children prefer bright colors. However, it is in their overuse that they become tiring to the senses of the children and teachers who spend their day in the presence of things that contain too many intense colors. From a relational point of view, the problem is that overstimulating environments promote crankiness and hyperarousal in children. Instead, teachers should do what they can to create a balance of natural and artificial materials, soft colors, pleasant tactile qualities, and careful lighting, which together soothe the senses at the same time as they stimulate them. It is easy to collect things from nature to enhance the environment (e.g., tree branches, feathers, pinecones, smooth stones) that are safe for infants and toddlers to handle. Living plants (nonpoisonous) can be placed in hanging baskets or high shelves to add beauty and calm. Water in an aquarium or colored bottle offers a fluid element. The natural colors balance the ones inherent in the manufactured materials and furnishings. Natural light should be used wherever possible. Artificial lighting should not be uniform and monotonous. The lightscape can be made lively by means of variations in intensity, coloration, and filtering.

Promote Complex Exploration and Social Play

Relationship-based spaces support the whole system of relationships in a program. They invite complex social play by providing places for children to interact in small groups without interruption. As described in Chapter 9, infants and toddlers function at a higher level in a small group than they do in a large one. Therefore, it is good to find a place in the classroom or yard where small groups can go for special play. In small groups of children who know one another well, play often takes the form of games in which children join together in a common familiar theme (e.g., tag, follow the leader, do what I do).

Learning areas of the classroom serve to limit numbers of children and promote complex social play. In addition, protected areas (e.g., a mattress on the floor surrounded by curtains) allow children places to get away from the larger group either by themselves or in groups of two or three. The classroom should be stocked with materials that invite imagination and flexibility (Gandini & Topal, 1999). This can happen by offering throughout the environment open-ended materials that can be used in many ways. Cardboard, cloth, and other undefined materials encourage children to combine things in a variety of ways and engage in pretend play. The color insert provides many examples of these strategies.

Provide Spaces that Inform, Document, and Teach

The infant and toddler classroom, as described in Chapter 6, should be a space for documentation that records observations, informs, and teaches. The entryway in particular is an important place for communication between parents and teachers. On a nearby table, two-way communication notebooks or envelopes help parents and teachers send messages or pictures back and forth. Inside the classroom, a holding wall is useful for providing an easy and convenient place to tack up pieces saved from an ongoing theme for reference and study. Various vertical surfaces (e.g., walls, windows, cabinets, appliances) can be places to tape documentation. A low bookshelf for the diaries, albums, and flipbooks telling the stories of past activities and events provides a library often visited by the children and teachers.

Box 7.3 provides a list of questions to assess a program's environment from a child's perspective.

BOX 7.3.
Questions to ask yourself about the environment

Put yourself in the shoes of the infants and toddlers who spend their days in your space. Use the statements below, from a child's perspective, to assess your space. Write the number of each statement in all the places on your floor plan—both indoors and outdoors—where you are confident the statement is true.

1. I can see who I am and what I like to do in your program and at home.

2. There are soft comfortable places where my tired mommy, daddy, grandma, or auntie can sit and talk with me and my teacher.

3. Soft colors, diffused lighting, and wonderful smells and sounds stimulate my senses.

4. The natural world can be found here for me to explore inside and out.

5. There is something sparkly, shadowy, or wondrous and magical here.

6. My teacher leaves out a special object each day so I can keep trying to figure out more about its properties and how it works.

7. There are materials here that make me want to play pretend with my friends.

8. I can feel strong and daring and be physically active here.

9. I see signs and pictures that my teachers and family talk to me about.

10. I get to know lots of friendly adults and find out about all the places around here outside my classroom.

Adapted from *Designs for Living and Learning: Transforming Early Childhood Environments*, by Deb Curtis and Margie Carter. Copyright © 2003 by Deb Curtis and Margie Carter, Reprinted with permission of Redleaf Press, St. Paul, MN, www.redleafpress.org.

OUTDOOR ENVIRONMENTS
FOR INFANTS AND TODDLERS

Educators and parents around the world are becoming concerned that many children today spend little time outdoors and have only a small connection with nature. Children need such connections and a chance to spend slow, unhurried time exploring the plants, animals, sights, sounds, textures, and formations of the outdoors. Infants and toddlers get off on the wrong foot if sedentary patterns are set early and children develop a dislike or even fear of the natural environment.

The good news is that early childhood educators can make a big difference; there are many ways to improve the outdoor environment and weave nature education throughout the whole curriculum (e.g., Benson & Leeper Miller, 2008; Torquati & Barber, 2005; Williams, 2008). Table 7.1 gives many examples of activities that can be done with children in the outdoors. These activities can be conducted in any program, whether center or home based, but are easiest to do in an outdoor environment especially designed to connect young children to the natural world.

Table 7.1. Things to do in the outdoor environment: Connecting infants and toddlers to the natural world

Curriculum domain	Sample activities
Social and emotional development	Explore the textures, smells, and sounds of nature while developing a sense of comfort and wonder with the environment
	Begin to develop relationships with adults and peers through a safe exploration of the outdoor environment
	Develop curiosity in the natural environment through hands-on experiences
	Develop respect for the living things in the natural world (e.g., learning to step around growing plants, touch flowers gently)
Approaches to learning	Demonstrate curiosity in the natural environment through hands-on experiences
	Explore the textures, smells, and sounds of nature
	Develop initiative through free play and exploration outside
	Try several different methods to solve a problem
Health and physical development	Experience the safe and enjoyable conduct of indoor routines moved outdoors (e.g., eating and napping)
	Taste healthy things from nature (e.g., tomatoes grown in the garden)
	Experience all of the seasons and types of weather safely and enjoyably
	Experience a variety of natural surfaces (e.g., walk/crawl in dirt, grass, sand)

Table 7.1. *(continued)*

Curriculum domain	Sample activities
Language and literacy	Increase vocabulary by referring to items in nature by names
	Use your language carefully and strategically (Don't bombard with language and labels but instead provide rich expansions and elaborations on child's interests.)
	Use space-relational words such as *over, around, big, small, near,* and *far* when referencing nature
	Observe a child's eyes and body closely and, during pauses in the child's action, jump in to describe what you think might be their experience (e.g., of dirt, grass, stones, leaves, trees, animals, insects)
Science	Focus attention on sounds and sensory opportunities children encounter
	Focus attention on cause-effect relationships they encounter
	Select items in nature and sort them by size or color or some other dimensions
	Explore physical features of the outdoor environment (e.g., bark on trees, smell of flowers, feel of grass on feet) and help children express what they are feeling through facial expressions, words, signs, or gestures (e.g., imitate the sounds of nature)
	Explore the way animals fit into their natural environments (e.g., the color of insects matches where they live)
	Explore changes in nature and create connections and associations (e.g., it gets cold in winter and sometimes snows; there is frost on the leaves)
Mathematics	Identify and compare dimensions of objects (e.g., a branch is smaller than a tree, flowers are bigger than an ant)
	Count leaves, sticks, rocks, clouds, nuts, and flowers
	Notice what happens when things are added or subtracted (e.g., more water coming into a tub, more leaves falling from a tree)
	Show how one large object can be broken down into smaller pieces (e.g., a stick can be broken into several small pieces)
Creative arts	Notice with children the beauty of nature and observe what catches their attention and appreciation
	Experience familiar materials with guidance in the outdoors (e.g., water, playdough, clay, finger paints, nontoxic shaving cream) and expand learning by adding these materials to the natural world
	Experience new textures such as pine cones, bark, sand, and leaves
	Enjoy movement and music activities outside (e.g., imitating the motion of a tree or ant, the shape of a flower, the sound of a honey bee or song bird)

Adapted from the Nebraska Early Learning Guidelines Connecting Children to Nature Supplement (http://ectc.nde.ne.gov/ELG/nature_education.pdf). This is a product of the Nebraska Department of Education's Early Childhood Training Center.

Note: The sample activities integrate nature education with learning in the traditional subject matter domains.

In designing an outdoor environment, the same simple principles apply to all of the early childhood years (National Arbor Day Foundation, 2007). Because the resulting environment is so radically different from the traditional playground (dominated by its giant play structure and flat, uniform ground surface), it may even be renamed as a *playscape, outdoor classroom,* or *nature park*. The outdoor space is divided into clearly marked areas identified by a sign or other visual clue. The recommended areas include the following:

- Entry feature
- Open area for large-motor activities
- Climbing and crawling area
- "Messy materials" area
- Building area
- Music and movement area
- Garden and/or greenhouse
- Gathering area
- Storage places
- Water area
- Dirt-digging area
- Sand area
- Wheeled-toy area
- Area for swings or other dynamic equipment such as hammocks

Rusty Keeler, a landscape architect, described such an infant and toddler playscape that he designed for a not-for-profit child care in Skaneateles, New York (Keeler, 2008). For babies (0–12 months), a soft rubber crawl pad extended into a walking and crawling path. Smooth metal arches were placed along the path for the babies to pull up on. One of the arches featured hanging chimes that children could clink and tinkle. Also along the trail was a small sand area with a storage bench for sand buckets and scoopers. A small trellis with a bench swing provided a cozy area. The toddler area was set off from the infant area by a small hedgerow of thick shrubs. The toddler area offered a more challenging layout, including a looping track for riding toys, tunnel, herb garden, benches, water feature, hill slide, and large sand area with room for groups of children to work on giant sand and water projects. Looking at the photos in Keeler's book, one gains a sense of his vision for children, which he described as follows:

> We can do it. We can create extraordinary places for young children to discover themselves and the world around them. We can create places for children that

tickle the imagination and surprise the senses. We can make places for children of all abilities to interact with nature as they play on the planet. We can craft these spaces with love, collaboration, and care. (2008, p. 18).

Similar inspiring areas are found in the "nature explore classroom" in programs such as the Child Saving Institute in Omaha, Nebraska. The photo essay "Nature Explore Classrooms for Infants and Toddlers" in the color insert illustrates children from the Child Saving Institute playing in the different areas. The environment promotes many of the relationship-based principles because it is welcoming and inviting, meets individual needs, soothes and stimulates the senses, and invites complex exploration and social play.

SUMMARY

A visitor to any program for infants and toddlers immediately sizes up the messages that the environment gives about the educational choices and the quality of caregiving being provided to the children. When the environment is drab and dismal—or conversely, when it is overstimulating and harshly plastic—it seems to say that feelings are not important in this place. For the reader who thinks that comment is too critical, consider being a young child (or teacher) spending many hours a day in a place that is physically depressing or hyperarousing.

The environment instead can become the most visible way that educators convey their deep caring and respect for the children. Using a welcoming layout that fosters encounters, communication, and relationships, it suggests a "sense of we." The arrangement of the furnishings and learning materials encourages children to make discoveries and choices and solve problems. Attention to detail—the color of the walls, the shape and feel of the furniture, the arrangement of objects, the smells and soft music—suggests concern with every aspect of the child's thoughts and feelings. The walls and windows through which light pours speak through all of the photos and words they contain about the life of the classroom and what the children are doing and learning. In the words of Loris Malaguzzi, founder of the Reggio Emilia educational programs,

> We value space because of its power to organize, promote pleasant relationships among people of different ages, create a handsome environment, provide changes, promote choices and activity, and its potential for sparking all kinds of social, affective, and cognitive learning. All of this contributes to a sense of well-being and security in children. We also think as it has been said that the space has to be a sort of aquarium that mirrors the ideas, values, attitudes, and cultures of the people who live within it. (quoted in Gandini, 1988, p. 177)

With such pro-environment values and intentions, an amazing thing begins to happen. The children's program space goes from being simply a beautiful ballroom in which the children and adults gather to dance in relationship, to becoming itself almost a living thing. It takes on force and personality as if it is another dance partner for the children, inviting them to enter into layer upon layer of significant associations with people, places, and things in the beautiful, surprising, and beckoning world around us.

RESOURCES

Benson, J., & Leeper Miller, J. (2008). Experiences in nature: A pathway to standards. *Young Children, 63*(4), 22–29.

Curtis, D., & Carter, M. (2003). *Designs for living and learning: Transforming early childhood environments.* St. Paul, MN: Redleaf Press.

Gandini, L. (1988). Educational and caring spaces. In C.P. Edwards, L. Gandini, & G. Forman (Eds.), *The hundred languages of children: The Reggio Emilia approach, advanced reflections* (2nd ed., pp. 161–178). Greenwich, CT: Ablex.

Greenman, J. (Ed.). (2005, May). Environments that support exploration and learning. *Beyond the journal: Young children on the web.* Retrieved December 1, 2008, from http://journal.naeyc.org/btj/200505/

McHenry, J.D., & Buerk, K.J. (2008). Infants and toddlers meet the natural world. *Young Children, 63*(1), 40–41.

CHAPTER 8

Staying in Step

Supporting Relationships with Families

Dawn and Carey are the parents of 15-month-old Ava. Ava has been in two child care centers already and is now entering home child care because, as Dawn says, "The relationship piece was not right in either place. In the first center, the teachers were warm and responsive, but Ava had three teachers by the time she was 14 months of age." Carol was baby Ava's first teacher. But when Ava learned to crawl she was moved to the next room…without Carol. Before Dawn and Ava had adjusted to the next teacher fully, it was time to move again. Dawn then chose another program, but there the teachers lacked the engaging interactions she had seen at the first center. Dawn and Carey clearly value a relationship-based approach, although perhaps they would not have been able to articulate that when they began their child care experiences.

Jessica and Bill are the parents of Louis, now age 4 months. They are selecting their first child care program and are looking for a caregiver who is experienced but also a great relater. They say there is an elusive quality of relating that they know they will recognize when

147

they see it. They want someone who they can relate to comfortably but also who relates well to the baby. Some potential caregivers talk to them but not to Louis. Others turn right to Louis but seem to ignore the parents' needs to connect. In addition to looking for someone who relates both to them and their child, Jessica and Bill also want someone who will talk with them about their parenting decisions. They wonder if they will find someone who relates to both them and their baby.

In this chapter, we remind the reader of the prime importance of parents to the development of infants. Thus, we return to the dances in a relationship-based model that support the child's primary relationship with parents. Just as a lively ball encompasses many dances, our approach also supports several kinds of dances. The triangle schematic in Figure 1.1 laid out all the combinations of dances considered important in a relationship-based infant and toddler program and includes dances between teachers and parents.

How can a teacher support these dances in the context of a relationship-based program? To answer this question, we first briefly review literature on teacher–parent relationships and parenting support. Then, we identify a number of concerns that parents express and the principles that organize the partnership with parents in a relationship-based program. These principles take into account the two major relationship dances we address in this chapter: the dance between teachers and parents and the dance of teachers supporting parents in their parenting role.

A BRIEF REVIEW OF LITERATURE ON PARENT–TEACHER RELATIONSHIPS AND SUPPORT FOR PARENTING IN CENTERS

Excellent American early childhood programs have long emphasized the importance of good relationships with parents (Elicker, Noppe, Noppe, & Fortner-Wood, 1997; Galinsky, 1990). Infant programs in Italy also provide excellent models for close partnership with parents (Gandini & Edwards, 2001). A good parent and teacher relationship appears to be an important underpinning for supportive teacher–child relationships in an infant and toddler center-based care setting. For example, Owen, Ware, and Barfoot (2002) found that increased mother and teacher communications were associated with increased supportiveness and sensitivity between teacher and child, and Smith and Hubbard (1988) found modest but significant relations between teacher–parent interaction and children's adaptation to child care. It follows that parent–teacher communication helps the teacher to better know and respond to the child, who can't fully speak for him-or herself, although studies to date typically document correlation not causality (Shpancer, 2002). That is, we do not know whether the parent–teacher relationship causes the teacher–child relationship sensitivity or if teachers who relate better to parents are also more capable in relating to children.

There also are alternative ways to characterize the parent role in infant and toddler programs. Some program leaders recommend adopting a business model and characterizing parents as customers. Customer service models emphasize problem solving, exceeding expectations, and listening to parents. This model provides guidance for when parents have complaints by emphasizing the opportunity of program improvement from parent feedback (Franklin, 2004).

While a customer service model may emphasize relationships, a relationship-oriented model views the roles of parents and teachers as partners, with parents and teachers collaborating with one another (Elicker et al., 1997). Tasks shift under such a model; for example, it becomes important for teachers and parents to truly understand the different roles and perceptions teachers and parents have of the other. Galinsky (1994) illustrated four sets of deep feelings of which both teachers and parents should be aware:

1. Parents may feel that they are the only ones capable of caring for the child. They may feel possessive or slightly jealous of other caregivers. Teachers also have strong feelings of attachment toward the child and may be surprised if a parent does not recognize that.

2. Parents may have deep and sometimes unstated expectations for care that may or may not match the teacher's beliefs about quality.

3. Feelings about separation may be intense for both parent and child. Separation from children may engender parents' own previous fears about loss. Parents also may leave their children abruptly because the separation is overly painful for them.

4. Parents may feel judged by teachers because many parents do not differentiate their children's behaviors from themselves at this early stage.

In a relationship-based program, teachers and parents move toward trust and communication that provides support for these very deeply held feelings. Trust both grows from and furthers mutual respect and communication between parents and teachers as parents and teachers validate each other's role, experience, and importance in the child's life (Mason & Duberstein, 1992).

Partnership with parents may be attained developmentally. Gonzalez-Mena and Eyer (2007) proposed three stages of relating to parents:

• Stage 1 is a "caregiver as savior stage" in which the caregiver relates mostly to the children. Caregivers may even see themselves as saving children from their parents.

- In Stage 2, the caregivers come to see the parents as clients. However, they may still be working to change parents and see themselves as superior in their knowledge of children and development to parents.

- In Stage 3, the teacher is a partner to the parent. Teachers supplement and support parents. Parent and teacher share in the care of the child and engage in mutual relationship with open communication, even when conflicts arise.

Stage 3 is similar to the parent–teacher relationship dance we refer to in this book. It is also reflective of the National Association for the Education of Young Children's (2007) Program Standard 7, which is focused on family and community partnerships and is consistent with the type of support emphasized for parents in the Head Start Performance Standards (U.S. Department of Health and Human Services, 2002).

There have been more studies focused on the features and effects of parent–teacher relationships, our first theme in this chapter, than on how center-based programs support parenting, our second theme. There is evidence that high-quality center-based experiences or positive teacher–child relationships can compensate to some extent for poor-quality home environments or poor relationships between children and parents, but research provides less guidance for how child care programs support parents in their parenting role (Shpancer, 2002). While there is conventional wisdom on the topic, perhaps the best evidence for center-based programs supplementing parenting comes from intervention programs such as Early Head Start that provide parent education together with social services during regular home visits (U.S. Department of Health and Human Services, 2002).

WHAT PARENTS WANT AND NEED TO KNOW

Our opening vignettes illustrated some of the concerns that parents have about relationships in child care. It may be helpful for teachers, students, and directors to reflect on the feelings of parents about relationships in child care. It may also be helpful for parents to recognize the universality of common questions of parents. A parent may have a number of questions:

- How does my child's teacher interact with me?

- Can I count on the teacher to relate to me as a partner?

- How will the teacher support me as a parent?

- How does the teacher relate to my child?

- Can I count on the teacher to be supportive and attentive to my child?

- Can the teacher–child relationship become so important to my child that it replaces my own in importance?

- What does it mean when a program says they follow a relationship model?

- How is that different from what other programs do?

- How do I stay informed and in tune with the practices being carried out in the program?

- How can I have input into the practices and values of the program?

- How do I ensure that practices and values of the program are consistent with the values of our family?

PRINCIPLES OF RELATIONSHIP-BASED PROGRAMS

To address a parent's concerns, we identify eight principles of relationship-based approaches for including parents (see Box 8.1). The discussion of these principles is supplemented with suggested language for teachers and directors to use when interacting with parents. This will aid in the teacher's discussion of each of these aspects of the program's relationship-based approach with parents.

BOX 8.1.
Principles for parent–teacher relationships

The following are principles for parent–teacher relationships in relationship-based programs:

1. Relationships with parents are valued and cultivated. Parents and teachers are partners.

2. In relationship-based programs, teachers and directors provide support and information about parenting.

3. In relationship-based programs, teachers seek to form a closer relationship with the child, providing a secure base during child care. They recognize that such a relationship supports the child's development and does not interfere with the relationship with parents.

4. Relationship-based programs provide parents with extensive information about the program as well as about their own child.

5. Relationship-based programs build community among the parents.

6. Relationship-based programs value the contributions of parents to the program overall.

7. Relationship-based programs seek continuity between family values and program offerings.

8. Relationship-based programs articulate relationship-oriented principles and practices to parents.

Be Partners

What are parents looking for in a partnership? Our experience is that parents may differ in what they want in their relationship with their child's teacher, but primarily they want a teacher who relates comfortably with them as well as with their child. They want a teacher who greets them as well as the child. Some teachers and parents become very good friends (or may even be good friends before the caregiving relationship begins), but it is not necessary to be close friends to have a good teacher–parent relationship. What is important is that information flows openly and comfortably—that there is a sense of trust. Parents want a teacher who is open and forthcoming about the child's experiences throughout the day, who volunteers information about the child, and who conveys this information thoroughly and consistently.

When teachers are partners with parents, each contributes to the partnership by sharing information the other needs from their respective portions of the child's day. For example, if the child was up in the night, the parent conveys this information because it might mean that the child is becoming ill. If the child took a shorter than usual nap at the center, this information is conveyed to the parent because the child may be ready for bed sooner than usual. Shared information extends to play and development. If the child was delighted in his or her image in the mirror, this is also shared—because perhaps the parents will want to have some mirror play as well.

Teachers should take the lead in this two-way communication. For example, teachers may say to parents, "I like it when you tell me about his breakfast. It helps me know what he might be ready for when he is here." Teachers should also be responsive when the parent initiates because the teacher and parent are truly engaged in a partnership. Box 8.2 provides additional examples of specific strategies that successful relationship-based programs have used to strengthen communication and relationships with parents. Box 8.3 illustrates a measure that has been used in many child care settings to assess the quality of relationships between parents and teachers.

Provide Support and Information About Parenting

Most parents are continuously seeking information about parenting. However, parents may not seek this information from the teacher until a strong relationship of trust is built. Parents may perceive judgment if teachers have a vestige of Stage 1 or Stage 2 visions of parents as described previously (Gonzalez-Mena & Eyer, 2007). Thus, to provide support for parenting, teachers truly need to have embraced the idea that they are partners (Stage 3). Some parents may continue to be concerned that the teacher may judge their parenting skills. However, most parents worry less about this as the partnership grows. They then may welcome the opportunity to have a dialogue about the many decisions of parenting.

BOX 8.2.
Promoting parent–teacher communication

The following are specific suggestions for promoting parent–teacher communication that some programs have found helpful. Every program finds its own methods for communicating with parents. What is important is that parents feel they are in a relationship and that information about the infant flows between the parent and teacher every day. Other communication strategies supplement the daily communication.

- *Daily notes to which both the parents and teachers contribute.* Parents tell about the child's feeding and early morning experiences; teachers continue this throughout the day. Teachers write about the child's feeding, sleeping, and elimination but also about the child's mood and activities of the day.

- *Formal parent–teacher conferences on an annual or semiannual basis.* These may or may not be preceded by a developmental report about the child's progress.

- *Monthly goals for the child.* These are always based on the child's interest and emerging development. They are developed jointly by the parent and teacher.

- *Weekly or monthly parent read-and-play sessions.* Schedule these sessions in a center common area to promote parent–child interaction before children leave for home.

- *Staff scheduling so that parents see the same teachers every day— morning and afternoon.* Relationship-based programs structure the schedules of primary caregivers so that parents communicate with the primary caregiver every day. In addition, caregivers for both drop off and pick up are the same every day. For example, the primary caregiver may arrive at the center at 7 a.m. every day and see the parents at drop off time. If the primary caregiver leaves before children are picked up by their parents, a second consistent caregiver may round out the day. It is important that this person is the same every day. Traditional programs may "group" the children as numbers go down, but the benefit of communication with the parents is diminished under this scenario. When this happens, the child may have two or three teachers in the waning hours of the day. With so many messengers to pass information through, important messages about the child's experiences may not be transmitted.

- *Teachers communicate (call, text, or e-mail) with parents at home or at work to convey an important happening during the day.* Teachers call parents when they have a concern (e.g., child seems fussy but has no fever).

BOX 8.3.
The Parent–Caregiver Relationship Scale

The parent–caregiver relationship is often considered an important aspect of infant child care quality, yet no valid research instrument has been available to assess this relationship. The Parent-Caregiver Relationship Scale (PCRS) was developed as a measure of the perceived quality of the relationship between the parents and the child care provider ("caregiver") of an infant or toddler. A study assessed the practicality and validity of the PCRS for use in child development and child care research.

The study focused on parents and child care providers who shared the care of infants or toddlers (2–24 months of age) and who had been in their current child care placement for at least 2 months. The PCRS was developed by reviewing the existing literature and talking with parents and caregivers. A total of 35 scale items was created; parallel versions were written for parents and caregivers. The items reflected many perceived qualities of the parent–caregiver relationship, including trust/confidence, open communication, respect, caring, competence, collaboration, shared values, and affiliation/liking.

Based on analysis of the questionnaires of the 217 study participants, it was concluded that the PCRS is a promising and usable research instrument. PCRS respondents rated their relationships using all five scale points on 17 of the PCRS items (1 = strongly disagree to 5 = strongly agree). They used 3 or 4 points on the other items. The average overall ratings were high (4.17 for parents and 4.31 for caregivers), suggesting that most respondents viewed their relationships quite positively. Both parent and caregiver versions of the PCRS proved to be reliable, both in terms of internal consistency and stability over time.

When the PCRS items were factor analyzed, three subscales were found to be interpretable for parents and caregivers. For parents, the subscales were confidence, collaboration, and affiliation. For caregivers, the subscales were confidence, collaboration, and caring. On the basis of these analyses, it was concluded that parents and caregivers had perceptions that were structured similarly in some ways and differently in other ways. For example, parents seemed to consider friendship (affiliation) with the caregiver as a separate and distinct aspect of the relationship, yet caregivers seemed to include friendship as an aspect of collaboration with the parent.

When correlations between the PCRS and other measures of the child care setting were examined, some expected links were found, but only for center-based care. Parent–caregiver relationships were rated more positively by both parents and caregivers when children were in

Box 8.3 (continued)

center care more hours per week. Parents who rated their relationship with the caregiver more positively also reported higher overall satisfaction with the child care center arrangement. Positive perceptions of the relationship with the parent were also most common in caregivers who had high satisfaction with their working conditions and who have positive perceptions of parents in general.

Adapted by Jim Elicker, Associate Professor of Child Development and Family Studies, Purdue University, from Elicker, J., Noppe, I.C., Noppe, L.D., & Fortner-Wood, C. (1997). The Parent Caregiver Relationship Scale: Rounding out the relationship system in infant child care. *Early Education and Development, 8*(1), 83–100. Reprinted with permission of the publisher (Taylor & Francis, http://www.informaworld.com).

Parents often want a teacher who can offer suggestions but also affirm them in the parenting role. Some parents may not want dialogue about their parenting decisions—they may consider this their domain—but will welcome articles or speakers on topics relating to parenting (e.g., how to support children's emotional development or toilet learning).

When speaking with a parent, the teacher may say, "Several of the parents have been asking about language development. Of course, every child is unique and develops at his or her own pace, but we thought it might be interesting to have a parent meeting focused on language development. Would you like that?" A higher stage of development is necessary for teachers to convey a sense of partnership to parents when an aspect of the program is to enhance parenting. However, one way around this concern is to realize that all parents need information and support. It is not disrespectful to convey the types of information that parents may not have had access to. Box 8.4 provides additional strategies to support the parenting dance.

Form a Close Relationship with the Child

Parents may worry that a teacher will pay less attention to their children than they do, or that the teacher may miss important cues their children are sending. On the other hand, a parent may be confused about how close the child's relationship with the teacher should be. When parents understand that children benefit from a secure relationship with the teacher, they usually become free to embrace a strong teacher–child relationship. Sometimes a parent worries that the teacher may become more important to the child than the parent. The parent may see the child performing tasks for the teacher not seen at home or may not see the child misbehave in school. Thus, the parent may erroneously conclude that the child prefers the teacher; however, this is usually not the case. Sometimes teachers misread the meaning of these behaviors as well.

BOX 8.4.
Promoting the parent–child relationship dance

There are a number of ways that relationship-based programs can promote the parent–child dance. Here are some specific strategies:

- *Encourage specific activities at home.* One program helped parents
  create literacy notebooks for reporting about the emerging language
  and fun things the child and parent did at home around literacy.
  Another program emphasized doing a specific activity at home each
  month. This program had a potluck dinner to show parents how to
  introduce the activity. Then, the teacher inquired throughout the
  month about how the activity was going.

- *Focus intentionally on the child's relationships.* One program shared
  the teacher's and parent's responses on the Attachment Q Sort
  (Waters & Deane, 1985) in a guided conference. The director guided
  the parent and teacher through a conversation focused on how the
  child was the same and different in each relationship with the aim of
  helping both to be open to ways to promote secure relationships.
  For example, one parent noted that she thought her child was "not
  cuddly" but the teacher noted that sitting on her lap was something
  the child was very likely to do at school. The parent concluded,
  "Perhaps she would like me to cuddle with her more or to have more
  contact comfort." While expertise is needed to share in this way, the
  general idea of sharing about the positive aspects of parent–child
  and teacher–child relationships can be more widely adopted.

- *Measure relationship qualities.* Some Early Head Start programs
  are now using the Toddler Attachment Sort-45 (TAS-45) as a much
  simpler measure of parent–child attachment security than the Q
  Sort referred to above. The measure also assesses "hot spots" of
  children's competency, including the child's warmth, cuddliness,
  and cooperativeness as well as the child's avoidance of others and
  demandingness (Kirkland, Bimler, Drawneek, McKim, & Scholmerich,
  2004).

- *Offer parent education meetings.* Periodic parent meetings may
  discuss an important area of parent interest, such as toilet learning
  or promoting pro-social behaviors. These programs might feature a
  well-known speaker, a local expert, or simply allow parents to share
  their recommended practices. Some may choose to follow a parenting education curriculum.

- *Think of teachers as models for parents.* The Early Head Start
  Research and Evaluation Project found that parents improved in infant
  and toddler center-based programs more than the control groups in
  specific behaviors—even when they did not receive home visits for
  parenting education. Parents of infants in Early Head Start centers

Box 8.4 *(continued)*

had higher Home Observation for Measurement of the Environment (HOME) scores[1], played with their children more, and spanked less than parents of control group children—probably because they saw teachers focusing on providing a stimulating environment, playing with children, and using other techniques besides spanking.

- *Conduct home visits.* The Early Head Start Research and Evaluation Project found greatest gains among low-income parents and children when center-based services were combined with regular home visits. Through these home visits in mixed-model programs, families received family support services as needed but also continued to focus on parenting as appropriate to each stage of their child's development. The Early Head Start parents in these mixed-model programs were more supportive and less detached of their children in interactions, provided more supportive assistance during a teaching task, read to their children more, and spanked less. Home visitors emphasized the importance of a supportive, involved, and nonpunitive relationship with children, which teachers also modeled. For more information on the Early Head Start Research and Evaluation Project, visit http://www.acf.hhs.gov/programs/opre/ehs/ehs_resrch/index.html.

- *Provide family support services for parents.* Two-generation programs, such as Early Head Start, provide family support services in areas such as mental health, nutrition, health, housing, and employment. Parents who are struggling with mental health issues will have a difficult time responding to and optimizing the developmental opportunities for a vigorous, active, growing infant or toddler. While most infant programs do not have resources for formal parent support services, many times they can provide referrals to parents in need or link to programs that do provide these services.

- *Provide support services for children.* Similarly, children need health and dental screening and services. Some may need disability services, and families may need support in accessing them. An infant's disability may be first detected by the infant care teacher. A relationship-based program partners with the parent through the challenging but potentially uplifting process of referring a child for special diagnosis, identification, and sometimes treatment. When attending an infant and toddler program, parents may confront for the first time the difference between the child they envisioned and the child they have. Relationship-based programs can provide support and acceptance throughout this process.

[1]While HOME scores and rates of spanking were not significantly different between program and control groups, due to the small number of sites, effect sizes of .19 for each showed these were meaningful differences.

Most children readily form secondary attachments. However, studies have shown that secondary attachments do not detract from the primary attachment with parents. One study of primary and secondary attachments found that, when stressed, children demonstrated strong attachment to both parents and their caregivers but retained unique and special responses to parents (Fox, 1977). Regarding misbehavior, most children also do misbehave from time to time and may misbehave more at home than in the center. This may be a good thing—demonstrating that the child feels safe enough to let down his or her guard—and should not be taken as a cue that the child loves the teacher more than the parent. Of course, parents and teachers are both always examining their own practices to ensure that their interactions and environments support children's best responses. A director may say to a parent, "Sophie is forming a close relationship with her teacher. I can tell because she plays so well when the teacher is in the room. She has a great relationship with you, too. We feel really good when children have two sets of great relationships—at home and at school!"

Provide Parents with Information About the Program

Because relationships with parents are so important, relationship-based programs take many steps to ensure that parents are well informed. Newsletters, bulletin boards, web pages, photo-documented displays about activities (e.g., the children's trip to the hen house, child of the week, what the children did with the pumpkins donated by one of the families) are in abundance. Parents are informed about policies, but also, importantly, about the fun and learning occurring in the center. Parents should always be welcome to visit—anytime and without announcement. For example, parents may stay for lunch or go on a walk with the children. Parents know all the children in the group and the program's routine so they can talk with their children about the day, environment, and friends and can model positive relationships with other children and teachers. A director may say to a parent, "Please feel free to drop in *any* time. Our goal is for you to feel totally comfortable about James's care, so come visit so you can see what happens during the day—and you can see how well he gets along here."

Build Community Among the Parents

Parent–parent relationships further extend the purposes of the relationship-based program. They are facilitated by such activities as programs and discussions about parenting, potluck suppers, family nights, come-to-lunch day, and story hour. It is a good thing when parents know each other and support one another out of school. For example, children may sometimes play together during vacations, parents may organize food for the parents of a new baby, or families may talk informally about toilet learning. By providing a space for more than one parent to sit (see Chapter 7), the program further facilitates interactions between the parents of children within the program. Often, parents in relationship-based programs express the view that the other parents are their main support community. This gives them a feeling of security and well-being as parents (that they are able to pass on to their children). A teacher may say to the parents, "We have a new baby coming into our program, so I would like to have a get-together with all the parents in a couple of weeks to welcome his family."

Value the Contributions of Parents

Relationship-based programs invite parents to be on advisory boards and are not reluctant to hear their opinions about practices and improvements. Such programs feature open communication and value the discourse and liveliness found in an open community. Mechanisms for parent input are well established. Parents may complete annual surveys about the program, there may be elected representatives on advisory boards or policy councils, or parents may represent the program in the larger community. Parents may then mobilize to make improvements or enlarge the program offerings; for example, parents in one rela-tionship-based program organized to repaint the equipment on the playground. A director may say to the parents, "Thanks to our fabulous parents for the beautiful new playground! Thanks to Martin for the paint, thanks to Jessie and Marcia for donating the brushes, and thanks to everyone else for all their hard work!"

Seek Continuity Between
Family Values and Program Offerings

Relationships are more readily formed when everyone feels comfortable and "at home" in the setting. Early childhood educators have consistently found that par-ents are most comfortable when there are teachers of their own nationality or who speak their language. Importantly, these parents are likely to believe that their children will be more comfortable and relate more easily if spoken to in their own language or cared for by someone who is of a similar nationality. There are many examples of more subtle ways that programs can promote cultural and values continuity. Chapter 3 provided an example of a survey that can be used to learn more about parenting beliefs and practices.

Parenting beliefs come up continuously in regard to the care of infants and toddlers. In fact, most aspects of infant and toddler caregiving are rooted in traditions—often strong and deeply held—about how children are to be tended. Thus, teachers in a relationship-based program provide information and reasons for the decisions they make. They continuously learn what parents prefer in prac-tice and learn about how parents do things at home. When the relationship is good, much of this information is shared informally. Both parent and teacher learn from each other as they seek a balance on caregiving practices. Teachers also take steps to affirm the culture and values of families within their program. Food from a minority culture may be featured as refreshments for family night or with older toddlers. Books telling about the children's cultures send a message to both parents and children that these cultures and their traditions are valued. To learn more about how parents feel about values, a director might say, "We are doing a semiannual survey so we can be sure we know how you feel about all the practices. This will help us be most responsive to your needs and provide the best environment for your baby. Thanks for taking time to fill out this survey!"

Articulate Relationship-Oriented Principles and Practices to Parents

Many program directors explain their emphasis on relationships to parents before the children enroll. Some directors talk to parents about the importance of attachments, telling them that secondary attachments to teachers are encouraged and that having two sets of relationships strengthens the child's early social, emotional, and other forms of development. They may tell parents about the studies that showed infants and toddlers consistently turned to parents for support when they were stressed (Fox, 1977); this reassures parents about the strong connections children have to them. These directors emphasize the subtle learning and emotional regulation that takes place within the protection of relationships. Parents readily grasp that open communication and relationships with the teachers and other parents contributes in a natural way to this culture of relationships. A director may say at this time, "We want you to know how important our parents are, so please come to talk with me *any time* about how you are feeling and what you think your baby needs."

SUMMARY

Good relationships between parents and teachers support the dances between teachers and children and between parents and their children. Infants and toddlers must rely on the important adults in their lives to communicate well with one another and develop a trusting, informative relationship. This allows the children to experience a sense of continuity from home to child care and from child care to home. In a program that emphasizes relationships, the teacher–parent relationship is one of partnership. Parents are viewed as partners rather than as customers or clients. Even when the program emphasizes teaching parents about parenting, the spirit remains one of respect and partnership. The partnership centers on the child and relies on mutual respect, information sharing, inclusiveness, and a sense of community. It requires that the purposes and principles of the overall relationship-oriented program be communicated clearly to parents so they understand the importance of relationships (with both parents and teachers) to infants and understand the many steps that the program takes to provide their children with these safe and secure relationships. However, the partnership also requires that the program understand the parents' cultural and personal values. The teacher and parent should mutually engage in the very human task of sharing deeply felt views and daily information in a spirit of supporting the well-being of the child they both care about so much.

CHAPTER 9

Lots of Little Feet

Supporting Peer Relationships

Francie is a 24-month-old girl who notices a new toddler in her group, still crying softly after his mother has left. She watches him closely and then goes over to him. "Don't cry, Michael," she says. "Don't cry any more. Your Mommy will come back." Michael stops crying and begins to feel more comfortable in the toddler center.

Niles is an 18-month-old boy in a toddler group. He admires several older children and likes to follow them around. One Monday morning, Niles comes in with a new idea: He carefully goes around the room and in turn pushes each of the older boys so that they fall over. They each look surprised and then just pop back up and keep playing. The teachers confer and have a laugh together. Their theory is that Niles has decided he wants to be "top dog" for a change. Because Niles does not hurt anyone and the behavior soon ceases, the teachers do not intervene other than to monitor Niles closely.

These opening anecdotes are a good place to begin a discussion of peer relationships in infants and toddlers. They show how far children come in just a few years, as well as why adults need to carefully monitor them and provide continual support. This chapter first describes what is known about the development and benefits of peer relationships during the first 3 years of life, then considers what teachers can do to support this development.

ARE PEER RELATIONSHIPS BENEFICIAL FOR INFANT AND TODDLER DEVELOPMENT?

The importance of early peer relations for social and cognitive development has been an increasing subject of recent research. During most of the 20th century, research focused on the mother–child relationship. It was not until the 1970s that attention turned to infants' peer relationships. Since then, however, interesting questions have been raised about whether children younger than 3 years need (or even prefer) to have playmates of their own age, as well as the possible special benefits of such interaction.

A *peer* is defined as someone who is a developmental age mate. The term is vague and simply refers to a person who is roughly equal to another in ability, age, status, or other relevant characteristic. When we talk about peer interaction in this chapter, we are referring mainly to children's relationships with others in their child care group, or else to their relationships at home or in the neighborhood with other children who are approximately their age and developmental level.

Age of Access to Peer Relations

The development of peer relationships has been studied in primates and human beings of diverse cultures. Melvin Konner (1975), an anthropologist, reviewed all of the information and concluded that for most human groups (and also for primate species), it is not typical for infants to spend much time in exclusively same-age peer groups (e.g., infant or toddler classroom). Instead, it is more common for youngsters to interact either in caregiving situations, in which a juvenile looks after an infant who is usually a close relative, or in playgroup settings, in which a multi-age cluster of family children and neighbors gather together to play (with the older children loosely watching out for the little ones). For example, in the hunter-gathers of the Kalahari Desert of sub-Saharan Africa that he studied, Konner observed how infants spent their days on the backs of their mothers, but toddlers instead were deemed competent enough to "tag along" and join in the local multi-age playgroup. These people lived and dwelled in small bands of families who wandered together, hunting game animals and gathering nuts and vegetables to eat. The children's playgroups typically consisted of all the children available—often six to eight children, boys and girls, ranging in age from infancy through adolescence. In their playgroups, children were seen to do much observation and imitation of adult subsistence activity, pretend subsistence play, and rough and tumble.

Similar findings have been found in many studies of child development around the world (Edwards, deGuzman, Brown, & Kumru, 2006). The findings seem to suggest that infants and toddlers get plenty of contact with other children in most places, but it is usually in a family or household setting and not necessarily with strict age mates—more commonly with a special child caregiver or else in the mixed company of all the little boys and girls who are playing together. In most cultural settings, infants spend their days in a safe, bounded space centered on the emotional and physical presence of the mother or caregiver (e.g., grandmother, older sibling, father).

Chapter 3 described some Kenyan mothers with heavy workloads who relied on their elder children for help with child care, housework, and subsistence activity. These mothers carried their babies on their backs as they did their work or else turned to their older children who were assigned as "child nurses" to help them out. When infants got too big and heavy to be carried around all day, they were turned over to the playgroup, with the oldest child officially in charge. Infants and toddlers also had some contact with peers outside their immediate household when their mothers went on visits around the community or to market, or when they joined other women in a collective work group in someone's garden.

Across cultural communities, the infants and toddlers with the most opportunity to observe and make contact with a variety of other children are those from settlements with the greatest density of people and/or where women have most freedom of movement. Not until the preschool age do young children typically gain free access to their entire yard, homestead, and neighboring areas (Edwards & Liu, 2002). At about age 5 years, children become empowered to independently wander and, if bold enough, venture out to explore other areas considered safe— the "free-range childhood" described by nature educators such as Richard Louv (2006). Often, there are enough age mates for children to break into boys' and girls' groups. These same-sex playgroups are very common in many communities.

Cultural differences in children's autonomy and access to peer relations becomes quite visible around age 5 years—more so than for infants and toddlers. However, in communities like the United States where neighbors are not usually kinfolk and households consist of nuclear families, even older children continue to be confined in their free exploration outdoors. Roads filled with traffic and strangers pose real danger. Parents may have to make plans for their children to play with anyone other than a sibling. Similarly, in the urban areas of Africa, families are often crammed into housing estates where people have come from many different ethnic and language groups from all over the country. They feel like strangers to one another and worry that their children may fight and start family hostilities. Mothers restrict their toddlers' and preschoolers' freedom of movement and try to keep them within family groups only (Whiting & Edwards, 1988).

In contrast, in compact rural villages where trust is high, toddlers and preschoolers continue to have much more autonomy. For example, in parts of rural Mexico, yards are small, houses are open, and children feel free to wander throughout the village. As they play in large groups, toddlers are monitored by any adults living nearby, who keep a watchful eye and feel responsible to break up fights or tell children what to do when the need arises.

The traditional world of childhood has been turned upside down by modern conditions of urban life. School has transformed middle childhood in almost all of the world's societies today. The comparable effects of child care and preschool on infants and toddlers in the contemporary world must be considered. For example, throughout North America and Northern Europe today, women have become essential contributors to family income. The increasing use of preschools, organized playgroups, and child care arrangements has brought the age of access to peer relations down near the beginning of life.

To provide a flavor of what life is like for many infants and toddlers today, we can look at the findings of a study conducted of children of working or student parents in Amherst, Massachusetts (Edwards, Logue, Loehr, & Roth, 1986, 1987). The 38 children were infants and toddlers ages 2–30 months. Half of the children attended a high-quality, university-based infant and toddler program for 15–20 hours per week; the other half also had mothers who were working or studying at least half-time, but these children were cared for in home-based arrangements (e.g., by fathers, family child care providers, babysitters). Spot observations were conducted by telephone and equally distributed across morning, afternoon, and evening time periods, 7 days per week over 8 months, thus providing a detailed picture of the ecology of the children's lives.

Initial interviews had revealed that most parents, whether they used center- or home-based supplementary care, strongly valued early peer contacts for children. Almost all parents saw some kind of peer experience especially beneficial (or even necessary) at the toddler age. The center-care group had 3 times as much contact with nonfamily members as did the home-care group; however, combining groups, a total of about one fifth of their observations included a family child and one fifth included a nonfamily peer. Life experience for this sample of contemporary American infants and toddlers therefore resembles that of older children in the cross-cultural observations. Such early and intense contact with nonfamily peers represents a new kind of experience for many infants and toddlers today and puts new pressure on adults to help the children deal with it.

Development of Peer Interaction

It seems that young children are ready for peer interaction. Recent studies of infants and toddlers indicate that they are sociable very early in life, behaving in ways that bring about or sustain friendly interpersonal contact (Eckerman & Peterman, 2004). A clear developmental progression can be seen. In the early months of life, infants show interest in one another. They look intensely at the other child, come close, and contact the play material the other child is using. Frequently, they smile, vocalize, and touch or pat the other child. Sometimes they take toys away or push, but these behaviors are much less frequent than those that can be called sociable. However, it is difficult for infants to generate long sequences of peer interaction or to coordinate their actions with one another.

True peer interaction skills emerge during the second year of life. They are greatly facilitated by the children knowing each other well and by the presence of an adult who helps them learn to use their words or to notice the other child's feelings and responses. Toddlers are usually very motivated to play with other children. Having accomplished the developmental work involved in establishing reciprocity with their mother and other primary caregivers, they now begin to display an appetite for establishing strong and lasting relationships—attachments and friendships—with other people. Mueller and Cohen (1986) referred to "peer hunger" as first seen during the toddler period, but perhaps it is more of a friendship hunger—a desire to have fun and exciting relationships with other little people like oneself and therefore gain new kinds of social experience, skill, knowledge, and confidence. Adults, especially parents, play key roles in mediating toddlers' entry into these wider social relationships and in influencing the emotional responses, communicative styles, and social repertories that children bring to forming meaningful and sustainable relationships and associations. Adults may also help by protecting children's friendships, supervising play, or coaching them in skills such as entering a group, sharing toys and space, and dealing with conflicts and disputes that arise by using words or friendly gestures, finding another toy, or seeking adult help.

Skilled toddler peer interaction is a very joyful thing to witness (see Box 9.1). In small groups of two to four children who know one another well, interaction often takes the form of games in which children join together in a common familiar theme (e.g., tag, Follow the Leader). At first, their interaction takes the form of chains, in which two or more children imitate one another in loose sequences. A little later, children begin to engage in true role reversal, in which one child and another take turns (e.g., rolling a ball back and forth). Often, children invent their own special rituals, such as shouting a certain word that makes them all laugh, rolling a ball back and forth, or running in a certain way around a particular tree. Friends seem to find pleasure in one another's company and seek to be close during meals, naps, or storytime. Children are ecstatic if their parents get them together to play in the home setting. Here is a conversation overheard between two 3-year-old friends who attended a toddler center together:

Nathan, upon seeing his best friend, Sam, after vacation: "Sam! I didn't see you for a
   long time."
Sam: "I was at my Granny's house."
Nathan: "Someone told me you were at your grandmother's."
Sam: "Did you want me?"
Nathan: "I wanted you a lot of times. I missed you." (Edwards, 1986, p. 116)

BOX 9.1.
Cooperative coordinated action between toddlers

The following is an example of cooperative coordinated action between two 32-month-old children. Each child's actions are listed in sequential order with verbalizations in quotation marks.

Child 1	Child 2
Joins peer at playhouse.	
	Sits on floor of playhouse.
Sits beside peer.	
	Throws ball out window and says, "I want to throw, okay?"
Says, "Okay." Throws ball out window.	
	Retrieves ball. Says, "I better get some."
Enters house, saying, "I go back in." Sits down.	
	Sits down. Says, "You next to me." Holds ball up to throw. Says, "Throw this ball."
Holds ball up to throw. Throws ball out the window.	
	Throws ball out the door. Says, "Watch." Retrieves ball. Says, "I get it."
Retrieves ball. Says, "I got it."	
	Enters house. Says, "I got it. I go back in."
Enters house. Says, "Back in."	
	Sits down.
Sits down.	

Adapted from Eckerman, C.O., & Peterman, K. (2004). Peers and infant social/communicative development. In G. Bremmer & A. Fogel (Eds.), *Blackwell handbook of infant development* (pp. 326–350). Reproduced with permission of Blackwell Publishing Ltd.

We believe that many 2-year-old children feel the same way about their special friends—even if they can't express it in words.

Value and Function of Early Peer Relationships

What do peer relationships mean to infants and toddlers? What benefits do they serve? We believe that early peer relations support the human goal of *mutuality*—

of being with others and joining in, sharing in joint attention and emotional sharing. The psychologist Colwyn Trevarthen (1995) has written of the child's desire to produce meaning through emotional joining and the great pleasures the child feels when moving or communicating in synchrony and rhythm with others, thereby creating a "space of we."

The developmental outcomes of experiencing adequate mutuality are capacities for cooperation and companionship. During infancy, mutuality comes from eye-to-eye contact and being physically close. During toddlerhood, if children have the opportunities and adult support, they also develop mutuality by participating in peer group games and expressive activities involving singing, shouting, clapping, and hand motions. They eagerly join in with dancing, chanting, marching, and chasing. These ancient and joyful forms of play create heightened emotion through the use of synchrony, rhythm, and/or patterned turn taking and alternation. During toddlerhood, children's feelings of mutuality grow into full-blown capacities for kindness and empathy under the right conditions. Quann and Wien (2006) documented three types of concerned care in a toddler classroom, which they called *proximal empathy* (when a child noticed a nearby child becoming distressed and coming to help), *altruistic empathy* (when a child noticed a child from afar becoming distressing and coming to help), and *self-corrective empathy* (when a child offered concerned care after causing distress in another child).

So what do these peer relationships really mean to the children? Can infants and toddlers form true attachments to peers, or are their friendships easily replaced and of only casual significance? We cannot know because children do not have the language to tell us, but by toddlerhood, it seems that friendships can offer children emotional security and comfort and be a very important part of why they like to come to their infant and toddler group. When children enter the center in the morning, they may look first to see if their best friends have arrived and greet them enthusiastically. They notice when their friends are absent and say their names. They are willing to go home with their friends' parents and stay at their house, perhaps even overnight. Sometimes sets of families become close friends through their children. Making the transition to a new classroom or program goes much more smoothly if a child does so with a close and familiar peer. In all of these ways, it appears that friendships can be very important to children starting in the second year. When these relationships are formed, they should be treated with respect and regard by teachers and parents, like the close friendships of older children.

SUPPORTING PEER RELATIONSHIPS

We have identified seven principles of relationship-based approaches for promoting friendships and meaningful associations among infants and toddlers in group care, which are listed in Box 9.2. Each of these principles are addressed in turn. We provide suggested strategies for practices that help children gain social skills

---

BOX 9.2.
Principles for supporting peers

The following are principles for supporting peers in relationship-based programs:

1. Help children learn others' names and encourage a group atmosphere of friendly greetings and courtesy

2. Provide spaces for small group interaction to balance spaces and times for large group interaction

3. Coach children in social skills they need for peer interaction, such as entering a group and using their words to resolve conflicts

4. Notice what objects, routines, and places become especially significant to children and support these "peer rituals"

5. Recognize special friendships that emerge in the group and allow them to flourish, along with a general spirit of inclusiveness

6. Encourage out-of-center connections between children and families, and support continuity of relationships across transitions to new classrooms when possible

7. Examine your own values about children's peer relationships and friendships

---

needed, as well as suggested language for teachers and directors to use when interacting with parents to aid discussions.

Use Names, Friendly Greetings, and Courtesy

The atmosphere in a children's program is one of the things over which the teachers have the most control and can have an immediate impact in a positive way. Children love it when they come into an environment that promotes recognition and visibility (e.g., seeing a photo display with all of their group's faces and names, beginning group time with a name song). Right away, instead of feeling impersonal and anonymous, their experience of coming into a program is individualized. They learn and rehearse the other children's names, connections, favorite things, and preferences, and they feel welcomed every day to the social life in the group. Everyone likes to hear his or her name said. The teacher can model to the children the practice of always saying that name along with a greeting to mark comings and goings. How those words are uttered makes a big difference. Children can easily learn to "have a smile in their voices" when they say someone's name along with *hi* or *bye-bye*. Similarly, polite words like *please* and *thank you* make people feel genuinely good; they are not just empty courtesies. Children who learn to notice other children and know their names are much more likely to make social overtures toward them.

Provide Spaces for Small Groups

Infants and toddlers in group care spend much of their time all together in their classroom or outdoor area. Therefore, it is important to provide spaces that encourage small group interaction. The level of children's social play is often much more complex in a group of three or four than in a larger group because it is easier for them to attend closely to another child's action and coordinate with it when not so many others are present. Thus, the turn taking of coordinated peer interaction is mostly seen in small group interaction.

In our toddler center at the University of Massachusetts, where the second author (Carolyn Pope Edwards) was once director, numerous learning centers were provided throughout the room that encouraged small group interaction, including a reading area with a crib mattress and pillows; a kitchen role-play and dress-up area; and an area with shelves containing manipulatives, puzzles, and sorting toys that rotated according to children's interests. These learning areas provided the partial seclusion needed for children to focus on their play with materials in the company of a few children and perhaps one of the adults. Down the hall was a small observation room used for special studies by researchers. A small group was often taken there for about 20 minutes of play. The children seemed to revel in the time by themselves and played with great pleasure, even inventing imitation games.

Coach Children in Social Skills

Children need help in learning all the skills they need to engage in sustained social interaction. Things that seem automatic for preschool children are just being learned during toddlerhood. Adults can really help through modeling and coaching, but they need to be careful not to be too directive and intrusive, which will actually slow down the process of the children acquiring their own skills. Observing carefully before intervening is almost always recommended, along with trying to hold back as long as possible to see if the children can solve the situation for themselves (see Box 9.3).

For a child who has particular difficulties with social play, there are many positive ways to intervene (Landy, 2002). The teacher can do the following:

- Coach the child to learn and use other children's names, which gets the other children's attention better and predisposes them positively to accept the child

- Coach the child on words to use in a situation, such as, "Can I play too?"

BOX 9.3.
To intervene or not intervene

This story is also shown in the color insert. We repeat it here to provoke thinking about when a teacher should intervene in toddler interaction.

———————————

Sofia, a 2-year-old girl, was out on the playground with her child care group. She discovered a leaf on the ground. She picked it up with her fingers and investigated it, then lifted it up to her face as if wondering about the texture. She took the leaf and put it in her hands squeezing it together. Then, she went around calling insistently for her best friend, "Kya, where Kya?" until she found her.

"Look, Kya," she said as she pushed the leaf toward Kya's face and then led Kya over to where she had found the leaf. When they got there, Kya reached toward the plant and touched a leaf. Sofia took her own leaf and laid it down on the plant. Kya and Sofia looked at each other and smiled.

They continued to explore, with Sofia saying, "Look, Kya," as she explored a new part and Kya saying, "Here, 'Fia," as she handed Sofia a new part of the plant. Then, Kya began to reach up high to a different leaf. She pulled the branch down close to her face and tried to lick it, but Sofia stopped her.

"No, Kya! No!" directed Sofia. She wanted her friend to explore, but not by tasting. Kya stopped licking the plant, and the two girls continued to play together.

Do you think the teacher should have intervened as soon as she saw Kya starting to lick the plant? If she had done so, then she would have interrupted the play and not let the girls solve it for themselves. By holding back, she saw what the girls were able to do for themselves. Impressed, the teacher shared the episode with her colleagues and the girls' parents. They had some good discussions about the children's development of self-regulation and language, as well as their deep interest in the natural world.

Adapted from Benson, J., & Leeper Miller, J. (2008). Experiences in nature: A pathway to standards. *Young Children, 63*(4), 22–29. Reprinted with permission from the National Association for the Education of Young Children.

- Help the child see to the connection between the child's action and another's responses

- Coach the child to respond to others' invitations

- Suggest some ways for the child to enter the group and join the play

- Show the child how to join the flow of the play so as not to disrupt it (e.g., helping a frustrated child at the edge of a circle enter quietly holding on to the teacher's hand or sitting on the teacher's lap)

- Show the child how to sit and watch a moment, then do something appropriate to join the play

- Encourage a rejected child to try again (e.g., "Let's see if you get on this truck if you can ride along with the others.")

When learned during the toddler years, all of these skills have a tremendous effect on social skills and may be one of the greatest gifts a teacher can give. They will set a child on a positive course toward a happy childhood with lots of friends and playmates.

Support Peer Culture

Shared meaning is what makes friendships important to human beings of any age—it brings people together in the first place and holds them together through the passage of time. When the children in a group create their own little rituals around particular objects, routines, or places, they are forming important relationships with one another. They may have particular ways that they insist on doing things, or certain songs or words they like to hear repeated at the beginnings and ends of activities. The children may develop special places they go to and scripts of action they follow there. They invent cues for group laughter so that when one child shouts the cue, everyone follows enthusiastically. Such rituals are an aspect of group life that make the experience more consistent, coherent, and emotionally safe for children by providing soothing or enjoyable repetition of gestures, actions, and words. Through rituals, children establish stable boundaries around the flux of changing events. At the same time, they also provide numerous possibilities for creative embellishment in which children can "interpret, produce, display, and extend a wide range of social knowledge" (Corsaro, 2003, p. 28) and thus invent their own particular peer culture.

Teachers can do many things to help children create shared memory and peer rituals. They can smile when they recognize a ritual and label it with language to help the children understand what they are doing (e.g., "You all really love to play on the pillows after lunch, don't you?"). Or, teachers can read and reread a favorite book and help children find props to act it out, perhaps taking some photos to discuss with them.

Supporting a collective fantasy life fosters shared memory (and cognitive development) along with peer relationships. The Italian centers of Pistoia are especially skilled in this way of working (Galardini & Giovannini, 2001). For example, puppet theater has a central place in every infant and toddler center (see Box 9.4). Through puppets and fairytales, children are supported by teachers to invent imaginary roles together and thus get in touch with their emotions, including those of fear and anger. Year after year, children and teachers create and

---

BOX 9.4.
Using puppets to aid transition

The following story is from the library teacher at Filastrocca ("Nursery Rhymes") Preschool in Pistoia, Italy. She speaks about how she uses puppets to help toddlers make the transition into the center.

We have worked out a strategy that makes the children feel at home and introduces another familiar, reassuring presence in our school. On the first day of school, the youngest children form a circle with the small chairs where everybody, adults and children, meet to talk, sing and tell a little story, and welcome the character friend, Hannibal Mouse. Who is Hannibal? He is a funny little puppet, made of soft fabric and dressed like a child, who often comes to visit school in the morning. Hannibal Mouse is not merely a puppet animated by the adult hand; rather, he becomes a friend who is able to emotionally engage children and create moments of anticipation and joy. He is funny and brings surprises. He knows the children's names and can draw out the quietest children. He tells about stories of daily life, his misfortunes, his adventures with his wife, Caroline, and maybe it's those detailed stories that make him so close to the children's experiences. They live, through his words, events similar to theirs, and they have fun and they are reassured. He provides a common element to the collective memory of each group of children, enriching imagination and stimulating verbal and listening skills.

Hannibal corresponds by letter with the children using a mailbox near the youngest children's classroom. Parents also play along and bring to school presents for Hannibal, such as small clothes and toys. They have become their children's secretaries and advise them in preparing letters for Hannibal. Sometimes they are also "accomplices" and write response message from Hannibal which they place in the mailbox or on their child's bed.

From an interview with Carolyn Pope Edwards and Lella Gandini.

recreate a cast of characters that the children adore: the Little Gray Mouse, Rainbow Magician, and Prezzemolina ("Little Parsley Head"). The children thus become actors in a play of their own creation rich with meaning.

In the parent handbook of one of the Pistoia preschools, a quotation is found from a 5-year-old girl as she thinks back on her first days in the school: "I remember that rascal Hannibal Mouse and his wife Caroline, who used to make a lot of bad jokes. I'm wondering, what happened to my pacifier?" It seems interesting that as she remembers her favorite puppets, she recalls happy laughter and then has an association to her old transitional object, her pacifier. Now she has moved on, obviously, but how significant these experiences must have been for her.

Support Children's Friendships

Every year in our toddler group at the University of Massachusetts, we saw close friendships emerge among pairs or small groups of older children. Our group of 12 children ranged in age from about 13–20 months at the beginning of the program. The children stayed together for a full school year before going on to preschool programs around town. It was usually among the children older than 18 months that the best friendships emerged. Often, we saw that two sets of pairs would come together for rich play; for example, a pair of girls and a pair of boys or, alternatively, a gang of buddies would emerge containing three or four or five children. These special friendships were powerful and intense. They looked like family attachments in many ways. The children engaged in highly involved play with one another at the center. They looked for each other first upon arrival but were not exclusionary of others. All the oldest children became part of the pack of buddies. When younger children wanted to play, they were included, too.

The group of best friends added character to the larger group and often invented the special games and rituals that the whole class came to join. They acted as leaders to others so that teachers could move the whole group along by mobilizing some friends first, or get everyone involved in a new activity by drawing in a couple of these older children. The teachers' role in supporting these friendships was primarily to appreciate and recognize them. They told the parents of the friendships and explained why they are important, as well as how they indicate the children's advancing social skills. They also helped the older children learn to watch out for and include young children safely in their play. Teachers listened with delight to the parents' tales of what the children did together on weekends. They also approved of the parents' plans to try to keep their children together for another year when they made the transition to a new program.

Encourage Out-of-Center Connections

Friendships that cross over between home and center are not always possible, given home locations, neighborhood safety, transportation systems, family values about sociability, and many other factors that influence the formation of social networks. Yet, when feasible, these forms of bonds are highly meaningful to both parents and children. Teachers can promote them by providing lists of names, addresses, and telephone numbers—when proper consent and permission are obtained. Parents thereby may gain new friends to compare notes and ideas with, while children gain opportunities to refine their social skills far beyond what is possible in the public setting alone. In our experience, when families become close to one another through the child care system, they often stay connected for years. Children form much deeper and more elaborate meanings about their experience that may become part of their cognitive working models about relationships: "I am someone who has friends, and who is a friend. My whole family is part of my friendships from school." Likewise, when children can make the transition to a new classroom or program with a familiar friend, the continuity across time gives them a psychological boost to get through transitions successfully. Greater coherence and continuity between home and school experience—and across time—strengthen the learning that takes place in both settings and help parents become more informed and articulate advocates as their children enter formal schooling.

Promoting connections among families, especially across time, can be a struggle because families have many competing priorities. We once explored this topic through a cross-cultural study of parents' feelings about young children's friendships, bringing together researchers from the United States, Norway, Turkey, and South Korea. We wanted to explore how parents today from diverse communities think about their young children's first interactions and relationships with people from outside the family (Aukrust, Edwards, Kumru, Knoche, & Kim, 2003). The study came about because we noticed that parents from different cultural backgrounds seemed to have different values about how best to mediate children's social relationships; no agreed-upon "right way" for doing it exists. Instead, parents (and researchers) respond in various culturally mediated ways to choices as they bring up their children. We wondered how this plays out as parents face the issue of helping their children move out from the safety of the family unit into the life of the community around them. How do parents today in different societies think they should help their young children learn to deal with neighbors, teachers, classmates, and other community members from outside the family? For example, should they focus on giving their preschool children experiences that help them learn to form and maintain close ties with a few, very close individuals, who will become best friends for years to come? Or, instead, should they provide experiences that foster a friendly and less intimate style of interaction with a diverse succession of new people? Questions like these are particularly challenging for parents in modern societies with high mobility and density of populations. We therefore realized that parents bring many different cognitive models to the issues related to young children's contact with other children in public settings such as child care and preschool.

Find Out About Your Values

Questions about young children's friendships are stimulating to discuss in a group, as they get to the heart of what young children need emotionally from other people. We developed a survey questionnaire (see Figure 9.1) and used it with parents whose children were ages 3–5 and in preschool or child care. Many of the questions address parents' values about how invested and lasting, versus casual and

What Are Your Beliefs About
Friendships Among Young Children?

For each of the six statements below, please choose an answer to complete the sentence according to your beliefs about the social and emotional needs of children.

1. What young children today need most is

   a. Confidence to meet and communicate with new people in new situations.

   b. Capacity to form deep, meaningful relationships that provide security and continuity.

2. Communication skills come from

   a. Learning to make oneself understood to people who do not understand immediately.

   b. Having many conversations with a few people whom the child knows well.

3. Young children should have true attachment relationships with adults

   a. Only at home, not at preschool or child care.

   b. At home but also at preschool or child care as a basis for secure learning there.

4. Young children need

   a. Time together with a variety of people from different backgrounds and cultures.

   b. To get to know a few people well and become part of a close group.

5. Young children need

   a. Playmates, but at this age it is not important whether they develop into close friends.

   b. Friendships that will last and continue into the years to come.

6. At any age, it is important and useful to

   a. Make friends quickly and easily.

   b. Hold onto close, best friends and have a few people you can really trust.

Figure 9.1. Survey questionnaire to determine beliefs about young children's friendships. Choice A is the *casual/brief* choice. Choice B is the *invested/lasting* choice. (In research use, the order was randomized.) (Adapted from Aukrust, V., Edwards, C.P., Kumru, A., Knoche, L, & Kim, M. (2003). Young children's extended relationships in school: Parental ethnotheories in four communities, in Norway, United States, Turkey, and Korea. *International Journal of Behavior Development, 27*(6), 481–494.)

brief, young children's friendships are. We have found that they prove to be a good discussion tool for any group of parents, teachers, or student teachers.

The questionnaire is an excellent discussion tool because it is easy to see the positive value of both sides of every choice; however, depending on where parents' preferences lie, they may make different kinds of judgments for their children. For example, if they think children most need to learn skills for making new friends quickly and easily, and likewise for meeting and communicating with new people in new situations, they might not think it is so difficult for a child to change child care situations and to make the transition without a familiar friend. On the other hand, if parents think childhood is about getting to know a few people well and becoming part of a close group, and likewise for forming friendships that will last and continue into the years to come, then they might want to maximize stability over time and continuity of relationships across a transition for a child. In our research study, we found significant cultural differences for many of the questions, with American parents tending to be higher in choosing on the casual/brief answers. At the opposite extreme, the Norwegian parents choose the invested/ lasting options. However, Norwegians are as individualistic and equality oriented as Americans; they just have different values about the importance of close, lasting relationships. They also organize their preschools and elementary schools so that children stay with the same teacher and classmates for 3–6 years at a time.

SUMMARY

Sense of belonging has to do with being part of a social group—a community of place, kinship, values, memories, and shared experience. Children want to get out on that dance floor of extended relationships and move in time with partners who are their same size and shape. Their early experiences of group belonging may have just as much to do with peer interactions as with attachment feelings to adults. Relationship-dancing as part of a group provides the child with an important part of self-identity—whether the society places its highest priorities on collectivism or individualism. Through sharing with peers, children appropriate cultural tools and skills of language, communication, and friendship. Rituals, songs, stories, and routines are the concrete expression of group belonging.

Teachers can help children develop firm and satisfying peer relations through such simple strategies as encouraging children to learn others' names, providing spaces for small group interaction, coaching children in social skills, acknowledging their rituals, supporting their special friendships, and encouraging out-of-center connections between children and families. Gradually, as the dance between peers becomes smooth and familiar, the children themselves encourage each other to try out more complex steps and learn how to dance to new compositions, beats, and tempos. The dance partnership widens as children try out new partners and as new friends are added to their group. As each child alternates dancing sometimes with one or two partners and sometimes with many, the dance itself becomes a story about who the child has been and who the child is becoming—a reciprocal self created through close relationships.

RESOURCES

Corsaro, W.A. (2003*). "We're friends, right?: Inside kids' culture.* Washington, DC: Joseph Henry Press.

Landy, S. (2002). *Pathways to competence: Encouraging healthy social and emotional development in young children.* Baltimore: Paul H. Brookes Publishing Co.

Quann, V., & Wien, C.A. (2006). The visible empathy of infants and toddlers. *Young Children, 61*(4), 22–29. Available online at http://journal.naeyc.org/btj/200607/Quann709BTJ.asp

CHAPTER 10

Closing the Circle

Supporting Teachers and Administrators

Kristi was a teacher in a traditional (non-relationship-based) infant and toddler program. In this program, children graduated to another teacher when they learned to crawl and again when they became toddlers. Kristi was the teacher in the "in-between" room, so crawlers came to her and then left when they became sturdy walkers at around 18 months of age. Children entered her room at a time when stranger anxiety was at its peak and left when they still needed to rely on the teacher as a secure base for exploration. They often cried quite a bit during the transitions and were comforted when the previous teacher came to visit. Kristi left the child care program because she said it was too hard to "watch the babies and parents go through these transitions" and she wondered if they were doing harm. She felt torn and decided it "just wasn't worth it."

Maria is an infant and toddler teacher in an Early Head Start program that keeps children and teachers together throughout the infant and toddler years. Her program states it practices "continuity" (keeping children and teachers together through some or all of the infant and toddler years) and "primary caregiving" (whereby a consistent teacher provides primary care for a small number of children). Maria proudly refers to the toddlers she has had in her care for the past 2 years as "her toddlers." She is deeply in tune with these toddlers and their parents; she feels satisfaction in her work each day and with herself as an infant and toddler teacher. Because she plans to be an infant and toddler teacher for a long time, Maria is investing time in training. She completed the Program for Infant Toddler Care (program of training developed by WestEd and the California Department of Education) and is now pursuing college credit at a local community college, taking a course in infant development. The relationship-based model of her program complements Maria's commitment and deepening professional development.

FOCUS ON TEACHERS AND ADMINISTRATORS

The stories in the chapter opener draw our attention to the teachers and administrators who carry out a relationship-based program. Remember Figure 1.1, which showed the triangle of relationships? One corner was devoted to the staff, including teachers and administrators. This chapter considers questions that teachers and administrators may have about a relationship-based program. We introduce a set of principles to guide administrators in implementing a relationship-based program with teachers, as well as another dimension of the layered approach to relationships—the relationships teachers have with one another.

Setting the stage for the program among the staff is vitally important to the success of a relationship-based program. In many ways, the principles of relating to children and parents we discussed in the other chapters also extend to the staff. For teachers to feel comfortable in their relationships with children and parents, they need to feel a sense of safety and caring within the program, both from administrators and among fellow teachers. Many teachers have identified benefits that a relationship-based program has for them, as well as concerns of which administrators should be aware.

Relationship-Based Programs from a Teacher's Point of View

Teachers are able to derive a number of benefits from a relationship-based program once it is up and running smoothly, including a feeling that they can invest in the children and families they are assigned to, a rhythm that applies to their employment, and a feeling of being grounded in their work. Teachers may also have concerns that need to be addressed, which may include a fear of getting too attached to children and families, anticipated grief for when the 0–3 years are over and a child moves onto preschool, fear that they may not be able to connect to all of their children and/or parents, and concern they will be better at working with children of some ages than with children of other ages. This chapter elaborates on each one in turn.

Benefits are often felt rather quickly after implementing a relationship-based approach. Teachers often welcome the knowledge that they will be with a group of children for an extended period of time. This approach allows them to invest in their relationships with the children and try different ways of getting to know the child's family. Teachers plan and gauge classroom activities to the rhythms of infancy and toddlerhood. As the relationship-based program settles into place, one can observe that the staff seems to settle as well. Teachers know what they will be doing for several years, so they concentrate on doing it well. They do not need to focus so much on who their new children will be and whether they can meet the children's needs, as can be the case when there is a great deal of change.

On the other hand, teachers may have some concerns. Some teachers think that they should not become "too attached" to the children they care for because they will cause the child or parent discomfort. When a child cries upon separating from a beloved teacher, these teachers interpret such behavior as negative and seek to teach the child not to be "so dependent." Such a teacher needs to understand how the attachment system works. By now, it must be clear that they also can be helped to see that the child's secure attachment to a teacher only supplements a secure attachment the child has with parents. If the parent–child relationship is not secure, the child's overall development also is served in a positive way by having a secure relationship with the teacher. Moreover, if the child has a secure relationship with the teacher but not the parent, the child may gain interaction skills with the teacher that can be helpful in building a better relationship with the parent.

Other teachers may anticipate grief when the separation with the child comes. Certainly the grief that accompanies separation when children graduate is real, but teachers are professionals. Children gain a strong base and good memories of relationships from the relationships they have with infant and toddler teachers. The concern of some teachers regarding not being able to connect with all children often turns out to be more imagined than actual. In our experience, most teachers are able to connect with most of their children and parents, given support and an emphasis on honesty and openness in relating.

One objection to relationship-based or continuity models is that teachers may have become accustomed to thinking of themselves as a particular type of teacher (e.g., a teacher of 2-year-old children) and they may resist working with children of other ages. In one study of continuity in Louisiana, infant teachers particularly resisted working with toddlers (Aguillard, Pierce, Benedict, & Burns, 2005). Our experience with this issue is that it is helpful to work gently and gradually with teachers to make this shift. Give the teacher of 2-year-old children time to work with the young infants or ask the teacher of young infants how he or she would feel about moving with a child of whom the teacher is particularly fond. Such actions will help these teachers make the transition to a new way of doing business. Typically, we have found that teachers' strong feelings about the specific children they care for supercede strong feelings about being a certain type of teacher. That is, good relationships often trump preconceived ideas about working with a particular age of child.

Relationship-Based Programs from an Administrator's View

As is true for teachers, the administrators may have views of benefits, including a feeling of stability in staffing over time and "groundedness" about the program. Concerns of administrators may include worry about hiring and supporting staff who can carry out a relationship-based program and the administrative energy needed to calculate where children and teachers will be located in time and in the facility.

In our experience, a relationship-based model radically diminishes turnover, especially among full-time core staff when continuity with children and families increased. Certainly, if turnover diminishes, administrators can also experience the settling in of the program and turn attention to building the program. However, administrators do worry about finding teachers who can carry out the program. There is also a particular pressure to hire well given all the assumptions about the importance of relationships. Directors may also fear that they will spend all their time "doing the math" as to when children will be ready for moves. It is realistic to convey that the relationship-based program requires the director to plan matriculation carefully (e.g., when the young babies will be ready for the crawlers' room, when the crawlers will be ready for the walkers' room). However, planning for matriculation tends to become easier with experience.

Principles for Supporting a Relationship-Based Program

We have identified a number of principles that will aid a program in planning for teacher and administrative support for a relationship-based program (see Box 10.1). We think that many of these principles address some of the concerns and build on the benefits discussed in the previous sections.

Hire Teachers Who Are Good at Relating   We assume that the program desires to keep teachers and infants together in a consistent fashion. Who should those teachers be? It is vital to hire teachers who are emotionally healthy. As Fraiberg and colleagues (1975) said so eloquently, everyone brings

> ## BOX 10.1.
> ## Principles for supporting
> ## a relationship-based program
>
> The following principles may be helpful for administrators to consider as they plan a relationship-based program:
>
> 1. Hire teachers who are good at relating.
>
> 2. Help teachers think about the commitment to the infant and toddler period and make the plan for continuity clear to the teachers.
>
> 3. Help teachers plan professional development in rhythm with their children's development.
>
> 4. Consider teacher and parent preferences for assignments.
>
> 5. Support teachers in relationship building.
>
> 6. Use principles and consistent assignments for part-time staff (e.g., afternoon teachers) so that their assignments have continuity.
>
> 7. Give teachers autonomy (e.g., funds) for redesigning spaces to make a new room "their own."
>
> 8. Provide one-to-one support for each teacher regularly.
>
> 9. Develop a system for planning ahead for room changes and accepting new children.
>
> 10. Plan for the end of a cycle well in advance of its completion. Have rituals for children, parents, and teachers and acknowledge both the celebration and grief.
>
> 11. Develop flexible procedures for visiting new and former beloved teachers.

ghosts from the nursery to adulthood. The patterns of relating that were received when teachers were very young children are carried—usually unconsciously—into their own ways of relating to infants and toddlers. Teachers who have received sensitive and responsive caregiving already know the rhythms of responsiveness. When they think about responding to babies, they automatically want to respond in a sensitive way.

The Donald O. Clifton Child Development Center in Omaha, Nebraska, has developed for its own use a formal process of selecting teachers who are good at forming relationships. The process is based on the proprietary principles that the Gallup Organization uses in consultation with elementary and secondary schools for teacher selection (see http://www.Gallup.com). The Early Childhood Perceiver identifies a number of themes that help to identify the kinds of teachers who are likely to be responsive to infants and toddlers, such as "rapport drive," "individualized perception," "empathy," and "parent communication." Scores on the Early Childhood Perceiver correlate significantly with the Teacher–Child Attachment Q Sort scores ($r = .65$; Raikes, 1994). While it is not necessary to have a formal interview such as this one, it is useful to keep in mind the qualities that a person who has had healthy relationships is likely to bring to teaching: empathy, a desire to form rapport with children, connectedness, an ability to see children as individuals, and a desire for good relationships with parents. Other programs have identified similar relationship characteristics they seek in teachers and have developed scenarios about which to query prospective teachers.

Some programs have had difficulty establishing a relationship-based infant and toddler program. One reason that this approach can fail is that directors may have difficulty hiring or retaining teachers well suited for it (Aguillard et al., 2005). Sometimes the approach fails because the wrong teachers are hired. For example, some people seek to work in early childhood because they have lacked fulfillment of their own emotional needs. Teachers who want children to cling to them out of their own unfulfilled needs for belonging will not be able to allow children to come and go in the healthy ways that secure base–promoting teachers are able to do. They will find it difficult to give children what they need to develop a balance of security and autonomy. Healthy attachments allow these very interrelated qualities to develop in combination with each other.

Does every teacher need to have had a healthy relationship with his or her own parents? No, but if a teacher has had a positive relationship with his or her parents, it is a good beginning. Although that fact does not guarantee that the teacher has all the necessary qualities, it helps to provide a positive foundation for infant and toddler teaching. Teachers who lacked such a positive beginning can be good teachers if they have had positive relationships subsequently, or if they have become aware of the patterns in relationships they have experienced and seek consciously and skillfully to do something different. As Mary Main has shown, the early caregiving one receives is not immutable (Wallin, 2007). She finds that awareness of the patterns coincides more with how adults interact as parents versus how they were parented themselves. Thus, it is possible, through later positive relationships and reflection, for early inappropriate caregiving to be improved on in the next generation.

Help Teachers Think About the Commitment to the Infant and Toddler Years
When a teacher begins with a group of infants and toddlers, a supervisor can help the teacher develop a clear and realistic concept about the period of time for the commitment. A supervisor might ask, "Are you able to make a commitment to the children and their parents for nearly 3 years, to the best of your knowledge?" Things come up in people's lives that cannot be anticipated, so not every teacher who makes such a commitment will be able to fulfill the promise. However, most teachers appreciate this guidance to

think realistically about the future. Sometimes, early childhood teachers do not have long-term plans; asking this question helps them think more intentionally about career plans. At this point, a supervisor can help the teacher further understand the implications of relationships for early infant and toddler development and why the program has adopted its approach to emphasizing relationships.

A number of reasons exist to enter into this good-faith agreement. First of all, parents who have enrolled in a relationship-based program expect it. Espousing a philosophy that pertains to providing a secure base means that program staff believe this continuity is better for the babies. Certainly, it is consistent with the philosophy that fewer disruptions will provide fewer stressful moments for the babies. Other staff can also build a set of expectations around beliefs that teachers will be with their babies throughout the time period that the continuity model is employed.

If a teacher honestly does not know whether such a commitment can be made, a supervisor can decide whether to go ahead and "give the teacher a family." Such a teacher may benefit from floating or substituting while considering whether he or she is able to make a longer-term commitment.

Help Teachers Plan Professional Development
It is not difficult to plan professional development in ways that coincide with developmental transitions that occur within a relationship-based program. For example, a teacher may plan to explore other employment opportunities when his or her children graduate to preschool. Children's natural transitions create natural transitions for adults who care for them. Infant and toddler teachers in relationship-based programs where teachers stay with children from program entry until age 3 years can thus plan their work in 3-year cycles. Such planning ensures stability for children and families for a known period of time and gives structure to the teacher's plans as well. Some teachers may choose to take a break after children graduate and then come back to work with "a new family." These options provide a more orderly and predictable way to organize an infant and toddler program than the more usual approach, by which turnover may be unpredictable.

Consider Teacher and Parent Preferences for Assignments
For relationships to work well, it is important to realize that people may relate better to some individuals than to others. Although it is important to treat all parents and children with care and respect, some consideration of the types of personalities that are likely to work together is appropriate, particularly in matching teachers and parents.

Parents may have worked with a teacher when they had an older child and may request that their younger child be with this teacher as well. Whenever possible, it is a good idea to honor these preferences because they are often deeply held. In a less relationship-oriented setting, a parent may hear something like, "Mrs. Jones, *all* of our teachers are fine teachers. You will be happy with any of our teachers. We will not be able to honor your preference." It is not always true that parents will be happy with every teacher or that every teacher will be able to work equally well with every parent. Because the relationships matter so much and operate at a deep intuitive level, it is possible that parents could resent not being with the teacher they chose. However, despite all good intentions, granting preferences is not always possible, and matching personalities that meld cannot be perfectly anticipated. In these cases, teachers and parents can be supported to "reach out as far as it takes" to establish their relationship. This guide, first suggested by Greenspan and Greenspan (1985), is a good one for working with infants. They suggest that all teachers and parents should use it to establish a positive relationship with children, but it is also a good guide for working with the parents.

Support Relationship Building   Administrators play a role in supporting relationships between parents and teachers and in helping teachers build relationships with children. Administrators may model good interactions with parents or even facilitate a conference between them, particularly if the child is having adjustment problems or one relationship seems not to be secure. Administrators can tune into the teacher–child relationships and help the teacher think of ways to build relationships with each child.

At the Donald O. Clifton Child Development Center, when the first author (Helen Raikes) was co-director, the process of relationship building was formalized by using the Waters and Deane (1985) Attachment Q Sort. As noted previously, the director met with teachers and parents to discuss the components of the relationships each had with the child to see if teacher and parent could learn from one another. These were relationship-building conferences that also served to strengthen both the parent and teacher relationships with the child and helped the director to know the nature of each relationship on a fairly deep level. If relationships needed support, the director became aware of children's needs for support. For example, one item on the Q sort queries if the child stands and cries upon separation rather than following the teacher. A child who does so may need support in developing efficacy. The director could subsequently work with the teacher to find ways to build the child's confidence. Less formal ways of supporting teacher–child and parent–child relationships are likely more common.

Use Principles and Consistent Assignments for Part-Time Staff   Many teachers start the day early so they are present when their children arrive in the morning. However, some children may stay longer than a teacher's workday. To fill this gap, most programs hire part-time teachers who work late in the afternoon until the center closes. We suggest that administrators hire a consistent teacher for part-time work with each group of children so that the teacher who leaves is handing off to the same person every day and the parent sees the same person every day at pick-up time. If the continuity model involves teachers and children moving to new rooms, the part-time teacher should move with the full-time teacher and her group of children when children move to a new room.

Give Teachers Autonomy for Redesigning Spaces

In some continuity models, the teacher and children move into a new room when the children reach a particular age or readiness. For example, a teacher and his or her group of children may move from an infant room into a toddler room. When this is done, we recommend that the teacher be given latitude in deep cleaning, rearranging, and purchasing new materials in conjunction with the move so that the room feels like the teacher's own. This ownership will create a deeper grounding for the teacher and enable the teacher to be more effective with the children and families. Other continuity models involve assigning a teacher or two to a room, with teachers staying in this space through the infant and toddler years. In this case, it is also a good idea to give the teachers autonomy and some resources for planning and designing the space.

Provide One-to-One Support for Each Teacher Regularly

There are many ways to support teachers. Certainly, seeing them on a daily basis is important. One good approach is to make rounds in the early morning and again in mid-afternoon, at which time the director can be apprised of any problems and share new information. At one center, feedback from parent evaluations was provided on a quarterly basis. This was accompanied by a conference with each teacher about the feedback. At the time of the conference, the director also reviewed each teacher's individualized notebooks (one for each child) and discussed the teacher's professional goals for the next time period. Completing this cycle and meeting standards was accompanied by a bonus provided by the employer. The conference provided a time to process concerns and victories and supported general relationship building. From time to time, groups of teachers or individuals were taken out to lunch or a special event was scheduled. Maintaining a positive relationship with each teacher should be a priority of the director.

Develop a System for Planning Ahead

Many infant and toddler programs have long waiting lists, with families placing themselves on the lists almost as soon as parents know they are expecting a new baby. It does take considerable advance planning to determine when there will be openings and how children will progress through the system. Transparency and consistent expectations about moves will be helpful to all. Teachers like to know if they are changing rooms and like considerable advance time for preparing children and parents (and themselves) for the moves. Of course, there are things in the child care world that simply cannot be anticipated. When a new child is applying to be in the center, discussing whether to accept the new child with the teacher is a good idea.

Plan for the End of a Cycle   When a cycle is complete (e.g., when children are ready to graduate into the preschool program), it is important to acknowledge the transition and to honor both the celebration and the grief. Have rituals for children, parents, and teachers. Some programs like to have graduation ceremonies; others celebrate more informally in developmentally appropriate ways with a picnic or party. Rituals to visit preschool help parents and children. It is important for the director to acknowledge the teacher's feelings of joy and sadness. It is certainly appropriate to recognize the teacher for the very important role played in the children's early years. Some teachers embrace this time as an opportunity to reexamine their career goals, but others may simply feel sad and miss the babies who have been in their care so long. Acknowledging the feelings will help teachers process them as they realize their roles in the growth continuum of developing youngsters. Teacher and parent grief can play off each other. Parents may feel particularly secure with the infant and toddler teacher, so they are reluctant to move on and may also be sad that the child's infancy is over. The director has an important role in being available to help all the parties process these important transition feelings.

Develop Flexible Procedures for Visiting Teachers   It is reasonable for parents and children to want to visit the former teacher after they have moved to a new level (e.g., preschool). In some traditional programs, children are forbidden to visit their former teacher, who also is discouraged from coming into the new room after the children have made the transition. When children move to preschool with their family of peers and have been well oriented, they often do quite well. Parents and children may want to visit the former teacher. Teachers and parents alike can negotiate these transitions by being sensitive and flexible. In some programs, it works better to formalize the visits, perhaps by having a daily time when visiting the former room is a choice.

THE TEACHER–TEACHER COMMUNITY

In Figure 1.1, we emphasized within-group relationships among teachers, parents, and children. Here we focus briefly on supporting teacher–teacher relationships. There are many ways to support building positive relationships among staff—using group problem solving (listening to teachers), recognizing teachers, encouraging teachers to help one another, hosting social and other events, and creating a climate of respect and support.

Using Group Problem Solving: Listening to Teachers

In a child care setting, and particularly in an infant and toddler setting, a great deal of time is focused on emotions and functions that are quite basic. It, therefore, is natural that parents and teachers will feel quite deeply about certain things. For example, teachers may have deeply held but different ideas about a daily schedule, such as how individualized the nap schedule should be. Using problems and disagreements as learning experiences helps to build community. Teachers involved can be brought together to discuss their assumptions and alternative solutions. Whenever possible, the director should convey confidence that teachers can generate solutions and the director can support teachers' communication with one another. If teachers suggest a solution that is outside the program's usual practices, it can be a good idea to respond with flexibility to reinforce the initiative on the part of the teachers.

Recognizing Teachers

Most infant and toddler teachers are not in the business for recognition. However, nearly everyone feels encouraged when excellent practices are highlighted (and recognizing good practices tends to reinforce them). For example, when children are experiencing a series of illnesses, when the teachers cannot take the children outdoors due to inclement weather, or if the children in general are more fussy, teachers can sometimes become discouraged. Recognition can help convey a sense that they are doing a good job—just what they should be doing—and help them keep their spirits up.

Encouraging Teachers to Help One Another

Teachers in many infant and toddler communities become quite close to one another and often help one another. In a program that is built around relationships, it is important for the director to be aware of the reciprocity of these relationships. For example, if a teacher consistently does not return during the time allotted for a break, the trust and reciprocity such a model requires is undermined. Thus, directors should be aware of how teachers help one another and encourage and acknowledge the acts that support the reciprocity often seen in caring communities.

Hosting Social and Other Events

Taking teachers out to lunch (or covering for them so they can go with each other), having a regular event that is appealing (e.g., with door prizes), gift exchanges, bridal or baby showers, and birthday parties are all events that help to build community among the staff. Many teachers tend to bond with one another when they attend early childhood conferences. This is an especially great opportunity when the conference is out of town. It may afford opportunities to present, to gain college credit, or even to take one's first airplane ride with friendly colleagues.

Creating a Climate of Caring and Respect

Infant and toddler directors seeking to implement a relationship-based program are often told to "do unto others as you would have them do unto others." Thus, directors will do well to treat teachers as they would like for them to treat parents and children. More than any other feature, this modeling builds the very core of the relationship-based approach. The empathy with which the director responds to the teacher who is not feeling well, the encouragement to teachers who need support in solving their differences, and the belief teachers have in the director's caring and consistency in decision making will transmit into the program more generally.

SUMMARY

This chapter focused on beliefs and concerns both teachers and directors have about a relationship-based program. Eleven principles that apply to working with teachers were presented. We also presented a number of suggestions for supporting the community of teachers within a program. Our experiences with relationship-based infant and toddler programs have taught us that respectful attention to relationships between the director and teachers forms a basis for how the teachers will relate to the parents and children—and thus the overall success of the program.

References

Abramson, S. (2007). Co-inquiry: Documentation, communication, action. *Young Children Beyond the Journal.* Retrieved December 1, 2008, from http://journal.naeyc. org/btj/vp/pdf/voices_abramson_co-inquiry.pdf

Aguillard, A.E., Pierce, S.H., Benedict, J.H., & Burts, D.C. (2005). Barriers to implementation of continuity of care practices in child care centers. *Early Childhood Research Quarterly, 20*(3), 329–344.

Ainsworth, M.D.S. (1967). *Infancy in Uganda: Infant care and the growth of love.* Baltimore: John Hopkins University Press.

Ainsworth, M.D.S. (1979). Attachment as related to mother–infant interaction. In J.S. Rosenblatt, R.A. Hinde, C. Beer, & M. Busnel (Eds.), *Advances in the study of behavior* (Vol. 9). San Diego: Academic Press.

Ainsworth, M.D.S., & Bell, S. (1970). Attachment, exploration and separation: Illustrated by behavior of one year olds in a strange situation. *Child Development, 41,* 49–67.

Ainsworth, M.D.S., Blehar, M.C., Waters, E., & Wall, S. (1978). *Patterns of attachment: A psychological study of the strange situation.* Hillsdale, NJ: Lawrence Erlbaum Associates.

Arnett, J. (1989). Caregivers in day-care centers: Does training matter? *Journal of Applied Developmental Psychology, 10,* 541–552.

Aukrust, V., Edwards, C.P., Kumru, A., Knoche, L, & Kim, M. (2003). Young children's extended relationships in school: Parental ethnotheories in four communities, in Norway, United States, Turkey, and Korea. *International Journal of Behavior Development, 27*(6), 481–494.

Baker, A.C., & Manfredi/Petitt, L.A. (2004). *Relationships: The heart of quality care.* Washington, DC: National Association for the Education of Young Children.

Baldwin, D.A. (1995). Understanding the link between joint attention and language. In C. Moore & P. Dunham (Eds.), *Joint attention: Its origins and role in development* (pp. 131–158). Mahwah, NJ: Lawrence Erlbaum Associates.

Baldwin, J.M. (1897). *Social and ethical interpretations in mental development.* New York: Macmillan.

Barnas, M.V., & Cummings, E.M. (1997). Caregiver stability and toddlers' attachment-related behaviors toward caregivers in day care. *Infant Behavior and Development, 52,* 51–53.

Bell, R., & Ainsworth, M.D.S. (1972). Infant crying and maternal responsiveness. *Child Development, 43,* 1171–1190.

Benson, J., & Leeper Miller, J. (2008). Experiences in nature: A pathway to standards. *Young Children, 63*(4), 22–29.

Blehar, M.C., Lieberman, A.F., & Ainsworth, M.D. (1977). Early face-to-face interaction and its relation to later infant–mother attachment. *Child Development, 48,* 182–194.

Booth, C.L., Kelly, J.F., Spieker, S.J., & Zuckerman, T.G. (2003). Toddlers' attachment security to child-care providers: The Safe and Secure Scale. *Early Education and Development, 14*(1), 83–100.

Bove, C. (1999). Welcoming the child into infant care: Perspectives from Italy. *Young Children, 54*(2), 32–34.

Bove, C. (2001). Inserimento: A strategy for delicately beginning relationships and communications. In L. Gandini & C.P. Edwards (Eds.), *Bambini: The Italian approach to infant/toddler care* (pp. 109–123). New York: Teachers College Press.

Bowlby, J. (1944). Forty-four juvenile thieves: Their characters and home life. *International Journal of Psycho-Analysis, 25,* 19–52, 107–127.

Bowlby, J. (1951). *Maternal care and mental health.* Geneva: World Health Organization.

Bowlby, J. (1969). *Attachment* (Vol. 1). London: Hogarth Press.

Bowlby, J. (1973). *Separation: Anxiety and anger* (Vol. 2). London: Hogarth Press.

Bowlby, J. (1980). *Loss: Sadness and depression* (Vol. 3). London: Hogarth Press.

Braungart-Rieker, J., Garwood, M.M., & Stifter, C.A. (1997). Compliance and noncompliance: The roles of maternal control and child temperament. *Journal of Applied Developmental Psychology, 18,* 411–428.

Brazelton, T.B. (1992). *Touchpoints.* Reading, MA: Addison-Wesley.

Brazelton, T.B., & Cramer, B.G. (1989). *The earliest relationship.* Reading, MA: Addison-Wesley.

Brown-Dupaul, J., Keyes, T., & Segatti, L. (2001). Using documentation panels to communicate with families. *Childhood Education, 77*(4), 209–213.

Burrington, B., & Sortino, S. (2004). In our real world: An anatomy of documentation. In J. Hendrick (Ed.), *Next steps toward teaching the Reggio way: Accepting the challenge to change* (pp. 224–237). Upper Saddle River, NJ: Prentice Hall.

Caldera, Y.M., Huston, A.C., & O'Brien, M. (1989). Social interactions and play preferences of parents and toddlers with feminine, masculine, and neutral toys. *Child Development, 60,* 70–76.

Cassibba, R., Van IJzendoorn, M.H., & D'Odorico, L. (2000). Attachment and play in child care centers: Reliability and validity of the attachment Q-sort for mothers and professional caregivers in Italy. *International Journal of Behavioral Development, 24*(2), 241–255.

Cassidy, J. (1988). Child–mother attachment and the self in six-year-olds. *Child Development, 59*(1), 121–134.

Center on the Developing Child at Harvard University. (2007). *A science-based framework for early childhood policy: Using evidence to improve outcomes in learning, behavior, and health for vulnerable children.* Retrieved December 1, 2008, from http://www. developingchild.harvard.edu

Chisolm, J.S. (1981). Residence patterns and the environment of mother–infant interaction among the Navaho. In T.M. Field, A.M. Sostek, P. Vietze, & P.H. Leiderman (Eds.), *Culture and early interactions* (pp. 3–20). Mahwah, NJ: Lawrence Erlbaum Associates.

Chisolm, J.S. (1989). Biology, culture, and the development of temperament: A Navaho example. In J.K. Nugent, B.M. Lester, & T.B. Brazelton (Eds.), *The cultural context of infancy: Vol. 1. Biology, culture, and infant development* (pp. 341–366). Norwood, NJ: Ablex.

Clark, R., Hyde, J.S., Essex, M.J., & Klein, M.H. (1997). Length of maternity leave and quality of mother–infant interactions. *Child Development, 68,* 364–383.

Cohn, J.F., & Tronick, E.Z. (1983). Three-month-old infants' reaction to simulated maternal depression. *Child Development, 54,* 185–193.

Cohn, J.F., & Tronick, E.Z. (1988). Mother–infant face-to-face interaction: Influence is bidirectional and unrelated to periodic cycles in either partner's behavior. *Developmental Psychology, 24*(3), 386–392.

Copple, C., & Bredekamp, S. (2008). *Developmentally appropriate practice in early childhood programs.* Washington, DC: National Association for the Education of Young Children.

Corsaro, W.A. (2003). *"We're friends, right?": Inside kids' culture.* Washington, DC: Joseph Henry Press.

Cotton, J., Edwards, C.P., Zhao, W., & Gelabert, J.M. (2007). Nurturing care for China's orphaned children. *Young Children, 62*(6), 58–62. Available online at http://journal. naeyc.org/btj/200711/pdf/BTJEdwards.pdf

Cox Suarez, S. (2006). Making learning visible through documentation: Creating a culture of inquiry among preservice teachers. *The New Educator, 2*(1), 33–35.

Crockenberg, S.C., & Litman, C. (1990). Autonomy as competence in 2-year-olds: Maternal correlates of child defiance, compliance, and self-assertion. *Developmental Psychology, 26*, 961–971.

Cryer, D., Hurwitz, S., & Wolery, M. (2000). Continuity of caregiver for infant and toddlers in center-based care: Report on a survey of center practices. *Early Childhood Research Quarterly, 15 (4),* 497-514.

Curtis, D., & Carter, M. (2003). *Designs for living and learning: Transforming early childhood environments.* St. Paul, MN: Redleaf Press.

Curtis, D., & Carter, M. (2006). *Visionary infant and toddler program environments.* Riverside, CA: Harvest Resources.

Dahlberg, G., Moss, P., & Pence, A. (1999). *Beyond quality in early childhood education and care: Postmodern perspectives.* London: Falmer Press.

David, M., & Appell, G. (2001). *Lóczy: An unusual approach to mothering.* Budapest, Hungary: Association Pikler-Lóczy for Young Children. Available from Resources for Infant Educarers, http:// www.rie.org

Denham, S.A., Mitchell-Copeland, J., Strandberg, K., Auerbach, S., & Blair, K. (1997). Parental contributions to preschoolers' emotional competence: Direct and indirect effects. *Motivation and Emotion, 21*(1), 65–86.

Dieter, J.N., Field, T., Hernandez-Reif, M., Emory, E.K., & Redzepi, M. (2003). Stable preterm infants gain more weight and sleep less after five days of massage therapy. *Journal of Pediatric Psychology, 28*, 403–411.

Doherty, D.A. (2004). The relational rights of children in our care. In J. Hendrick (Ed.), *Next steps toward teaching the Reggio way: Accepting the challenge to change* (pp. 122–134). Upper Saddle River, NJ: Prentice Hall.

Donovan, W.L., Leavitt, L.A., & Walsh, R.O. (2000). Maternal illusory control predicts socialization strategies and toddler compliance. *Developmental Psychology, 36*, 402–411.

Dowdney, L., & Pickles, A.R. (1991). Expression of negative affect within disciplinary encounters: Is there dyadic reciprocity? *Developmental Psychology, 27*, 606–617.

Dubin, E.R., & Dubin, R. (1963). The authority inception period in socialization. *Child Development, 34*, 885–898.

Eckerman, C.O., & Peterman, K. (2004). Peers and infant social/communicative development. In G. Bremmer & A. Fogel (Eds.), *Blackwell handbook of infant development* (pp. 326–350). Malden, MA: Blackwell Publishing.

Edwards, C.P. (1986). *Promoting social and moral development in young children: Creative approaches for the classroom.* New York: Teachers College.

Edwards, C.P. (1989). The transition from infancy to early childhood: A difficult transition, and a difficult theory. In V.R. Bricker & G.H. Gossen (Eds.), *Ethnographic encounters in Southern Mesoamerica: Essays in honor of Evon Z. Vogt, Jr.* (pp. 167–175). Austin: University of Texas.

Edwards, C.P. (2004). Caregiving through a relationship lens. In J. Hendrick (Ed.), *Next steps toward teaching the Reggio way: Accepting the challenge to change* (pp. 114–121). Upper Saddle River, NJ: Prentice Hall.

Edwards, C.P., Churchill, S., Gabriel, M., Heaton, R., Jones-Branch, J., Marvin, C., et al. (2007). Students learn about documentation throughout their training program. *Early Childhood Research and Practice, 10*(2). Retrieved December 1, 2008, from http://ecrp.uiuc.edu/v9n2/edwards.html

Edwards, C.P., deGuzman, M.T., Brown, J., & Kumru, A. (2006). Children's social behaviors and peer interactions in diverse cultures. In X. Chen, D. French, & B. Schneider (Eds.), *Peer relations in cultural context* (pp. 23–51). New York: Cambridge University Press.

Edwards, C.P., & Gandini, L. (2001). Research as a partnership for learning together: Studying the growth of relationships inside the *nido*. In L. Gandini & C.P. Edwards (Eds.), *Bambini: The Italian approach to infant/toddler care* (pp. 181–199). New York: Teachers College Press.

Edwards, C.P., Gandini, L., & Giovannini, D. (1996). The contrasting developmental expectations of parents and early childhood teachers in two cultural communities. In S. Harkness & C. Super (Eds.), *Parents' cultural belief systems* (pp. 270–288). New York: Guilford.

Edwards, C.P., Gandini, L., Peon-Casanova, L., & Danielson, J. (2003). *Bambini: Early care and education in Pistoia, Italy, a child-friendly city* [Video]. Lincoln, NE: Great Plains National.

Edwards, C.P., & Liu, W. (2002). Parenting toddlers. In M.L. Bornstein (Ed.), *Handbook of parenting: Vol. I. Children and parenting* (2nd ed., pp. 45–72). Mahwah, NJ: Lawrence Erlbaum Associates.

Edwards, C.P., Logue, M.E., Loehr, S., & Roth, S. (1986). The influence of model infant group care on parent/child interaction at home. *Early Childhood Research Quarterly, 1,* 317–332.

Edwards, C.P., Logue, M.E., Loehr, S., & Roth, S. (1987). The effects of day care participation on parent/infant interaction at home. *American Journal of Orthopsychiatry, 57,* 33–36.

Edwards, C.P., & Raikes, H. (2002). Extending the dance: Relationship-based approaches to infant-toddler care and education. *Young Children, 57*(4), 10–17.

Edwards, C.P., & Rinaldi, C. (Eds.). (2008). *The diary of Laura: Perspectives on a Reggio Emilia diary.* Minneapolis, MN: Redleaf Press.

Edwards, C.P., & Whiting, B.B. (1993). "Mother, older sibling, and me": The overlapping roles of caregivers and companions in the social world of two- to three-year-olds in Ngeca, Kenya. In K. MacDonald (Ed.), *Parent–child play: Descriptions and implications* (pp. 305–329). Albany: State University of New York Press.

Edwards, C.P., & Whiting, B.B. (2004). *Ngecha: A Kenyan village in a time of rapid social change.* Lincoln: University of Nebraska Press.

Elicker, J., Noppe, I.C., Noppe, L.D., & Fortner-Wood, C. (1997). The Parent Caregiver Relationship Scale: Rounding out the relationship system in infant child care. *Early Education and Development, 8*(1), 83–100.

Emde, R. (1996). Thinking about intervention and improving socio-emotional development. *Zero to Three*, August/September, 11–16.

Epstein, A.S. (2007). *The intentional teacher: Choosing the best strategies for young children's learning*. Washington, DC: National Association for the Education of Young Children.

Erickson, J. (1991). *Patterns in preschool relationships: The effect of teacher–child attachment on peer competence*. Unpublished master's thesis, University of Nebraska–Lincoln.

Erickson, M., Sroufe, A.L., & Egeland, B. (1985). The relationship between quality of attachment and behavior problems in a high-risk sample. *Monographs of the Society for Research in Child Development, 50*, 147–166.

Erikson, E. (1950). *Childhood and society*. New York: Norton.

Etaugh, C., Grinnell, K., & Etaugh, A. (1989). Development of gender labeling: Effect of age of pictured children. *Sex Roles, 21*, 769–773.

Evans, K. (Ed.). (2003). *For the children: The Half the Sky Foundation's guide to infant nurture, child care, and preschool education in China's social welfare institutions*. Berkeley, CA: Half the Sky Foundation.

Fagot, B.I. (1995). Psychosocial and cognitive determinants of early gender-role behavior. *Annual Review of Sex Research, 6*, 1–31.

Family and Medical Leave Act (FMLA) of 1993, PL 103-3, 5 U.S.C. §§ 6381 *et seq.*, 29 U.S.C. §§ 2601 *et seq.*

Fox, N. (1977). Attachment of kibbutz infant to mother and metapelet. *Child Development, 48*, 1228–1239.

Fraiberg, S., Edelson, E., & Shapiro, V. (1975). Ghosts in the nursery: A psychoanalytic approach to the problem of impaired infant–mother relationships. *Journal of the American Academy of Child Psychiatry, XIV*, 387–421.

Franklin, W.H. (2004). Who cares? Eight principles for dealing with customers. In Child Care Information Exchange (Eds.), *Parent relations: Building an active partnership* (pp. 3–6). Redmond, WA: Child Care Information Exchange.

Freud, S. (1903/1953). *Three essays on the theory of sexuality*. In J. Strachey (Ed. & Trans.), *The standard edition of the complete psychological works of Sigmund Freud* (Vol. 7, pp. 1550–1669). London: Hogarth.

Furrow, D., Nelson, K., & Benedict, H. (1979). Mother's speech to children and syntactic development: Some simple relationships. *Journal of Child Language, 6*, 423–442.

Fyfe, B., Hovey, S.M., & Strange, J. (2004). Thinking with parents about learning. In J. Hendrick (Ed.), *Next steps toward teaching the Reggio way: Accepting the challenge to change* (pp. 96–105). Upper Saddle River, NJ: Prentice Hall.

Galardini, A., & Giovannini, D. (2001). Pistoia: Creating a dynamic, open system to serve children, families, and communities. In L. Gandini & C.P. Edwards (Eds.), *Bambini: The Italian approach to infant/toddler care* (pp. 89–108). New York: Teachers College Press.

Galinsky, E. (1990). Why are some parent/teacher partnerships clouded with difficulties? *Young Children, 45*(5), 2–39.

Galinsky, E. (1994). How parents and teachers see each other. In Child Care Information Exchange (Eds.), *Parent relations: Building an active partnership*, (pp. 7–9). Redmond, WA: Child Care Information Exchange.

Gandini, L. (1988). Educational and caring spaces. In C.P. Edwards, L. Gandini, & G. Forman (Eds.), *The Hundred Languages of Children: The Reggio Emilia Approach, Advanced Reflections* (2nd ed., pp. 161–178). Greenwich, CT: Ablex.

Gandini, L. (2001). Reggio Emilia: Experiencing life in an infant-toddler center. Interview with Cristina Bondavalli. In L. Gandini & C.P. Edwards (Eds.), *Bambini: The*

Italian approach to infant/toddler care (pp. 55–66). New York: Teachers College Press.

Gandini, L., & Edwards, C. (Eds.). (2001). *Bambini: The Italian approach to infant/toddler care.* New York: Teachers College Press.

Gandini, L., & Goldhaber, J. (2001). Two reflections about documentation. In L. Gandini & C.P. Edwards (Eds.), *Bambini: The Italian approach to infant/toddler care* (pp. 124–145). New York: Teachers College Press.

Gandini, L., & Topal, C. (1999). *Beautiful stuff: Learning with found materials.* Worcester, MA: Davis Press.

Giovannini, D. (2001). Traces of childhood: A child's diary. In L. Gandini & C.P. Edwards (Eds.), *Bambini: The Italian approach to infant/toddler care* (pp. 146–151). New York: Teachers College Press.

Goldhaber, J., & Smith, D. (2002). The development of documentation strategies to support teacher reflection, inquiry, and collaboration. In V.R. Fu, A.J. Stremmel, & L.T. Hill (Eds.), *Teaching and learning: Collaborative exploration of the Reggio Emilia approach* (pp. 147–160). Upper Saddle River, NJ: Prentice Hall.

Gonzalez-Mena, J., & Eyer, D.W. (2007). *Infants, toddlers, and caregivers* (7th ed.). New York: McGraw Hill.

Goossens, F., & van IJzendoorn, M.H. (1990). Quality of infants' attachment to professional caregivers: Relation to infant–parent attachment and day-care characteristics. *Child Development, 61*(3), 832–837.

Greenfield, P.M. (2004). *Weaving generations together: Evolving creativity in the Maya of Chiapas.* Santa Fe, NM: School of American Research Press.

Greenman, J. (1988). *Caring spaces, learning spaces: Children's environments that work.* Redmond, WA: Exchange Press.

Greenspan, S., & Greenspan, N.T. (1985). *First feelings: Milestones in the emotional development of your infant and child from birth to age 4.* New York: Viking Press.

Harkness, S., & Super, C. (Eds.). (1996). *Parents' cultural belief systems: Their origins, expressions, and consequences.* New York: Guilford.

Harlow, H. (1958). The nature of love. *The American Psychologist, 3,* 673–685.

Harlow, H. (1959). Love in infant monkeys. *Scientific American, 200*(6), 68–74.

Harlow, H., & Zimmerman, R. (1959). Affectional responses in the infant monkey. *Science, 130,* 431–432.

Harms, T., Cryer, D., & Clifford, R. (2006). *Infant Toddler Environment Rating Scale–Revised Edition.* New York: Teachers College Press.

Harms, T., Cryer, D., & Clifford, R. (2007). *Family Child Care Environment Rating Scale–Revised Edition.* New York: Teachers College Press.

Hart, B., & Risley, T.R. (1995). *Meaningful differences in the everyday experiences of young American children.* Baltimore: Paul H. Brookes Publishing Co.

Helm, J., Beneke, S., & Steinheimer, K. (1997). *Windows on learning: Documenting young children's work.* New York: Teachers College Press.

Helm, J., & Helm, A. (2006). *Building support for your school: How to use children's work to show learning.* New York: Teachers College Press.

Helm, J., & Katz, L. (2001). *Young investigators: The project approach in the early years.* New York: Teachers College Press.

Hewlett, B.S. (1991). *Intimate fathers: The nature and context of Aka Pygmy paternal infant care.* Ann Arbor: University of Michigan Press.

Hong, S., & Forman, G. (2000). What constitutes a good documentation panel and how to achieve it. *Canadian Children, 25*(2), 26–31.

Honig, A. (2002). *Secure relationships: Nurturing infant/toddler attachment in early care settings*. Washington, DC: National Association for the Education of Young Children.

Howes, C. (1999). Attachment relationships in the context of multiple caregivers. In J. Cassidy & P.R. Shaver (Eds.), *Handbook of attachment: Theory, research, and clinical applications* (pp. 671–687). New York: Guilford.

Howes, C., & Hamilton, C. (1992). Children's relationships with caregivers, mothers, and child care teachers. *Child Development, 63,* 859–866.

Howes, C., Hamilton, C.E., & Matheson, C.C. (1994). Children's relationships with peers: Differential associations with aspects of the teacher–child relationship. *Child Development, 65*(1), 253–263.

Howes, C., Matheson, C.C., & Hamilton, C.E. (1994). Maternal, teacher, and child care history and correlates of children's relationships with peers. *Child Development, 65*(1), 264–273.

Howes, C., & Smith, E.W. (1995a). Children and their caregivers: Profiles of relationships. *Social Development, 4 (1),* 44–61.

Howes, C., & Smith, E.W. (1995b). Relations among child care quality, teacher behavior, children's play activities, emotional security, and cognitive activity in child care. *Early Childhood Research Quarterly, 10*(4), 381–404.

Isabella, R., & Belsky, J. (1991). Interactional synchrony and the origins of infant–mother attachment: A replication study. *Child Development, 62,* 373–384.

Isbell, R., & Isbell, C. (2003). *The complete learning spaces book for infants and toddlers.* Beltsville, MD: Gryphon House.

Jones, E., & Nimmo, J. (1994). *Emergent curriculum.* Washington, DC: National Association for the Education of Young Children.

Josselson, R. (1996). *The space between us: Exploring the dimensions of human relationships.* Thousand Oaks, CA: Sage Publications.

Kagan, J. (1981). *The second year: The emergence of self-awareness.* Cambridge, MA: Harvard University Press.

Kaler, S.R., & Kopp, C. (1990). Compliance and comprehension in very young toddlers. *Child Development, 61,* 1997–2003.

Kaminsky, J.A. (2005). Reflections on *inserimento,* the process of welcoming children and parents into the infant-toddler center: An interview with Lella Gandini. *Innovations in Early Education: The International Reggio Exchange, 12*(2), Spring, 1–8.

Kantor, R., & Whaley, K.L. (1998). Existing frameworks and new ideas from our Reggio Emilia experience: Learning at a lab school with 2- to 4-year-old children. In C.P. Edwards, L. Gandini, & G. Forman (Eds.), *The hundred languages of children: The Reggio Emilia approach—advanced reflections* (pp. 313–333). Greenwich, CT: Ablex.

Katz, L.G., & Chard, S.C. (1996, April). The contribution of documentation to the quality of early childhood education. *ERIC Digest.* Retrieved December 1, 2008, from http://www.ericdigests.org/1996-4/quality.htm

Keeler, R. (2008). *Natural playscapes: Creating outdoor play environments for the soul.* Redmond, WA: Exchange Press.

Keller, H. (2002). Development as the interface between biology and culture: A conceptualization of early ontogenetic experiences. In H. Keller, Y.H. Poortinga, & A.

Scholmerich (Eds.), *Between culture and biology* (pp. 214–240). New York: Cambridge University Press.

Keller, H. (2007). *Cultures of infancy.* Mahwah, NJ: Lawrence Erlbaum Associates.

Keyser, J. (2006). *From parents to partners: Building a family-centered early childhood program.* Washington, DC: National Association for the Education of Young Children.

Kirkland, J., Bimler, D., Drawneek, A., McKim, M., & Scholmerich, A. (2004). An alternative approach for the analysis and interpretation of attachment sort items. *Early Child Development and Care, 174*(7–8), 701–719.

Kline, L.S. (2008). Documentation panel: The "Making Learning Visible" project. *Journal of Early Childhood Teacher Education, 29,* 70–80.

Kohlberg, L. (1966). A cognitive-developmental analysis of children's sex-role concepts and attitudes. In E.E. Maccoby (Ed.), *The development of sex differences* (pp. 82–173). Stanford, CA: Stanford University Press.

Konner, M. (1975). Relations among infants and juveniles in comparative perspective. In M. Lewis & L.A. Rosenblum (Eds.), *Friendship and peer relations* (pp. 99–129). New York: Wiley.

Kopp, C.B. (1982). The antecedents of self-regulation: A developmental perspective. *Developmental Psychology, 18,* 199–214.

Kopp, C.B. (1992). Emotional distress and control in young children. In N. Eisenberg & R.A. Fabes (Eds.), *Emotion and its regulation in early development* (pp. 41–56). San Francisco: Jossey-Bass.

Kuczynski, L., & Kochanska, G. (1990). Development of children's noncompliance strategies from toddlerhood to age 5. *Developmental Psychology, 26,* 398–408.

Kuczynski, L., Kochanska, G., Radke-Yarrow, M., & Girnius-Brown, O. (1987). A developmental interpretation of young children's noncompliance. *Developmental Psychology, 23,* 799–806.

Laakso, M.L., Poikkeus, A.M., & Lyytinen, P. (1999). Shared reading interaction in families with and without genetic risk for dyslexia: Implications for toddlers' language development. *Infant and Child Development, 8,* 179–195.

Landy, S. (2002). *Pathways to competence: Encouraging healthy social and emotional development in young children.* Baltimore: Paul H. Brookes Publishing Co.

LeeKeenan, D., & Edwards, C.P. (1992). Using the project approach with toddlers. *Young Children, 47*(4), 31–35.

LeVine, R.A., Dixon, S., LeVine, S., Richman, A., Leiderman, P.H., Keefer, C., et al. (1994). *Child care and culture: Lessons from Africa.* London: Cambridge University Press.

LeVine, R.A., & LeVine, B.B. (1963). *Nyansongo: A Gusii community in Kenya.* In B.B. Whiting (Ed.), *Six cultures: Studies of child rearing.* New York: John Wiley.

LeVine, R.A., Miller, P.M., & West, M.M. (Eds.). (1988). *Parental behavior in diverse societies.* San Francisco: Jossey Bass.

Lewis, M., & Brooks-Gunn, J. (1979). *Social cognition and the acquisition of self.* New York: Plenum.

Lewis, M., Sullivan, M., Stranger, C., & Weiss, M. (1989). Self development and self-conscious emotions. *Child Development, 60,* 146–156.

Lieberman, A.F. (1977). Preschoolers' competence with a peer: Relations with attachment and peer experience. *Child Development, 48,* 1277–1287.

Logue, M.E., Shelton, H., Cronkite, D., & Austin, J. (2007). Strengthening partnerships with families through toddlers' stories. *Young Children, 62*(2), 85–87.

Louv, R. (2006). *Last child in the woods: Saving our children from nature-deficit disorder.* Chapel Hill, NC: Algonquin Books.

Lynch, E.W., & Hanson, M.J. (2004). *Developing cross-cultural competence: A guide for working with children and their families* (3rd ed.). Baltimore: Paul H. Brookes Publishing Co.

Lytton, H. (1979). Disciplinary encounters between young boys and their mothers: Is there a contingency system? *Developmental Psychology, 15,* 256–268.

Maccoby, E.E. (1980). *Social development: Psychological growth and the parent–child relationship.* New York: Harcourt.

Maccoby, E.E. (1988). Gender as a social category. *Developmental Psychology, 24,* 755–765.

Maccoby, E.E. (1999). *The two sexes: Growing up apart, coming together.* Cambridge, MA: Harvard University Press.

Maccoby, E.E., & Martin, J.A. (1983). Socialization in the context of the family: Parent–child interaction. In P.H. Mussen (Series Ed.) & E.M. Hetherington (Vol. Ed.), *Handbook of child psychology: Vol. 4. Socialization, personality, and social development* (4th ed., pp. 1–101). New York: Wiley.

Mahler, M., Pine, F., & Bergman, A. (1975). *The psychological birth of the human infant.* New York: Basic Books.

Main, M., & Solomon, J. (1990). Procedures for identifying infants as disorganized/disoriented during the Ainsworth Strange Situation. In M. Greenberg, D. Cicchetti, & E.M. Cummings (Ed.), *Attachment in the preschool years: Theory, research, and intervention.* Chicago: University of Chicago Press.

Malaguzzi, L. (1998). History, ideas, and basic philosophy: An interview with Lella Gandini. In C.P. Edwards, L. Gandini, & G. Forman (Eds.), *The hundred languages of children: The Reggio Emilia approach—advanced reflections* (pp. 49–98). Greenwich, CT: Ablex.

Maretzki, T.W., & Maretzki, H. (1963). *Taira: An Okinawan village.* In B.B. Whiting (Ed.), *Six cultures: Studies of child rearing.* New York: John Wiley. (Reprinted as a separate volume, 1966)

Martin, C.A. (1993). New directions for investigating children's gender knowledge. *Developmental Review, 13,* 184–204.

Martini, M., & Kirkpatrick, J. (1981). Early interactions in the Marquesas Islands. In T.M. Field, A.M. Sostek, P. Vietze, & P.H. Leiderman (Eds.), *Culture and early interactions* (pp. 189–214). Mahwah, NJ: Lawrence Erlbaum Associates.

Mason, K., & Duberstein, L. (1992). Consequences of child care for parents' well-being. In A. Booth (Ed.), *Child care in the 1990s: Trends and consequences* (pp. 127–158). Mahwah, NJ: Lawrence Erlbaum Associates.

May, N., Kantor, R., & Sanderson, M. (2004). There it is! Exploring the permanence of objects and the power of self with infants and toddlers. In J. Hendrick (Ed.), *Next steps toward teaching the Reggio way: Accepting the challenge to change* (pp. 164–174). Upper Saddle River, NJ: Prentice Hall.

Meier, D.R., & Henderson, B. (2007). *Learning from young children in the classroom: The art and science of teacher research.* New York: Teachers College Press.

Meisels, S.J. (1995). *Performance assessment in early childhood education: The work sampling system.* ERIC EDO-PS-95-6. Retrieved December 1, 2008, from http://www.ericdigests.org

Meltzoff, A.N., & Moore, M.K. (1989). Imitation in newborn infants: Exploring the range of gestures imitated and the underlying mechanisms. *Developmental Psychology, 25,* 954–962.

Meltzoff, A.N., & Moore, M.K. (1992). Early imitation within a functional framework: The importance of person, identity, movement, and development. *Infant Behavior and Development, 15,* 479–505.

Miller, D. (2004). *More than play! Children learn important skills through visual-spatial work.* Retrieved December 1, 2008, from http://dimensionsfoundation.org/media/V_S_single_page_layout.pdf

Morelli, G.A., & Tronick, E.Z. (1991). Parenting and child development in the Efe foragers and Lese farmers of Zaire. In M.H. Bornstein (Ed.), *Cultural approaches to parenting* (pp. 91–113). Mahwah, NJ: Lawrence Erlbaum Associates.

Morrongiello, B.A., & Dawber, T. (1998). Toddlers' and mothers' behaviors in an injury-risk situation: Implications for sex differences in childhood injuries. *Journal of Applied Developmental Psychology, 19,* 625–639.

Mueller, E.C., & Cohen, D. (1986). Peer therapies and the little latency: A clinical perspective. In E.C. Mueller & C.R. Cooper (Eds.), *Process and outcome in peer relations* (pp. 161–183). San Diego: Academic Press.

National Arbor Day Foundation. (2007). *Learning with nature idea book: Creating nurturing outdoor spaces for children.* Lincoln, NE: Dimensions Educational Foundation.

National Association for the Education of Young Children. (2007). *Standard 7: NAEYC Accreditation Criteria for Families Standard.* Retrieved December 1, 2008, from http://www.naeyc.org/academy/standards/standard7/

National Scientific Council on the Developing Child. (2007). *The science of early childhood development: Closing the gap between what we know and what we do.* Available online at http//www.developingchild.net

Neugebauer, B. (2004, July/August). Cover story: Meet cover director, Nancy Rosenow. *Child Care Information Exchange,* 32–33.

Nsamenang, B. (2000). Issues in indigenous approaches to developmental research in sub-Saharan Africa. *International Society for the Study of Behavioral Development Newsletter, 38*(1), 1–2.

O'Connell, B., & Bretherington, I. (1984). Toddler's play, alone and with mother: The role of maternal guidance. In I. Bretherington (Ed.), *Symbolic play* (pp. 337–366). San Diego: Academic Press.

Oken-Wright, P. (2001). Documentation: Both mirror and light. *Innovations in early education: The international Reggio exchange, 8*(4), 5–15.

Oken-Wright, P., & Gravett, M. (2002). Big ideas and the essence of intent. In V.R. Fu, A.J. Stremmel, & L.T. Hill, *Teaching and learning: Collaborative exploration of the Reggio Emilia approach* (pp. 197–220). Upper Saddle, NJ: Prentice Hall.

Owen, M.T., Ware, A.M., & Barfoot, B. (2002). Caregiver–mother partnership behavior and the quality of caregiver–child and mother–child interactions. *Early Childhood Research Quarterly, 15*(3), 413–428.

Patterson, G.R. (1982). *Coercive family process.* Eugene, OR: Castalia Press.

Povinelli, D.J., & Simon, B.B. (1998). Young children's understanding of briefly versus extremely delayed images of the self: Emergence of the autobiographical stance. *Developmental Psychology, 34,* 188–194.

Power, T.G., & Chapieski, M.L. (1986). Childrearing and impulse control in toddlers: A naturalistic investigation. *Developmental Psychology, 22,* 271–275.

Quann, V., & Wien, C.A. (2006). The visible empathy of infants and toddlers. *Young Children, 61*(4), 22–29.

Raikes, H.H. (1993). The effect of time with teacher on infant–mother attachment. *Early Childhood Research Quarterly, 8*(3), 309–326.

Raikes, H.H. (1994). *Relations of the Early Childhood Perceiver to Attachment Q-Set ratings.* Unpublished manuscript.

Raikes, H., & McCall-Whitmer, J. (2006). *Beautiful Beginnings: A developmental curriculum for infants and toddlers.* Baltimore: Paul H. Brookes Publishing Co.

Raikes, H., Pan, B.A., Luze, G., Tamis-LeMonda, C., Brooks-Gunn, J., Constantine, J., et al. (2006). Mother–child bookreading in low-income families: Correlates and outcomes during the first three years of life. *Child Development, 77*(4), 924–953.

Reggio Children, Italy. (1996). *The little ones of silent movies.* Reggio Emilia, Italy: Reggio Children.

Reggio Children, Italy, and Harvard Project Zero. (2001). *Making learning visible: Children as individual and group learners.* Reggio Emilia, Italy: Reggio Children.

Reingold, H. (1982). Little children's participation in the work of adults: A nascent prosocial behavior. *Child Development, 53,* 114–125.

Reingold, H., Cook, K., & Kolowitz, V. (1987). Commands activate the behavior and pleasure of 2-year-old children. *Developmental Psychology, 23,* 146–151.

Rinaldi, C. (1998). Projected curriculum constructed through documentation—*progettazione*: An interview with Lella Gandini. In C.P. Edwards, L. Gandini, & G. Forman (Eds.), *The hundred languages of children: The Reggio Emilia approach—advanced reflections* (pp. 113–126). Greenwich, CT: Ablex.

Rinaldi, C. (2006). *In dialogue with Reggio Emilia: Listening, researching, and learning.* New York: Routledge.

Rogoff, B. (2003). *The cultural nature of human development.* New York: Oxford University.

Rosen, K., & Rothbaum, F. (1993). Quality of parental caregiving and security of attachment. *Developmental Psychology, 29,* 358–367.

Schoetzau, A. (1979). Effect of viewing distance on looking behavior in neonates. *International Journal of Behavioral Development, 2,* 121–131.

Shonkoff, J.P., & Phillips, D.A. (Eds.). (2000). *From neurons to neighborhoods: The science of early childhood development. Committee on Integrating the Science of Early Childhood Development.* Washington, DC: National Academies Press.

Shpancer, N. (2002). The home-daycare link: Mapping children's new world order. *Early Childhood Research Quarterly, 17*(3), 374–392.

Skeels, H. (1936). The relation of the foster home environment to the mental development of children placed in infancy. *Child Development, 7*(1), 1–5.

Smith, A.B., & Hubbard, P.M. (1988). The relationship between parent/staff communication and children's behavior in early childhood settings. *Early Childhood Development and Care, 35,* 13–28.

Smith, D., & Goldhaber, J. (2004). *Poking, pinching, and pretending: Documenting toddlers' explorations with clay.* St. Paul, MN: Redleaf Press.

Spitz, R. (1957). *No and yes: On the genesis of human communication.* New York: International Universities Press.

Spitz, R. (1965). *The first year of life.* New York: International Universities Press.

Sroufe, L.A. (1988). The role of infant-caregiver attachment in development. In J. Belsky & T. Nezworski (Eds.), *Clinical implications of attachment* (pp. 18–39). Mahwah, NJ: Lawrence Erlbaum Associates.

Stipek, D., Recchia, S., & McClintic, S. (1992). Self-evaluation in young children. *Monographs of the Society for Research in Child Development, 57*(Serial No. 226).

Sussna Klein, S. (2002). Infant and toddler care that recognizes their competence: Practices at the Pikler Institute. *Dimensions of Early Childhood: Journal of the Southern Early Childhood Association, 30*(2), 11–18.

Swadener, B.B., Kabiru, M., & Njenga, A. (2000). *Does the village still raise the child? A collaborative study of changing child-rearing and early education in Kenya.* Albany: State University of New York Press.

Thoman, E., & Browder, S. (1987). *Born dancing: How intuitive parents understand their baby's unspoken language.* New York: Harper & Row.

Thompson, R.A. (1999). Early attachment and later development. In J. Cassidy & P.R. Shaver (Eds.), *Handbook of attachment: Theory, research and clinical applications* (pp. 265–286). New York: Guilford.

Toda, S., & Fogel, A. (1993). Infant response to the still-face situation at 3 and 6 months. *Developmental Psychology, 29*(3), 532–538.

Torquati, J., & Barber, J. (2005). Dancing with trees: Infants and toddlers in the garden. *Young Children, 60*(3), 40–47.

Trevarthen, C. (1988). Universal cooperative motives: How infants begin to know the language and skills of the culture of their parents. In G. Jahoda & I.M. Lewis (Eds.), *Acquiring culture: Cross-cultural studies in child development* (pp. 37–90). Beckenham, UK: Croom Helm.

Trevarthen, C. (1995). The child's need to learn a culture. *Children and Society, 9*(1), 5–19.

Trevarthen, C. (2002, September). The musical lives of babies and families. *Zero to Three.*

Trevarthen, C., & Hubley, P. (1978). Secondary intersubjectivity: Confidence, confiding and acts of meaning in the first year. In A. Lock (Ed.), *Action, gesture, and symbol: The emergence of language* (pp. 183–227). San Diego: Academic Press.

Tronick, E. (1989). Emotions and emotional communication. *American Psychologist, 44,* 112–118.

Tronick, E.Z., Morelli, G.A., & Winn, S. (1987). Multiple caretaking of Efe (Pygmy) infants. *American Anthropologist, 89,* 96–106.

U.S. Department of Health and Human Services. (1994). *The statement of the Advisory Committee on Services to Families with Infants and Toddlers.* Washington, DC: Author.

U.S. Department of Health and Human Services. (2002). *Head Start program performance standards and other regulations. 45 C.F.T. 1301, 1302, 1303, 1304 and guidance 1305, 1306, 1308 and guidance.* Washington, DC: Government Printing Office.

Uzgiris, I.C., & Hunt, J.M. (1987). *Infant performance and experience: New findings with the ordinal scales.* Champaign: University of Illinois Press.

Van IJzendoorn, M.H., Sagi, A., & Lambermon, M.W.E. (1992). The multiple caregiver paradox: Some data from Holland and Israel. *Child Development, 66,* 209–223.

Vecchi, V. (1998). The role of the *atelierista*: An interview with Lella Gandini. In C.P. Edwards, L. Gandini, & G. Forman (Eds.), *The hundred languages of children: The Reggio Emilia approach—advanced reflections* (pp. 139–148). Greenwich, CT: Ablex.

Wallin, D.J. (2007). Mary Main: Mental representations, megacognition and the Adult Attachment Interview. In D.J. Wallin (Ed.), *Attachment in Psychotherapy* (pp. 25–42). New York: Guilford Press.

Waters, E., & Deane, K. (1985). Defining and assessing individual differences in attachment relationships: Q-methodology and the organization of behavior in infancy and early childhood. *Monographs of the Society for Research in Child Development, 50*(1-2, Serial No. 209).

Wein, C.A., Coates, A., Keating, B., & Bigelow, B. (2005). *Designing the environment to build connection to place.* Retrieved December 1, 2008, from http://journal.naeyc.org/btj/200505/05Wien.pdf

Weinraub, M., Clemens, L.P., Sockloff, A., Ethridge, T., Gracely, E., & Myers, B. (1984). The development of sex role stereotypes in the third year: Relationships to gender labeling, gender identity, sex-typed toy preference, and family characteristics. *Child Development, 55,* 1493–1503.

Weisner, T.S. (1984). Ecocultural niches of middle childhood: A cross-cultural perspective. In W.A. Collins (Ed.), *Development during middle childhood: The years from six to twelve* (pp. 335–369). Washington, DC: National Academies Press.

Weisner, T.S. (1987). Socialization for parenthood in sibling caretaking societies. In. J.B. Lancaster, J. Altmann, A.S. Rossi, & L.R. Sherrod (Ed.), *Parenting across the lifespan: Biosocial dimensions* (pp. 237–270). New York: Aldine de Gruyter.

Weisner, T. (1989). Cultural and universal aspects of social support for children: Evidence from the Abaluyia of Kenya. In D. Belle (Ed.), *Children's social networks and social supports* (pp. 70–90). New York: Wiley.

Weisner, T.S. (1996). The 5 to 7 transition as an ecocultural project. In A.J. Sameroff & M.M. Haith (Eds.), *The five to seven year shift* (pp. 295–328). Chicago: University of Chicago.

Weitzman, N., Birns, B., & Friend, R. (1985). Traditional and nontraditional mothers' communication with their daughters and sons. *Child Development, 56,* 894–898.

Wenar, C. (1982). On negativism. *Human Development, 25,* 1–23.

Westerman, M.A. (1990). Coordination of maternal directives with preschoolers' behavior in compliance-problem and healthy dyads. *Developmental Psychology, 26,* 621–630.

Whipple, R., & McCullough, S. (2005). The welcoming process. *Innovations in Early Education: The International Reggio Exchange, 12*(2), Spring, 9–16.

White, B. (1985). *The first three years of life* (Rev. ed.). Englewood Cliffs, NJ: Prentice Hall.

Whiting, B.B. (1983). The genesis of prosocial behavior. In D.L. Bridgeman (Ed.), *The nature of prosocial development: Interdisciplinary theories and strategies* (pp. 221–242). An Diego: Academic Press.

Whiting, B.B., & Edwards, C.P. (1988). *Children of different worlds: The formation of social behavior.* Cambridge, MA: Harvard University Press.

Whiting, B.B., & Whiting, J.W.M. (1975). *Children of six cultures: A psychocultural analysis.* Cambridge, MA: Harvard University Press.

Whiting, J. (1994). Environmental constraints on infant care. In E. Chasdi (Ed.), *Culture and human development: The selected papers of John Whiting* (pp. 107–134). New York: Cambridge University Press.

Williams, A.E. (2008). Exploring the natural world with infants and toddlers in an urban setting. *Young Children, 63*(1), 22–25.

Wolf, A.T. (2007). *Building relationships: A study of families, children and teachers.* Unpublished doctoral dissertation, University of Missouri, Kansas City.

Zahn-Waxler, C., Radke-Yarrow, M., & King, R.A. (1979). Child-rearing and children's prosocial initiations toward victims in distress. *Child Development, 50,* 319–330.

Zahn-Waxler, C., Radke-Yarrow, M., Wagner, E., & Chapman, M. (1992). Development of concern for others. *Developmental Psychology, 28,* 126–136.

Zhao, W. (2003, December). Lasting learning inspired by the Reggio Emilia philosophy: Professional development experience within the Chinese context. *Innovations in Early Education: The International Reggio Exchange.*

Zukow-Goldring, P. (1996). Sensitive caretaking fosters the comprehension of speech: When gestures speak louder than words. *Early Development and Parenting, 5*(4), 195–211.

Index

Page numbers followed by *b* indicate boxes; numbers followed by *f* indicate figures; and numbers followed by *t* indicate tables.

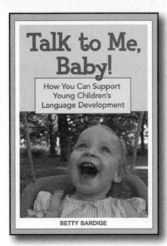